# Positive Tourism

Tourism affects millions of individuals, numerous societies and environments in multiple, nuanced and overlapping ways. While it can be viewed as a frivolous leisure pursuit or simply a large industry, with potentially destructive impacts, it might also be understood in terms of its effects on human fulfilment, the good life and greater well-being.

This book calls for positive tourism, principally grounded in theories from positive psychology (the study of what makes life worth living), and the development of a body of knowledge that explains what characterises optimal tourist experiences, what enables host communities to flourish and what encourages workers in tourism to thrive. Through original research studies reported in this international volume, we aim to develop this knowledge further. The intersections between ongoing and traditionally inspired applications of psychology in tourism and this new thrust in psychological inquiry promise to refresh and challenge tourism research.

This book will appeal to researchers and academics in tourism, leisure, positive psychology, management and related fields, as well as graduate students, professionals and policy makers.

**Sebastian Filep** is Senior Lecturer at the Tourism Department, University of Otago, New Zealand. He specialises in tourism and well-being research. He has published internationally in peer-reviewed academic journals and books on the topic of human well-being.

**Jennifer Laing** is Associate Professor in Management in the Department of Management and Marketing, La Trobe University, Australia. Her research interests include extraordinary tourist experiences, the role of events in society, travel narratives and wellness tourism. She has co-written five and edited two books on tourism and/or events.

**Mihaly Csikszentmihalyi** is Distinguished Professor of Psychology and Management and Founding Co-Director of the Quality of Life Research Centre, Claremont Graduate University, USA. He is noted for his work on happiness, but is best known as the architect of the notion of *flow*.

**Routledge Advances in Tourism**
Edited by Stephen Page
*School for Tourism, Bournemouth University*

For a full list of titles in this series, please visit www.routledge.com/series/SE0258

# Positive Tourism

Edited by Sebastian Filep, Jennifer
Laing and Mihaly Csikszentmihalyi

LONDON AND NEW YORK

First published 2017 by Routledge

2 Park Square, Milton Park, Abingdon, Oxfordshire OX14 4RN
52 Vanderbilt Avenue, New York, NY 10017

*Routledge is an imprint of the Taylor & Francis Group, an informa business*

First issued in paperback 2019

*British Library Cataloguing in Publication Data*
A catalogue record for this book is available from the British Library

*Library of Congress Cataloging-in-Publication Data*
Names: Filep, Sebastian, author. | Laing, Jennifer, 1967- author. |
    Csikszentmihalyi, Mihaly, author.
Title: Positive tourism / edited by Sebastian Filep, Jennifer Laing and
    Mihaly Csikszentmihalyi.
Description: Abingdon, Oxon ; New York : Routledge, is an imprint of the
    Taylor & Francis Group, an Informa Business, [2017] | Series: Routledge
    advances in tourism | Includes bibliographical references and index.
Identifiers: LCCN 2016020675| ISBN 9781138900653 (hbk) |
    ISBN 9781315707129 (ebk)
Subjects: LCSH: Tourism. | Tourism—Social aspects.
Classification: LCC G155.A1 P67 2017 | DDC 338.4/791—dc23
LC record available at https://lccn.loc.gov/2016020675

ISBN: 978-1-138-90065-3 (hbk)
ISBN: 978-0-367-36886-9 (pbk)

Typeset in Times New Roman
by Apex CoVantage, LLC

# Contents

# Figures

# Tables

# Contributors

**Deborah Che**, Lecturer in the School of Business and Tourism, Southern Cross University, Coolangatta, Australia. Email: deborah.che@scu.edu.au

**John Coffey**, Visiting Assistant Professor of Psychology in the Department of Psychology, The University of the South, Sewanee, USA. Email: jkcoffey2@gmail.com

**Mihaly Csikszentmihalyi**, Distinguished Professor of Psychology and Management and Founding Co-Director of the Quality of Life Research Centre, Claremont Graduate University, Claremont, CA, USA. Email: miska@cgu.edu; Mihaly.Csikszentmihalyi@cgu.edu

**Jessica de Bloom**, Research Fellow in the Institute for Advanced Social Research, Department of Psychology, School of Social Sciences and Humanities, University of Tampere, Finland. Email: jessica.de.bloom@uta.fi

**Sebastian Filep**, Senior Lecturer in the Department of Tourism, University of Otago, Dunedin, New Zealand. Email: sebastian.filep@otago.ac.nz

**Warwick Frost**, Associate Professor in the Department of Management and Marketing, La Trobe University, Melbourne, Australia. Email: w.frost@latrobe.edu.au

**Sabine Geurts**, Professor in the Behavioral Science Institute, Radboud University, Nijmegen, the Netherlands. Email: s.geurts@psych.ru.nl

**Chelsea Gill**, PhD Candidate in UQ Business School, The University of Queensland, Brisbane, Australia. Email: c.gill@uq.edu.au

**Troy D. Glover**, Professor in the Department of Recreation and Leisure Studies, University of Waterloo, Waterloo, Canada. Email: troy.glover@uwaterloo.ca

**Peita Hillman**, Lecturer in the School of International Tourism and Hospitality, International College of Management, Sydney (ICMS), Manly, Australia. Email: phillman@icms.edu.au

**Susan Houge Mackenzie**, Assistant Professor in Recreation, Parks, & Tourism Administration, California Polytechnic State University, San Luis Obispo, USA. Email: mackenzi@calpoly.edu

**John Kerr**, Adjunct Professor in the School of Kinesiology, University of British Columbia, Vancouver, Canada. Email: johnnkerrsportpsych@gmail.com

**Jennifer Laing**, Associate Professor in the Department of Management and Marketing, La Trobe University, Melbourne, Australia. Email: jennifer.laing@latrobe.edu.au

**Martin Lohmann**, Professor at Leuphana University of Lüneberg, Lüneburg, Germany. Email: lohmann@nit-kiel.de; m.lohmann@uni.leuphana.de

**Xavier Matteucci**, Research Associate and Adjunct Assistant Professor in the Department of Tourism and Service Management, MODUL University, Vienna, Austria. Email: xmatteucci@gmx.net; xavier.matteucci@modul.ac.at

**Brent D. Moyle**, Research Fellow in the Griffith Institute for Tourism, Griffith Business School, Griffith University, Southport, Australia. Email: b.moyle@griffith.edu.au

**Anja Pabel**, Lecturer in the School of Business and Law, Central Queensland University, Cairns, Australia. Email: a.pabel@cqu.edu.au

**Jan Packer**, Associate Professor and Principal Research Fellow – Tourism in UQ Business School, The University of Queensland, Brisbane, Australia. Email: j.packer@uq.edu.au

**Robert Saunders**, PhD Graduate of the Department of Management, Monash University, Caulfield, Australia. Email: srednuas@hotmail.com

**Cornelia Voigt**, Adjunct Research Fellow in Curtin Business School, Curtin University, Perth, Australia. Email: Cornelia.Voigt@curtin.edu.au

**Betty Weiler**, Professor and Director of Research, School of Business and Tourism, Southern Cross University, Coolangatta, Australia. Email: betty.weiler@scu.edu.au

# Foreword

Waiting in line to enter a new country or continent is a familiar experience for international travellers. Provided the right visas have been obtained and the background checks enacted by the gatekeeper reveal no nasty surprises, entry is usually straightforward. Then the pleasures of the visit begin. One can conceptualise positive tourism as an aspiring traveller, waiting to be accepted into the country of legitimate inquiry. Older relatives, such as tourist behaviour and sustainable tourism, have been given access a long time ago. They are now flourishing in the landscape of legitimate inquiry. But there are rumours that some other relatives, such as hopeful tourism and slow tourism, have been denied immediate access and are still waiting their turn.

Let us examine the case for the acceptance of positive tourism into the country of legitimate inquiry. Initially, a doubt, a possible confusion of identity, needs to be considered. Positive tourism does have a near namesake, positivism, whose style might raise alarm bells in the scrutiny for contemporary legitimacy. Positivism in tourism is an explicit and strong-minded adherence to an etic research approach. It is buttressed by a realistic ontology with an epistemology that demands a tight adherence to measured facts. It can be found cohabiting with tourism economics. This is not the heritage nor the growth path of the younger positive tourism. Instead, positive tourism, which is fundamentally about seeking to understand human well-being in the context of tourism and travel, has a highly prestigious family background.

In the last 15 years, positive psychology with an explicit emphasis on human flourishing has been developed as a solid and well-respected augmentation to long-standing psychology interests in ameliorating individual problems, deficits and difficulties. The research prowess, prestige and influence of the personnel in psychology, all of whom stressed these interests in building greater human happiness and subjective well-being, ensured the rapid international acceptance of positive psychology. Not insignificantly, for the task of establishing the legitimacy of positive tourism, Mihaly Csikszentmihalyi, one of the editors of this volume, is one of these prestigious psychologists.

The alignment of the research concepts and approaches in positive psychology to tourism has now been underway for a decade. The study topics of interest include the fulfilment of complex motivational patterns, the acquisition of skills, the positive emotional states, the durability of the health benefits of travel and the enduring value of tourism-derived memories. These individual concerns are united by the thread exploring the essential question: does tourism improve the life experience of those who travel? The themes of interest for positive tourism are accompanied by concepts and theories which underpin the new interests: mindfulness, flow, acts of kindness, humour, optimism, savouring and the broaden-and-build theory of emotions are examples. Both traditional and new tools to explore positive life-enhancing tourist experiences are appealing credentials in the application to be fully integrated into tourism research efforts. As the volume demonstrates, there are also recent research initiatives that explore positive psychology concepts with host communities and workers in tourism, which extend positive tourism beyond the study of individual tourist experience.

For this researcher, the case is clear. Positive tourism should be welcomed into the land of legitimate inquiry in the tourism field so that it can flourish while studying the very process of human flourishing.

Philip L. Pearce
Foundation Professor of Tourism
James Cook University, Australia.

# Acknowledgements

There are some people who have graced us with their kind assistance and without whom this volume would have been much harder to bring to completion. We are especially appreciative of help provided by Crystal Victoria Filep. Crystal has provided us with the following technical support: detailed corrections of grammar, spelling and English-language expression throughout the volume, reference checks (in-text citation checks, reference list corrections) and general formatting, as per *Routledge* guidelines. She has been instrumental in finalising the book project successfully. For their encouragement of this edited book initiative, we would also like to thank friends and colleagues at the Department of Tourism (University of Otago), the Department of Management and Marketing (La Trobe University) and the Quality of Life Research Centre (Claremont Graduate University).

Special thanks go to Professor Philip Pearce for his assistance with the review process and for his complimentary and well-crafted foreword. We are grateful for his words of encouragement of the positive tourism idea. Finally, the support of our immediate families has been critical to the completion of the project. We thank them for their patience and understanding.

# Part I

# Positive tourism

# 1   What is positive tourism? Why do we need it?

*Sebastian Filep, Jennifer Laing and Mihaly Csikszentmihalyi*

## Introduction

While acknowledging that not all influential and meaningful tourism knowledge is academic and scientific in nature (Liburd, 2012), the academic study of tourism has now arguably reached a level of maturity that is rich, diverse and highly useful to various stakeholders and in multiple ways at a global level. Academic tourism knowledge spans several decades of sustained empirical inquiry. This period of sustained tourism scholarship started during the Second World War and is now present in over 270 tourism and related academic journals. We seem to be living in an era of reflecting back on what we have produced in tourism studies and where the academic field may be heading in the future. Lai, Li and Scott (2015) have established that there has been a sustained focus over recent years on rethinking various forms of tourism knowledge (e.g. Xiao, Jafari, Cloke & Tribe, 2013; Xiao & Smith, 2006), but especially production of tourism knowledge (e.g. Franklin & Crang, 2001; Hall, 2004; Platenkamp & Botterill, 2013) and its subsequent consumption (e.g. Xiao & Smith, 2007). The production of tourism knowledge, it is argued, is important, as it naturally precedes the knowledge itself and its subsequent consumption. Among other factors, Lai *et al.* (2015) point to three important issues which have been found to influence the knowledge production process. These include the paradigm commitment (Hall, 2004; Platenkamp & Botterill, 2013), research methodology and methods (e.g. Ritchie, Burns & Palmer, 2005) and the disciplinary background of researchers involved in knowledge production (e.g. Tribe, 2004).

In this introductory chapter, we attempt to define what we mean by positive tourism. Following the work of Lai *et al.* (2015) on knowledge production factors, we start by first outlining our overarching philosophical and disciplinary paradigm. We then explain positive tourism's research methodology and introduce authors of this volume, noting their disciplinary and research backgrounds. While we recognise that our definition of positive tourism will be further shaped in the future, these factors allow us to come up with a broad and a basic definition for now. Following our explanation of what positive tourism is, we present an academic argument for the birth of positive tourism as a sub-field of tourism inquiry within which positive tourism topics and issues can be further explored.

The chapter concludes with a listing of key pillars which make up positive tourism and which align with the three broad sections of this book.

## What is positive tourism?

### *Defining our paradigm: humanism, humanistic and positive psychology*

The definition of what is 'positive' as opposed to what is 'negative' in human existence can be best understood by first explaining what is meant by humanism, an underlying philosophy which underpins this book. Most accounts have humanism beginning in fourteenth- and fifteenth-century Italy as a revolt against the scholasticism and authoritarianism of the medieval church. Arguably, one of the earliest proponents of humanism was Francesco Petrarca, known as Petrarch (1304–1374), who spearheaded a renewed interest in classics leading up to the rise of a special type of humanism, the Renaissance humanism. Others followed in Petrarch's footsteps – namely, Desiderius Erasmus, a Dutch humanist. Bullock (1985) has provided a precise explanation for what distinguishes humanism from other philosophical standpoints. The first is that human experience must itself be primary, and other realities can only be considered through this lens of human consciousness. The second characteristic of humanism is the value it places on the individual and respect for the freedom and dignity of the person, which it takes to provide a foundation for all other values and rights (Bullock, 1985). The third characteristic of humanism is an emphasis on ideas, reasoning and the plurality of perspectives through which the human spirit can be expressed. Viewing religion, science and art as fundamentally symbolic practices which embody the human hunger for meaning, humanists have typically accepted that there are many ways to the truth (Davidson, 2000).

These basic tenets of humanism have strongly influenced the development of psychology in the mid- to late-twentieth century – namely, humanistic psychology and later on positive psychology (Froh, 2004), which provide a theoretical foundation for the development of positive tourism. Rogers, Maslow, Murray, Allport and May are often considered key figures in humanistic psychology (Duckworth, Steen & Seligman, 2005). Humanistic psychologists have largely dealt with the questions of the good life, individual growth and achievements, authenticity and personal responsibility, suggesting explanations for the term 'positive'. Maslow's (1954) work on human needs, self-actualisation and fulfilment is especially seminal in the foundations of positive psychology, as Maslow himself introduced the term positive psychology to his readers. Building on the humanistic psychology foundations, theories specific to positive psychology have emerged in the new millennium: the broaden-and-build theory of positive emotions (Fredrickson, 2001), new theoretical models of human flourishing (Seligman, 2011), continuous innovation in the studies of optimal experiences or 'flow' (Csikszentmihalyi & Csikszentmihalyi, 2006), fresh perspectives on kindness and gratitude (Emmons & Crumpler, 2000), work on character strengths and virtues (Peterson, 2006) and many others. The aforementioned works are just a few examples of key literature in humanistic and positive psychology.

Positive psychology has been defined as 'the study of the conditions and processes that contribute to the flourishing or optimal functioning of people, groups and institutions' (Gable & Haidt, 2005, p. 103), or simply as the study of what makes life worth living (Seligman & Csikszentmihalyi, 2000). The history of the field has been introduced in detail to the tourism reader by Pearce, Filep and Ross (2011), and so the purpose here is not to re-introduce positive psychology. Briefly, however, philosophical roots of positive psychology can be traced back all the way to Ancient Greek philosophy, such as the writings of Aristotle on happiness and the good life. Central to these early roots is the concept of eudaimonia (*daimon* meaning 'the true self'). Eudaimonia has been defined as a higher state of flourishing that is shaped through self-development and self-realisation of the individual (Ryff & Singer, 1996). A core feature of eudaimonia is a humanist idea of striving toward excellence based on one's unique potential (Ryff & Singer, 1996) but positive psychology literature equally includes a significant body of knowledge on hedonic experiences (Fredrickson, 2001). Critiques of positive psychology in tourism studies have also emerged (Nawijn, 2016), and some of this criticism will be briefly addressed in the concluding chapter of this volume, while a more specific response to the criticism has also been produced (Filep, 2016). The ideas from positive psychology have multidisciplinary appeal and have been introduced in aligned fields to tourism, such as leisure (Freire, 2013) and recently event studies (Filep, Volic & Lee, 2015). Overall, it is clear that to understand what positive tourism means is to understand humanist philosophy as well as humanistic and positive psychology and what they stand for.

Warmoth, Resnick and Serlin (2007), however, remind us that the very concept of 'positive' (in positive psychology or elsewhere) makes sense in the wider context of lived human experiences, as positive is what is desirable – the category that can be studied experientially. This raises some methodological challenges, as experiential understandings of the world are subjective and hence require less objective measurements. For this reason, we adopt a type of epistemological pluralism in defining positive tourism. This pluralism aligns with pragmatism as our underlying research methodology.

## *Pragmatist research methodology*

Pragmatism is a philosophy based on the reflections of the Kantean/Fichte/Dilthey philosophical thought of the 'projection of our minds' (Laughlin, 1995, p. 72). While pragmatists agree with positivists and post-positivists about the existence of an external world independent of people's minds, the emphasis is placed on selecting explanations that best produce desired outcomes (Pansiri, 2005). In terms of the mode of inquiry, this means that pragmatism embraces pluralism by including the extremes normally espoused by positivism as well as those supported by interpretivists. The former emphasises quantitative methods as opposed to interpretivists' qualitative approaches. Both are welcome and encouraged under the parameters of positive tourism and qualitative and quantitative contributions can be found in this volume. By welcoming both quantitative and qualitative contributions, the tourism work, therefore, has a less positivist flavour than some of the highly empirical work which characterises much of mainstream (positive) psychology (Mruk, 2008). Tourism studies in this field (Filep & Pearce, 2014) have been characterised by Ryan (2015, p. 195) as works where 'psychometrics are generally absent, meaning that readers are spared from a series of partial least squares, structural equation models, and the like'. In this way, the tourism work on positive psychology avoids *methodolotry*, the idea of privileging qualitative over quantitative, and vice versa (Friedman, 2003). Multi-method assessments of happiness, well-being, human flourishing and satisfying life are all of interest to scholars in this field (Filep & Pearce, 2014) and well represent positive tourism.

### Positive tourism research community

Following Lai *et al.* (2015) on knowledge production factors, another core defining factor of positive tourism is the background of its researchers, primarily with disciplinary training and/or research interests in tourism, leisure, sport, recreation and positive, health and sport psychology. Researchers' backgrounds shape the definition of positive tourism as the researchers' own subjectivities and experiences and professional upbringings affect who they are and how they think and reason. The following is therefore a list of biographies of our authors, with reference to their professional backgrounds and affiliations.

Deborah Che, PhD, is Lecturer in the School of Business and Tourism at Southern Cross University, Australia. Her research interests include rural development, natural resource-based tourism (i.e. agritourism, ecotourism, hunting) development and marketing, cultural/heritage tourism and arts-based economic diversification strategies. A common theme in her research involves the interconnection between economic restructuring and shifting land uses. She has published in journals, including *Tourism Recreation Research, Tourism Geographies, Journal of Heritage Tourism, Tourism Review International, Geoforum, The Annals of the Association of American Geographers, The Professional Geographer* and *Agriculture and Human Values*. She is on the editorial board of *Tourism Geographies*.

John Coffey, PhD, MSW, is Assistant Professor at Sewanee: The University of the South, Tennessee, USA. He is the second person to earn a PhD in Positive Developmental Psychology. He earned his PhD at Claremont Graduate University and his MSW at the University of Michigan. He served on the board of the International Positive Psychology Association as the President of the Student Division. He has authored numerous research articles and presented internationally on ways to promote well-being while vacationing, in close relationships and in workplace and academic settings. John has consulted with a range of organizations and companies, such as Potentia and Happify, seeking to promote happiness and flourishing. In his spare time, he enjoys travelling to places near and far from home.

Mihaly Csikszentmihalyi, PhD, is Distinguished Professor of Psychology and Management and Founding Co-Director of the Quality of Life Research Center,

Claremont Graduate University, USA. He is noted for his work on happiness, but is best known as the architect of the notion of *flow*.

Jessica de Bloom, PhD, is a work and organizational psychologist and is employed as a research fellow at the Institute for Advanced Social Research at the University of Tampere, Finland. Her field of expertise concerns longitudinal, empirical research on stress, recovery and the effects of vacations on employee health, well-being and work performance. She serves on the editorial board of the *Scandinavian Journal of Work and Organizational Psychology*.

Sebastian Filep, PhD, is Senior Lecturer at the Tourism Department, University of Otago, New Zealand. He specialises in tourism and well-being research. He has published internationally in peer-reviewed academic journals and books on the topic of human well-being.

Warwick Frost, PhD, is Associate Professor in the Department of Management and Marketing at La Trobe University, Australia. His research interests include heritage, events, nature-based attractions and the interaction between media, popular culture and tourism. Warwick is a co-editor of the Routledge Advances in Events Research series and a member of the editorial board of *Journal of Heritage Tourism*. He has co-written five books, including *Commemorative Events: Memory, Identities, Conflict* (2013), *Imagining the American West through Film and Tourism* (2015) and *Gastronomy, Tourism and the Media* (forthcoming). Warwick has also edited *Tourism and Zoos: Conservation, Education, Entertainment?* (2011) and co-edited four books, including *National Parks and Tourism: International Perspectives on Development, Histories and Change* (2009) and *Rituals and Traditional Events in the Modern World* (2015).

Sabine Geurts, PhD, is a full professor of work and organizational psychology at the Behavioural Science Institute at Radboud University Nijmegen, the Netherlands. She is a Senior Researcher and Lecturer in occupational health psychology. Her scientific interests include work stress, recovery, sleep, working time arrangements and work-life balance. Geurts has published around 100 papers and book chapters in these areas, and she serves as a Consulting Editor for the journal *Work & Stress*. She is also head of the master's degree programme of Psychology of Work, Organization and Health.

Chelsea Gill is a research assistant and tutor at the University of Queensland Business School (Tourism Cluster), Australia. She is currently completing her PhD, which explores the restorative benefits of corporate retreats. Her research interests include restoration within the context of vacations, workplaces and religious organisations.

Troy D. Glover, PhD, is Director of the Healthy Communities Research Network, Professor in the Department of Recreation and Leisure Studies at the University of Waterloo, Canada, and a Fellow in the Academy of Leisure Sciences. His research explores the role(s) of leisure in advancing or deterring the realization of healthy communities. Accordingly, his research shifts the emphasis in leisure away from well-being derived through satisfaction and pleasure-seeking toward well-being derived through the development of social capital, community building and transformative place-making. His research favours a social ethic whereby community members are knowers of their own lived experiences with capabilities and entitlements to forward their own visions of a healthy community. Thus, Dr Glover's research is also aimed at engaging community members directly in dialogue to envision their aspirations for the future of their community.

Peita Hillman has been Lecturer in tourism at the International College of Management in Sydney since 2007. Peita is currently completing her master's by research in the School of Business and Tourism at Southern Cross University, Australia. Peita's research focuses on tourism and quality of life, with a particular focus on the well-being of local tourism industry employees.

Susan Houge Mackenzie, PhD, is Assistant Professor in Recreation, Parks and Tourism Administration at California Polytechnic State University, USA. She studies psychological aspects of adventure across tourism, recreation and education settings within positive psychology frameworks. Her research broadly focuses on how engaging in outdoor adventure enhances well-being. These interests are grounded in long-term experiences as a white-water guide and competitive sportsperson across four continents. Dr Houge Mackenzie's research has been applied across diverse domains, including sport psychology workshops, US Forest Service projects, risk management consulting in New Zealand and South America, and documentary films.

John Kerr, PhD, is Adjunct Professor of Sport and Exercise Psychology with the School of Kinesiology at the University of British Columbia, Canada. Previously, he held university positions in the United Kingdom, the Netherlands and Japan. He has published widely in psychology and sport and exercise psychology journals and is author, co-author or editor of ten psychology books, including *Violence in Rugby* (2012), *Rethinking Aggression and Violence in Sport* (2005), *Counselling Athletes: Applying Reversal Theory* (2001), *Experiencing Sport: Reversal Theory* (1999), *Motivation and Emotion in Sport* (1997) and *Understanding Soccer Hooliganism* (1994). He is a former high-level rugby player and coach.

Jennifer Laing, PhD, is Associate Professor in Management in the Department of Management and Marketing, La Trobe University, Australia. Her research interests include extraordinary tourist experiences, the role of events in society, travel narratives and wellness tourism. She has co-written five and edited two books on tourism and/or events.

Martin Lohmann, PhD, is Professor of Consumer Behaviour and Tourism Psychology at the Leuphana University of Lüneburg, Germany, Institute of Experimental Industrial Psychology – Lünelab – and Director of the NIT, Institute for Tourism and Recreational Research in Northern Europe, Kiel, Germany. He also teaches in the MBA Tourism Management programme at MODUL University, Vienna, Austria. The focus of Lohmann's work is on consumer behaviour in tourism and market research.

Xavier Matteucci, PhD, is a research associate in the Department of Tourism and Service Management at MODUL University Vienna, Austria. Xavier holds an MSc from the University of Surrey and a PhD from the Vienna University of Economics and Business. His research interests are primarily focused around tourism experiences, cultural tourism, quality of life and qualitative research methodologies. Xavier's recent work on tourists' experiences of flamenco has been published in *Annals of Tourism Research, Tourism Management* and *Leisure Studies*. His current research projects are related to the application of visual research methodologies in tourism.

Brent D. Moyle, PhD, currently works as a research fellow in the Griffith Institute for Tourism at Griffith University, Australia. Brent's research concentrates primarily on visitor management in natural and protected areas and the sustainable development of tourism destinations. Brent takes pride in his research being at the interface between theory and practice; he takes an interdisciplinary approach that applies a range of qualitative and quantitative methodologies. The outcomes of Brent's research have been published in over 20 international tourism research journals as well as book chapters, conference papers and reports to industry partners.

Anja Pabel, PhD, is Lecturer in tourism at Central Queensland University in Cairns, Australia. She holds a PhD in tourism from James Cook University, Australia. Her doctoral research investigated the role of humour in tourism settings. More specifically, she examined the ways in which humour influences the tourist experience in making tourists feel comfortable, connected and more mindful. These findings were considered from the perspective of positive psychology where humour itself is regarded as a character strength which contributes to people's well-being and happiness. Her main research interests are tourist behaviour, humour research and marine tourism.

Jan Packer, PhD, is a research fellow at the University of Queensland Business School, Australia. Her research focuses on applying principles from educational, environmental and positive psychology to understand and improve visitor experiences at natural and cultural tourism attractions such as museums, zoos and aquariums, botanic gardens, national parks, ecotourism and wildlife tourism attractions. She has a special interest in the quality-of-life outcomes of museum visits, and tourism and leisure more broadly.

Philip L. Pearce, PhD, is Foundation Professor of Tourism at James Cook University, Australia. He has published a number of books in tourism, including two sole author works on tourist behaviour in 2005 and 2011. He was the founding editor of *The Journal of Tourism Studies* (1990–2005). He is a frequent keynote speaker at tourism conferences, particularly in Asia. His special interest areas are tourist behaviour, notably tourist motivation and experience, tourism and communities, and tourism education and research.

Robert Saunders, PhD, is a researcher and consultant with more than 30 years' experience in park, wildlife and heritage management. He has particular interest in planning, communication and visitor experience, including their implications for both environmental protection and personal well-being. His 2014 PhD dissertation ('Steps Towards Change: Personal Transformation through Long-Distance Walking', Monash University) focused on the effects of long-distance walking on midlife adults. It identified attitudinal and behavioural change processes leading to the enhancement of well-being, as well as the emergence of pro-conservation and socially beneficial behaviours among participants.

Cornelia Voigt, PhD, is an adjunct research fellow at Curtin University, Perth, Australia. Her PhD thesis on wellness tourism was awarded the Sustainable Tourism CRC Sir Frank Moore Award for Excellence, an annual, national award acknowledging the best tourism thesis written each year. She co-edited the book *Wellness Tourism: A Destination Perspective* and has published a number of articles and book chapters in the field of wellness tourism. Her expertise in wellness tourism has led to the acquisition of competitive research grants and invited speeches at international conferences.

Betty Weiler, PhD, is a research professor in the School of Business and Tourism at Southern Cross University, Australia. Her 150 publications in international tourism research journals and other outlets have centred on the tourist experience, including the role of the tour guide and heritage and nature interpretation. Betty is known for her collaboration with and contribution to the management of protected areas, zoos and heritage attractions. More recently, her work has focused on managing visitors and influencing their on-site and post-visit behaviour.

Unfortunately, and for various reasons, not all scholars who may identify with positive tourism are found in this volume. The group of authors in this book, however, represent some of the key researchers in this field; nevertheless, we also recognise that not all of the contributors would explicitly label themselves as positive tourism academics.

In summary then, positive tourism is, broadly, a study of hedonic and eudaimonic human well-being and conditions (or various circumstances) for flourishing as they relate to individual tourists, members of host communities and tourism workers in diverse sectors of the tourism industry. Examples of the conditions for flourishing are types, or forms, of highly fulfilling tourist experiences (e.g. characteristics of meaningful tourist experiences); the nature of relationships between hosts and tourists (e.g. acts of kindness that build greater well-being); or the style of interactions between tourism workers and tourists (e.g. the role of co-creation of experiences for greater well-being). Positive tourism is a humanist-inspired study, principally grounded in theories, models and perspectives from psychology, especially positive psychology. Positive tourism knowledge is created through a diversity of approaches incorporating both quantitative and qualitative research methods, depending on research questions and research needs, which bridge strict divisions between positivism and interpretivism. Its research community members, due to their professional backgrounds, further situate positive tourism within the realm of tourism as a sub-set of leisure and the discipline of psychology.

## Why do we need positive tourism?

Broadly defining positive tourism is only one of the objectives of this chapter. A secondary, albeit no less important objective, is to briefly rationalise the value of positive tourism in the context of overall tourism scholarship. Over the years, tourism scholars have suggested that the field has matured enough to develop into some clearly delineated viewpoints or perspectives. These have been labelled tourism knowledge platforms. The platforms have been extensively outlined and discussed by scholars such as Jafari (2005) and Tribe (2008). Two bodies of tourism knowledge have especially been prominent: the *business* or the *advocacy* knowledge platform (Jafari, 2005) and the *cautionary*, social science knowledge platform (Jafari, 2005; Tribe, 2010). Tribe and Liburd (2016) recently presented a reconceptualised tourism knowledge system, surpassing the dichotomy between business and social science; however, they retain the belief that 'the business and social science of tourism dominate our knowledge production' (p. 58).

The first platform generally stresses the economic value of tourism development and the management practices and techniques that can most effectively be used to achieve this (Jafari, 2005). Much of the marketing, economics, management and related business literature on tourism would broadly fall under this umbrella. It reflects in part the historical evolution of many tourism studies programs, which are based within business schools or management or marketing departments and form part of business degrees (Morgan, 2004; Walle, 1997).

The second platform is typically championed by social scientists, especially, albeit not exclusively, sociologists, human geographers and anthropologists, for which 'a critical and analytical approach to the boosterism of a popular imagery has been paramount' (Pearce, 2009, p. 111). Within this platform, insightful and valuable research has emerged; however, negative, often dystopian views of tourists and tourism development are common. Tourism has been described as a

> spectre ... haunting our planet ... [that] ... can ruin landscapes, destroy communities, pollute the air and water, trivialise cultures, bring about uniformity and generally contribute to the continuing degradation of life on our planet.
>
> (Croall, 1995, p. 1)

In a similar vein, Poon (1993, p. 3) claimed that 'the tourism industry is in crisis ... a crisis of mass tourism; for it is mass tourism that has brought social, cultural, economic and environmental havoc in its wake'. While Poon acknowledged some benefits of tourism, these are limited to economic advantages such as 'foreign exchange, employment and incomes' (p. 290). The ultimate conclusion to these doomsday arguments is that 'tourism is toxic' (Pezzullo, 2007), in that 'tourism contaminates the people and the places where it occurs. Tourism corrodes. Tourism offends. Tourism exploits. In a sense, some might even conclude, tourism kills' (p. 2). More recently, Higgins-Desbiolles and Whyte (2013) have linked tourism to power imbalances and call for greater attention to 'tourism's role in supporting market hegemony – the force that is most destructive and oppressive' (2013, p. 431). They advocate a critical approach to tourism research in order to investigate 'global injustice and inequity' (p. 431).

Sharpley (2013) explains that the rhetoric employed in these commentaries has often been one in which tourism is *anthropomorphised* through arguments that tourism ultimately leads to 'bad' outcomes. Pezzullo (2007, p. 3) makes the same point, arguing that dislike of tourists 'is really a way to express a dislike for ourselves, our culture, and who we have become'. This has led both academics and journalists 'to engage in what might be referred to euphemistically as "tourism bashing", to give prominence to tourism as a destructive rather than constructive force' (Sharpley, 2013, p. 351). It is not a phenomenon limited to the tourism sphere. Dystopian views also dominate academic research on the modern city (Judd, 2005; Pow, 2015).

This is not to argue that tourism is a panacea for global ills. We fully agree with Sharpley that it 'would be naive, foolish or both to attempt to argue that the development of tourism – and, indeed, the behaviour of tourists – has not had negative consequences' (2013, p. 350). We also agree with Macbeth's (2013) view that it is important to explore tourism from two further platforms – sustainability and ethics. Research documenting such consequences is valuable and will undoubtedly continue into the future. Nevertheless, the potential of the human race to create better futures for itself and for others needs to be taken further into account. In response to the pessimism of the cautionary platform, its negativity, doom and gloom, we see scope for the development of positive tourism research grounded in positive psychology. The negative views often do not take into account the agency of human beings and their full potential (Croall, 1995; Higgins-Desbiolles & Whyte, 2013; Poon, 1993). A more nuanced and balanced debate should be encouraged (Pow, 2015), involving a diversity of approaches and perspectives (Bramwell & Lane, 2014; Sharpley, 2013).

Croall (1995), while outlining the problems inherent in encouraging tourism, provides a personal vignette that illustrates the potential that positive psychology may hold in helping us to unravel and understand some of the outcomes of tourism. His prose highlights the way in which travel can generate positive emotions and bring meaning and enrichment to our lives:

> The pace is about right: fast enough to let me relish the warm wind streaming against my face, slow enough to catch glimpses of the gorgeous green Devon countryside through gaps in the hedgerows. This, I decide, is the only way to travel. My hired mountain bike, yellow and mauve and bursting with gears, gives me a wonderful freedom to roam around this exquisite part of rural Devon. At one moment I'm riding smoothly along virtually empty country lanes around the village of Eggesford; the next I'm pedalling over the rugged paths of Flashdown Wood, matted with bluebells, and still steaming gently in the aftermath of the rain that fell earlier on this late spring morning. But my pleasure is not due simply to the delights of nature. In the village of Wembworthy I stop at a delightful small stone church set back from the roadside.

We side with Pritchard, Morgan and Ateljevic (2011) in arguing that a values-led humanist paradigm thinking in tourism is necessary. We believe that tourism inquiry must 'also include the anticipatory-utopian' unless we are to 'turn forever on the treadmills of somebody else's present' (Gregory, 2009, p. 285). This is not a new idea. As far back as 1986, Krippendorf argued for a vision of tourism as 'a true discovery, a place of experiences and learning, a means of human enrichment, a stimulus for a better reality and a better society. That is the utopian and idealistic framework on which one should build' (p. 530). Yet little has been done in the interim to heed his call. So there is much space for further development of humanist-inspired thinking and research agendas that will complement and, in some cases, challenge the dystopian scholarship in tourism. Within this development, there is an opportunity for psychology, as one of tourism's foundation disciplines, to play a greater role in helping us fulfil these goals.

## Conclusion

Clearly, multiple knowledge platforms have thus far emerged in tourism studies; however, one important knowledge platform is not yet sufficiently developed. We need a positive, humanist-inspired body of knowledge that explains what enables host communities to flourish, what encourages workers in tourism to thrive and what characterises optimal visitor experiences. The aim of building this knowledge platform is to establish conditions for human flourishing in tourism contexts and, ultimately, outline strategies for building greater human well-being. In this way, this new volume on *positive tourism*, principally grounded in theories from positive psychology (the study of what makes life worth living), serves as a way to introduce this new platform. The volume is divided into three areas of academic inquiry: positive tourist experiences, positive host communities and positive tourism workers – all separate pillars of positive tourism.

Readers will notice a heavy focus in the volume on a discussion of original research studies conducted by chapter authors. We have asked contributors to report on new research investigations to showcase their research in the field under the three positive tourism pillars. The book contains 13 contributions, mostly reporting on empirical studies conducted in different geographical regions of the world. The research-intensive feature of this edited volume follows the style of an earlier book on fulfilling tourist experiences through the lens of positive psychology (Filep & Pearce, 2014) and demonstrates the collective drive and enthusiasm by our research community to further advance positive tourism ideas.

## References

Bramwell, B., & Lane, B. (2014). The 'critical turn' and its implications for sustainable tourism research. *Journal of Sustainable Tourism*, 22(1), 1–8.
Bullock, A. (1985). *The humanist tradition in the West*. London: Thames and Hudson.
Croall, J. (1995). *Preserve or destroy: Tourism and the environment*. London: Calouste Gulbenkian Foundation.
Csikszentmihalyi, M., & Csikszentmihalyi, I. (Eds.). (2006). *A life worth living: Contributions to positive psychology*. New York: Oxford University Press.
Davidson, L. (2000). Philosophical foundations of humanistic psychology. *The Humanistic Psychologist*, 28(1–3), 7–31.
Duckworth, L., Steen, T., & Seligman, M. (2005). Positive psychology for clinical practice. *Annual Review of Clinical Psychology*, 1, 629–651.

Emmons, R., & Crumpler, C. (2000). Gratitude as human strength: Appraising the evidence. *Journal of Social and Clinical Psychology*, 19, 56–69.

Filep, S. (2016). Tourism and positive psychology critique: Too emotional? *Annals of Tourism Research*, 59, 113–115.

Filep, S., & Pearce, P. L. (Eds.). (2014). *Tourist experience and fulfilment: Insights from positive psychology*. New York: Routledge.

Filep, S., Volic, I., & Lee, I. (2015). On positive psychology of events. *Event Management*, 19, 495–507.

Franklin, A., & Crang, M. (2001). The trouble with tourism and travel theory? *Tourist Studies*, 1(1), 5–22.

Fredrickson, B. L. (2001). The role of positive emotions in positive psychology: The broaden-and-build theory of positive emotions. *American Psychologist*, 56(3), 218–226.

Freire, T. (Ed.). (2013). *Positive leisure science: From subjective experience to social contexts*. New York: Springer.

Friedman, H. (2003). Methodolotry and graphicacy. *American Psychologist*, 58, 817–818.

Froh, J. (2004, May/June). The history of positive psychology: Truth be told. *NYS Psychologist*, 16(3), 18–20.

Gable, S., & Haidt, J. (2005). What (and why) is positive psychology? *Review of General Psychology*, 9(2), 103–110.

Gregory, D. (2009). Geographical imagination. In D. Gregory, R. Johnston, G. Pratt, M. Watts & S. Whatmore (Eds.), *The dictionary of human geography* (5th ed.) (p. 285). Oxford: Wiley-Blackwell.

Hall, C. (2004). Reflexivity and tourism research. In J. Phillimore & L. Goodson (Eds.), *Qualitative research in tourism: Ontologies, epistemologies and methodologies* (pp. 137–155). London: Routledge.

Higgins-Desbiolles, F., & Whyte, K. (2013). No high hopes for hopeful tourism: A critical comment. *Annals of Tourism Research*, 40, 428–433.

Jafari, J. (2005). Bridging out, nesting afield: Powering a new platform. *Journal of Tourism Studies*, 16(2), 1–5.

Judd, D. (2005). Everything is always going to hell: Urban scholars as end-time prophets. *Urban Affairs Review*, 41(2), 119–131.

Krippendorf, J. (1986). Tourism in the system of industrial society. *Annals of Tourism Research*, 13(4), 393–414.

Lai, K., Li, J., & Scott, N. (2015). Tourism problemology: Reflexivity of knowledge making. *Annals of Tourism Research*, 51, 17–33.

Laughlin, R. (1995). Methodological themes: Empirical research in accounting alternative approaches and a case for 'middle-range' thinking. *Accounting, Auditing and Accountability Journal*, 8(1), 63–87.

Liburd, J. (2012). Tourism research 2.0. *Annals of Tourism Research*, 39(2), 883–907.

Macbeth, J. (2013). Tourism: The good, the bad and the sinner? *Tourism Recreation Research*, 38(3), 359–361.

Maslow, A. (1954). *Motivation and personality*. New York: Harper & Row Publishers.

Morgan, M. (2004). From production line to drama school: Higher education for the future of tourism. *International Journal of Contemporary Hospitality Management*, 16(2), 91–99.

Mruk, C. (2008). The psychology of self-esteem: A potential common ground for humanistic positive psychology and positivistic positive psychology. *Humanist Psychologist*, 36, 143–158.

Nawijn, J. (2016). Positive psychology in tourism: A critique. *Annals of Tourism Research,* 56, 151–153.

Pansiri, J. (2005). Pragmatism: A methodological approach to researching strategic alliances in tourism. *Tourism and Hospitality: Planning & Development,* 2(3), 191–206.

Pearce, P. (2009). Tourism research and the tropics: Further horizons. *Tourism Recreation Research,* 34(2), 107–121.

Pearce, P., Filep, S., & Ross, G. (2011). *Tourists, tourism and the good life.* New York: Routledge.

Peterson, C. (2006). *A primer in positive psychology.* Oxford: Oxford University Press.

Pezzullo, P. C. (2007). *Toxic tourism: Rhetorics of pollution, travel and environmental justice.* Tuscaloosa: University of Alabama Press.

Platenkamp, V., & Botterill, D. (2013). Critical realism, rationality and tourism knowledge. *Annals of Tourism Research,* 41, 110–129.

Poon, A. (1993). *Tourism, technology and competitive strategies.* Wallingford, UK: CABI.

Pow, C. P. (2015). Urban dystopia and epistemologies of hope. *Progress in Human Geography,* 39(4), 464–485.

Pritchard, A., Morgan, N., & Ateljevic, I. (2011). Hopeful tourism: A new transformative perspective. *Annals of Tourism Research,* 38(3), 941–963.

Ritchie, B. W., Burns, P. M., & Palmer, C. A. (Eds.). (2005). *Tourism research methods: Integrating theory with practice.* Wallingford, UK: CABI.

Ryan, C. (2015). Tourist experience and fulfilment: Insights from positive psychology: Book review. *Annals of Tourism Research,* 52, 195–196.

Ryff, C. D., & Singer, B. (1996). Psychological well-being: Meaning, measurement, and implications for psychotherapy research. *Psychotherapy and Psychosomatics,* 65(1), 14–23.

Seligman, M. E. (2011). *Flourish.* Sydney: Random House.

Seligman, M. E., & Csikszentmihalyi, M. (2000). Positive psychology: An introduction. *American Psychologist,* 55(1), 5–14.

Sharpley, R. (2013). In defence of tourism. *Tourism Recreation Research,* 38, 350–355.

Tribe, J. (2004). Knowing about tourism: Epistemological issues. In J. Phillimore & L. Goodson (Eds.), *Qualitative research in tourism* (pp. 46–62). London: Routledge.

Tribe, J. (2008). Tourism: A critical business. *Journal of Travel Research,* 46, 245–255.

Tribe, J. (2010). Tribes, territories and networks in the tourism academy. *Annals of Tourism Research,* 37(1), 7–33.

Tribe, J., & Liburd, J. (2016). The tourism knowledge system. *Annals of Tourism Research,* 57, 44–61.

Walle, A. (1997). Graduate education and research. *Annals of Tourism Research,* 24(3), 754–756.

Warmoth, A., Resnick, S., & Serlin, I. (2007). *Contributions of Humanistic Psychology to Positive Psychology.* Retrieved 3 April 2016 from State University of West Georgia: http://www.westga.edu/~psydept/os2/papers/serlin2.html

Xiao, H., Jafari, J., Cloke, P., & Tribe, J. (2013). Annals: 40–40 vision. *Annals of Tourism Research,* 40, 352–385.

Xiao, H., & Smith, S. (2006). The making of tourism research: Insights from a social sciences journal. *Annals of Tourism Research,* 33(2), 499–507.

Xiao, H., & Smith, S. (2007). The use of tourism knowledge: Research propositions. *Annals of Tourism Research,* 34(2), 310–331.

# Part II
# Positive tourist experiences

# 2  Meaningful vacation experiences

*Jan Packer and Chelsea Gill*

## Introduction

The concept of meaning has been a central topic in the positive psychology literature and is often considered an important factor associated with well-being, life
satisfaction and positive affect. Research in this area has explored the structure
of meaning (its components or levels), sources of meaning (including both external life domains and inner dimensions of self), the process of meaning making
(meaning detection as well as meaning construction) and the relationship between
meaning and well-being (Delle Fave, Brdar, Wissing & Vella-Brodrick, 2013).
According to Delle Fave *et al.* (2013), meaning is central to eudaimonic well-
being, while life satisfaction is more closely aligned with hedonic well-being,
although there is some overlap between the two.

Various domains of life, including work, standard of living, family, interpersonal
relationships, health, personal growth, leisure, spirituality, society and community
are considered sources of meaning, which vary in importance across the lifespan
(Delle Fave *et al.*, 2013). Steger and his colleagues (Steger *et al.*, 2013) reviewed
a range of qualitative, quantitative and mixed-method studies that have sought to
identify common sources of meaning, i.e. 'the specific aspects and domains of life
that people say they find meaningful or say that they use as a resource from which
to draw meaning' (p. 530). They concluded that there was some level of consensus regarding the most common sources of meaning and cited those identified by
Emmons (2003): relationships/intimacy, achievements/work, religion/spirituality
and self-transcendence/generativity.

Using an auto-photography technique, Steger *et al.* (2013) extended the findings
of previous research and provided a more detailed and nuanced understanding of
the things that make life meaningful. They identified 15 categories (nature, hobby/
leisure, relationships, pets, possessions, everyday necessities, religion, values,
education, technology, organisations/organised activities, physical environment,
future aspirations, occupation/work and self) and a miscellaneous group.

Of the aforementioned categories, relationships were found to be the most common source of meaning, along with hobby/leisure, nature and education. Steger
*et al.* (2013) included travel in the hobby/leisure category. Other researchers have
argued, however, that leisure at home should be viewed as a separate quality-of-life

domain from leisure away from home, i.e. vacations. Leiper (2004), for example, outlined several ways, some positive and some negative, in which tourism differs from other forms of leisure as a source of satisfying experiences. Dolnicar, Yanamandram and Cliff (2012) were able to demonstrate that respondents' ranking of the contribution that vacations made to their quality of life was almost equal to that of leisure and recreational experiences.

### Vacations and travel as a source of meaning

Increasingly, vacation time is recognised as a quality-of-life experience through which people (in the industrialised West) often define their lives (Darity, 2008). Vacations offer opportunities for social interaction, personal growth and identity development (Richards, 1999). Vacations are believed to offer a level of freedom that is not attainable in everyday life, thus allowing participants to not only escape the demands of everyday life but also to construct an alternative world (Darity, 2008) and an alternative, temporary identity (Stein, 2011). Because the vacation experience is seen as separate and different from everyday life, vacationers are able to enact different, but personally meaningful, roles within a new context (Stein, 2011). Vacations also provide the time and space for people to reflect on their lives, thus allowing the meaning and benefits gained from travel to be transferred back into their everyday lives in the form of 'new relationships, changed perspectives and different desires' (Wilson & Harris, 2006, p. 169).

Harrison (2003) addressed the question of what makes travel meaningful, using tourists' photographs, videos, journals and souvenirs to prompt memories and discussion. She identified four themes underlying people's reasons for travel, which reflect the meaning they invest in the experience: opportunity for human connection and/or intimacy, expression of a personal aesthetic, a way to explore and understand 'home' and an aid to make sense of the world. Based on qualitative analyses of tourists' diary, interview and open-ended questionnaire responses at three different destinations, Andereck, Bricker, Kerstetter and Nickerson (2006) identified three dimensions of meaning underlying tourists' reports of their experiences: the social aspects (interaction with others, sharing the experience with others), the environmental aspects (being in beautiful places, appreciating local heritage) and activities within those environments (learning about other places and times, experiencing renewal and escape). Using a phenomenological approach, Little and Schmidt (2006) explored the subjective spiritual experience of travel, including an enhanced awareness of self and other, a sense of connection and an intense sensation (emotional and physical reaction). As in Andereck *et al.'s* (2006) study, experiencing nature, cultural diversity and leisure activities were among the factors that together led to a memorable and meaningful experience. Little and Schmidt (2006) concluded that even mundane tourism experiences can inspire, engage and elicit significant meaning.

In summary, vacations in general and travel in particular provide focused opportunities for people to encounter many of the things that make everyday life meaningful (for example, relationships with others, encounters with nature and recreational activities). They can also provide the time, space and motivation for reflection and personal growth.

## Meaning and memory

In investigating travel and/or vacations as a source of meaning, researchers have mostly relied on participants' memories of their vacation experiences. This retrospective approach raises a question regarding the extent of the overlap between memorable experiences and meaningful experiences. Recent research on memorable tourism experiences has identified meaningfulness (defined as 'a sense of great value or significance') as one of seven dimensions that contribute to a tourism experience that is likely to be positively recalled (Kim, Ritchie & McCormick, 2012, p. 15). On the other hand, memorability is also likely to contribute to meaningfulness, as people reflect on and construct meanings around the experiences they remember.

Packer and Ballantyne (in press) argue that the remembered experience is one of the valued outcomes or take-away benefits of a visitor experience. The activities, events and environments in which visitors engage provide the opportunity for an experience, which is then interpreted, narrated and transformed into a meaningful memory or a reportable story. The place of meaning making is paramount in the process of constructing a remembered experience, but at the same time, the ongoing construction or reconstruction of meaning is built on the remembered experience. Photographs play an interesting role here, as they allow the remembered experience to be anchored to a specific place and time.

## Tourists' photographs: the capture, construction and communication of meaning

Photography is an integral component of the vacation experience and is commonly used by tourists as a means to capture memories which can then be used to extend the boundaries of the trip by sharing experiences with others, creating self-narratives and promoting a self-image (Stylianou-Lambert, 2012). Cederholm (2004, p. 236) found travellers often mentioned trying to 'catch the moment' or 'freeze and frame the experience' so that it could be preserved in time, thus providing a kind of 'proof' of the experience. Further, it has been argued that the act of photography itself is a performance that can be used for impression management to experiment, to experiment with or reconstruct identities (Belk & Yeh, 2011; Lo & McKercher, 2015). Photographs can thus be taken, preserved and shared to represent a place, an experience, a memory or an idealised self.

Botterill and Crompton (1996) highlighted the value of photographs as a medium for understanding different aspects of tourism, as the pictorial content of the photograph provides a point of departure for participants to describe and attribute meaning to the situation. Harper (2002) further defined and discussed the use of photo-elicitation as a research method that evokes not only information but also feelings and memories. According to Harper (2002, p. 23), photographs appear to capture the impossible: a person gone; an event past. That extraordinary sense of seeming to retrieve something that has disappeared belongs alone to the photograph, and it leads to deep and interesting talk.

Steger et al. (2013) pioneered the use of photography as a research method to explore sources of meaning in life. They distinguished between two approaches: auto-photography asks participants to take photographs of things that are important to them and to provide descriptions of the photographs; photo-elicitation uses photographs (which may be provided by the researcher or the participant) to prompt responses during an interview. These photograph-based techniques have some advantages over other methods. For example, they are less reliant on participants' ability to verbalise what makes life meaningful; they draw on cues from participants' own lives to prompt their responses; they are less reliant on culturally stereotyped sources of meaning; they provide a more direct and immediate record of the phenomena of interest; and they can convey emotion (Steger *et al.*, 2013).

## Aims and method

This research used a photograph-based method to explore the aspects of a vacation that people find meaningful. Steger *et al.'s* (2013) 15 categories were used as an initial framework for analysis of participants' narratives. The results illustrate how these everyday sources of meaning help to enrich vacation experiences, identify a number of other sources of meaning that are particularly important in the context of vacations and explore the vacation as a source of meaning in itself.

### *Participants and procedure*

A total of 77 participants were recruited through various means (30 responded to an advertisement in a university-wide staff newsletter; 24 responded to an invitation distributed at two Brisbane Travel Expos; 17 participants of other research projects agreed to participate; 6 responded to social media requests).

Participants were asked to choose five photographs that best represented their most meaningful vacation experiences. The photographs may have been taken by the participants or by someone else and could be from any of their past vacations. Participants were asked to respond to a web survey in which they briefly described what was depicted in each photograph and explained why the images were meaningful to them. There was an (optional) opportunity to upload each photograph. Participants were given one month after recruitment to complete the task. This approach gave participants the space and time to reflect on their vacations and to thoughtfully describe why each photograph was meaningful.

As part of the web survey, participants were able to peruse two example responses which demonstrated the level of reflection and detail that was sought from the instruction 'Please explain why this photograph is meaningful to you'.

**Sagavanirktok River in Alaska**

Photograph and reflection by Magdalena Zych, used with permission

The photograph shows the Sagavanirktok River from the Atigun Gorge, in the arctic in Alaska. I reached this place by hitchhiking for around 400 km from Fairbanks and then hiking for around 6 days in the mountains.

It was the first destination on my two-months-long trip to remote places in the northern-most part of Alaska, to Kamchatka and central Siberia. When the photograph was taken I was just amazed by the view, the sheer beauty of a meandering river which does not have a single bed but bifurcates in sandy braids and very slowly flows towards the Arctic Ocean, along many different routes at once. After the trip this view became for me a meta-phor of the many, and completely different, ways of life that I encountered during this trip. What is ironic is that most of the time all of us – people I encountered and me myself – thought that we are well aware of the differ-ences and understand them. But a conversation always revealed how naive our views most of the time are and how much there is to learn about things which we were taking for granted. Experiences of this trip very strongly changed my perspective in life and remain an important inspiration.

*Figure 2.1*  Example of a participant's response

They were also given five questions to help focus their reflections, although they were not expected to respond separately to these questions:

•   What were you thinking or feeling at the time the photograph was taken?
•   What were the associated events that made this vacation experience meaningful?
•   Has the photograph taken on new meanings since the time it was taken?
•   What do you feel or think as you look back on this photograph?
•   What does the photograph represent for you?

Figure 2.1 provides an example of one participant's entire response to one of her five photographs.

Demographic information was collected at the end of the survey. Participants who completed the survey (N = 72) received two movie vouchers to thank them for their contributions to the research. These 72 participants were predominantly female (76.4 per cent), spread fairly evenly across age groups from 20 to 60 years (2.8 per cent were under 20 years of age, 29.2 per cent aged 20–29, 26.4 per cent aged 30–39, 25 per cent aged 40–49, 16.7 per cent aged 50–59), had taken an average of 6.3 overseas trips and 8.4 domestic trips in the past ten years and travelled mostly for leisure (72.2 per cent) or a combination of work and leisure (26.4 per cent). An additional five participants did not complete the whole survey, but they did contribute a total of ten reflections, which have been included in the data analysis (yielding a total of 370 reflections). Of these, 64 per cent referred to international destinations. A total of 48,342 words of text were provided in response to the question, 'Please explain why this photograph is meaningful to you' (an average of 130 words per entry), and 324 photographs were uploaded.

## *Analysis*

The text responses regarding 'why this photograph is meaningful to you' were analysed in the following manner. Each response was examined using Steger *et al.'s* (2013) framework, and the categories represented in the response were identified. At least one of these predefined categories could be identified in the majority (97 per cent) of responses. The ways in which these 'everyday' sources of meaning enriched vacation experiences, and were intensified by the vacation context, were summarised descriptively, and frequency counts were used to identify the relative importance of the 15 categories. Sources of meaning that were not adequately represented by Steger *et al.'s* (2013) framework, but that were particularly important in the context of vacations, were also identified and described. Some themes were identified wherein the vacation itself was considered a source of meaning. Finally, participants' insights regarding photographs as a way of capturing meaning were also analysed.

## Results

### *How do everyday sources of meaning help to enrich vacation experiences?*

All 15 of Steger *et al.'s* (2013) categories representing common sources of meaning were present to some extent in participants' responses; however, their frequency of occurrence fell into three broad levels, as indicated in Table 2.1. In the following presentation of results, the ways in which each of the sources of meaning enriched and in turn was intensified by the vacation experience is described and illustrated using examples from participants' responses. (Participants' responses are presented using parentheses and single quote marks.)

### *Relationships (emotional connections with others)*

Relationships with both companions and hosts were often noted as meaningful aspects of vacations. ('Being with friends was what made it special'.) Participants

*Table 2.1* Frequency with which participants drew meaning from everyday sources in the context of a vacation

| Frequency with which source was mentioned | | Sources of meaning |
|---|---|---|
| **High frequency** | Mentioned as a source of meaning in approximately half of all responses | Relationships |
| **Moderate frequency** | Mentioned as a source of meaning in 10%–25% of responses | Nature<br>Everyday necessities<br>Education/learning<br>Physical environment<br>Values<br>Hobbies<br>Self |
| **Low frequency** | Mentioned as a source of meaning in fewer than 2% of responses | Religion<br>Pets<br>Technology<br>Future aspirations<br>Occupation/work<br>Possessions<br>Organisations |

reported that friendships and family bonds had been strengthened or 'cemented' through the sharing of experiences, the opportunities for deep and meaningful conversations and the need to work together as a team. In some cases, the vacation itself was an expression of the value of the relationship. ('It is a true form of friendship that people are prepared to travel the world to see each other'.) International vacations provide the opportunity to interact across cultures and language barriers, as well as to experience the hospitality of strangers. ('I will remember their generosity for the rest of my life and I'm still friends with them now'.)

### Nature (elements of the natural world)

Participants described vivid sensory experiences in nature, for example, recalling the softness of the water, the sound of the waves, the colours in the reef, the smell of the sunscreen and the taste of saltiness. They reported a sense of awe and wonder, peace and relaxation, reflection or contemplation, connection or reconnection with nature. Some reported that being in nature gave them a sense of perspective. ('How small are humans in comparison to these natural wonders?')

### Everyday necessities (e.g. food, money, sleep)

Everyday necessities often take on new meaning on vacation. Food in particular becomes an integral part of the experience of relaxing, spending time with friends or participating in the local culture. ('The holiday is also about eating local food and visiting markets and cooking local products'.) Money is necessary in order to travel. Having saved for some time to take a trip, or to be able to enjoy little luxuries while away, added to the meaning of the experience. ('It meant a lot to us as we were both still students and it had taken us a while to finally save up enough money to do a decent trip'.) Sleep is also a luxury that some types of vacation allow more than everyday life. ('This was the most relaxing holiday I have ever had. The children went to kids club during the day, if I chose to have a sleep I could'.)

## *Education (actively pursuing new skills, knowledge and insights)*

Although respondents rarely mentioned formal education or study as a source of meaning while on vacation, learning new skills, gaining knowledge and learning about life in general were benefits of travel that were highly valued. In particular, travel provided opportunities to learn about different cultures, histories, people and events. ('I appreciate seeing the differences in cultures and reflecting on the history that has made us who we are today'.) Some also found meaning in giving their children opportunities to learn. ('I hope that my kids learn to love the open spaces and serenity of nature rather than the dull concrete of the city'.)

## *Physical environment (a location that holds special meaning)*

Physical environments other than nature held meaning for many respondents. Being immersed in history, inspired by architecture or discovering an environment with special aesthetic appeal were all memorable experiences. Physical environments were imbued with meaning, as they were considered to represent more abstract ideas such as peace and chaos, change and permanence. The connection between the abstract ideas and the physical environments allowed personal reflections at a particular time and place to be captured and preserved. ('There is a feeling of permanence and strength of purpose there'. 'A tangible reminder of an iconic, peaceful and beautiful oasis among complete chaos'. 'It was a kind of marker for life to me . . . the feeling that everything is for its season'.)

## *Values (principles that are important to the participant)*

Vacations provided opportunities for people to reflect on their priorities in life and the things that were important to them. For some, these reflections were prompted by observations of different cultures or environments and often resulted in a commitment to take action. ('This was our first encounter with this reality and it made an impression on us both. For me, it was a greater commitment to support aid organisations'.) For others, being away from the daily routine, or being separated from family and friends served as a reminder of what was most important to them. ('It reminded me of all the friends I had back home in Australia at the time and that no matter the distance it is still possible to be great friends with them'.)

*Hobbies (activities pursued for pleasure)*

Vacations provide opportunities to engage in hobby or leisure activities that can only be accessed by travel – for example, mountain climbing, diving, surfing, skiing and snowboarding – or that take on new meaning during travel, such as photography. These often provide a sense of pride or achievement. ('I was very proud of my achievements on the ski field'.) Some activities are considered more acceptable or valid when on vacation, for instance, relaxing and spoiling oneself. ('We felt that we were able to be selfish for a little while and do whatever it was we wanted, just for us'.)

*Self (expressions of self-identity, self-acceptance, self-understanding or self-esteem)*

A number of respondents reported feeling proud of themselves as a result of their achievements while travelling. ('The effort to get to the top made the finish much more special and it felt like I had achieved something'.) Just being able to negotiate the many challenges that travel provides contributed to a sense of self-sufficiency, especially for those who were travelling alone. ('So proud of myself for travelling by myself'.) Although rarely expressed overtly, travel for many people became an expression of identity. ('This was the first time I have travelled internationally on my own. It kicked off my travel bug and my new title of global adventurer!')

*Religion (set of beliefs and practices followed)*

Although none of the respondents used the word 'pilgrimage', some spoke about places of spiritual significance, feeling a connection to faith, or being in awe of creation. ('The photo represents a coming together of family, faith and natural beauty – all of which are probably the most meaningful to me as a person'.)

*Pets (domestic animals kept as companions)*

Four of the 78 participants (5 per cent) mentioned a pet (always a dog) in at least one of their responses. The dog was considered part of the family, and taking the dog for walks was an enjoyable vacation activity. ('I think my Dog is awesome . . . he loves hanging with us; at the beach we can all have good family time together'.) Three participants spoke of vacations oriented around horses and horse-riding events.

*Technology (use of modern technology)*

Most mentions of technology as a source of meaning focused on being able to get away from the demands of work and modern communication technologies. Technology was mentioned twice as a positive tool for meaning making: once in relation to 'audio technology to help interpret the site' and once in relation to Facebook as a repository for vacation photographs. ('I like to keep a record of what we have done while on holiday. I post a few photos to Facebook and it makes a great place to reflect back on one's life'.)

*Future aspirations (plans, goals, careers)*

Some vacations help people to clarify their goals and aspirations regarding work, relationships and further travel. ('After this holiday I knew what I wanted to do – have my own property and live and work in the country'.)

*Occupation or work*

Occasionally, people described meaningful experiences that involved working holidays, or work intersecting with vacation in a meaningful way. ('This holiday was like a dream come true for me, as it combined my passion and love for my work, with a desire that originated from my childhood'.) Others found meaning in getting away from work, or in work as a means that makes travel possible.

*Possessions (material objects identified as important)*

Possessions were rarely mentioned as meaningful aspects of vacations – they were only mentioned if they were symbolic of an activity or achievement. ('Our new caravan . . . represents a new phase in our lives'.)

*Organisations (involvement in a specific group)*

Only one of the 370 responses mentioned a specific organisation. ('This photograph shows me . . . preparing to join the International Women's Day (IWD) march across the bridge . . . As a long time feminist and supporter and participant of International Women's Day events this was an unexpected delight'.)

## What other sources of meaning are particularly important in the context of vacations?

Sources of meaning that were particularly important in the context of vacations, but were not able to be classified using Steger *et al.'s* (2013) 15 categories, focused on various types of vacation experiences or environments that were perceived as meaningful by respondents. These included novel or unique experiences, escape from the everyday, idealised locations and favourite places.

*Novel or unique experiences*

Novel or unique experiences were among the most frequently cited sources of meaning. These included experiencing a different culture or lifestyle, a different climate, an ancient civilisation, a famous place, a place unknown to others, the smallest, largest, rarest, most remote, etc. Respondents used words such as 'mysterious', 'magical', 'eerie', 'fairy-tale', 'unreal', 'once-in-a-lifetime' and 'special' to describe these experiences that were clearly distinguished from everyday life. The element of surprise, unexpectedness or spontaneity also contributed to the memorability and meaningfulness of vacation experiences.

### Escape from the everyday

Respondents valued being able to get away from work, technology, busyness, stress, the city, other people and their normal routine. ('Work and all the related stresses of the city seemed far away'.)

### Idealised locations

The places they escaped to were sometimes idealised. ('I felt like I was in paradise'; 'like heaven on earth'; 'a dream come true'; 'a perfect day'.)

### Favourite places

For some respondents, their most meaningful vacations were not at exotic or novel locations, but rather at places that were familiar, where they felt a sense of attachment. ('I'd like to be going back to the same place . . . a place where I can feel safe and know what to expect. This photo makes me feel safe and secure'.)

### In what ways are vacations a source of meaning in themselves?

Although Steger *et al.* (2013) grouped travel and holidays as part of the leisure and miscellaneous sections (respectively) of their classification, in the current study, there was evidence in participants' responses that vacations might be considered a source of meaning in their own right, not only as a context within which other meaningful domains can be experienced. Participants spoke about vacations as milestone markers, vacations as remedy or reward, and vacations that had changed their lives.

### Vacations as milestone markers

Vacations were meaningful when they signalled the 'first time' the respondent had done something, seen something or spent time with someone. In fact, the word 'first' was used 161 times in the 370 responses. Also meaningful was the 'last time' they had been able to do something before life circumstances had changed, or the accomplishment of something they had 'always wanted to do'. Many reported having intentionally planned a vacation as a marker of a turning point or a new phase in their lives.

> This was my first overseas holiday by myself after getting a job, leaving home. It was the first place I had chosen to go. It was on a Contiki tour, so not entirely self-directed, but still a big step out into the world on my own.

*Vacations as remedy or reward*

Respondents had used vacations to reward themselves after a period of hard work or other life difficulties. Such vacations were often seen as contributing to the process of recovery or restoration.

> I had just finished 8 months of chemo and radiation and this trip was my reward.
>
> This was taken during our trip to Thailand after we had both finished our university degrees. This was a trip to celebrate many years of hard work and long hours studying.
>
> After separating from my husband of more than a decade, I needed to run away. To get out of my comfort zone, I signed up to travel from one side of the USA to the other – in a bus – with nine strangers. The highlight of my year was meeting and travelling with these amazing people. Without knowing it, they all have all changed my life.

*Life-changing vacations*

Respondents spoke of the life-changing impact of vacations on their motivation for living, understanding of themselves and others and commitment to contribute positively to the world. They used words such as inspiration, courage, and hope; having their eyes and minds opened; and seeing the world in a new way. Life-changing vacations were often those that involved having to face and overcome challenges and personal fears, and in the process reflecting on and learning lessons about life.

> This trip is one of the few experiences that I would confidently describe as life changing: we had to face new challenges every day, dealing with situations and people completely different from those we would be normally exposed to . . . My world-view afterwards was deeply shaped by this experience.
>
> I found in the experience a throwing off of the shackles of fear which have inhibited much of my life. Sort of a 'boldly going where no man (or woman) has gone before'. It was pretty liberating.
>
> This photo and the event represents overcoming my fears and going outside my comfort zone. When I look at the photo it reminds me that I'm capable of something if I put my mind to it.

## Photographs as a way of capturing meaning

As part of their reflections on the meaningful aspects of vacations represented by the photographs they had selected, several respondents commented on the important role played by the photograph itself as a reminder of the meaningful experience, a re-creation of the experience or a record of their lives.

*Photographs as a reminder*

Photographs capture not only images of places and people but also the thoughts, feelings and meanings associated with these places and people. Looking at the photograph serves as a reminder of relationships, experiences and insights – almost allowing the participant to transcend time and space.

> This photo is just one example of numerous I took . . . they all continue to remind of one of the most magnificent places on earth and all that I saw, felt and experienced there.
> It always reminds me of my loved family members that live so far away from me.

*Photographs as a re-creation*

Some photographs held so much meaning that they were given places of promi-nence, in the hope of re-creating the remembered experience, or making the experience part of everyday life.

> I feel happy when I look at this photograph – it's currently set as my desktop background, so it heralds significance for me. It brings me feelings of calm and acceptance . . . almost a meditative feeling on how amidst day to day life, there are these moments which are almost spiritual snapshots in time.

*Photographs as a record of life*

Although vacations represent only a small percentage of most people's lives, they provide a context in which photographs are almost ubiquitous. Thus for many, vacation photographs provide one of the only records they have of their lives and loved ones as they change and grow over time. For this reason, some photographs hold meaning beyond the vacation experience itself.

> I like to keep a record of what we have done while on holiday. I post a few photos to Facebook and it makes a great place to reflect back on one's life.
> Looking back I see a time in our life filled with wonder, and new learn-ings, children who bring so much laughter and joy to our life . . . This photo represents my world, my life.

## Discussion and conclusions

Using the photograph-based method, respondents were able to provide rich and thoughtful accounts of the ways in which they had found meaning in various aspects of their vacation experiences. All 15 of Steger *et al.'s* (2013) sources of meaning were present in the data, confirming that everyday sources of meaning both enrich and are enriched by the vacation context. Thus although vacation time is an extension of everyday life in which existing goals and values are maintained, it is also outside of everyday life, a kind of 'time out of time' (Falassi, 1987), when goals and values are able to be recalibrated. Participants' responses confirmed that vacations offer rich opportunities for social interaction, personal growth and identity development (Richards, 1999) and also provide a context for reflection on life (Wilson & Harris, 2006). Photographs enabled these meaningful moments to be captured in time, themselves becoming a source of meaning and a record of life.

As identified in previous research (Andereck *et al.*, 2006; Harrison, 2003), relationships were a significant source of meaning in the context of vacations, as in other life domains (Steger *et al.*, 2013). Although this study focused on meaning rather than motivation, the findings shed some light on the debate regarding whether tourists travel for the discovery of 'self' or search for the 'other' (Moscardo, Dann & McKercher, 2014). Overwhelmingly, the aspects that people mentioned most frequently as meaningful related to spending time with their travelling companions, which in Dann's conceptualisation (in Moscardo *et al.*, 2014) might be labelled the 'quest for other as brother' (p. 95). However, in those cases where respondents did refer to aspects of 'self', their responses clearly reflected a deeper level of meaning, involving overcoming challenges and developing self-esteem. These expressions were more in line with eudaimonic satisfaction or psychological well-being. Of course, Moscardo's conclusion that 'tourists primarily travel to discover themselves' carries the caveat that 'they are rarely likely to be conscious of this' (Moscardo *et al.*, 2014, p. 82). Thus it is not surprising that expressions of meaning focused on self were relatively infrequent in our data.

The twin ideas of tourism as an escape from the mundane and a search for novel experiences contributed new sources of meaning that had not been identified in other contexts. Gilbert and Abdullah's (2004) suggestion that vacations enhance a sense of happiness and well-being because they represent 'a distinct break from normal events' (p. 117) resonates well with our data. The search for novel or unique experiences is perhaps one of the motivations that can only be met, or can best be met, through tourism. Vacations offer abundant opportunities to encounter different environments, climates, cultures and lifestyles, and many respondents found meaning in doing something for the 'first time' or in seeing something that they considered 'special' or noteworthy in some way. These experiences contribute to the participants' social and human capital (Moscardo, 2009) as they provide resources for personal growth and also for enriching relationships. The claim that visitor experiences are the 'core product' or 'essence' of tourism (Prentice, Witt & Hamer, 1998; Tussyadiah, 2014) is thus well-supported in participants' responses.

Vacations were found to offer meaning in themselves, especially as participants used them as markers of significant life events or changes; for instance, a vacation often follows a wedding, a retirement or completion of a course of study. The vacation not only takes on the meanings associated with the significant event, but adds its own meaning as it contributes to a sense of reward or recovery, or the beginning of a new phase of life. Such occasions prompt reflective responses which the vacation provides. They contribute to the accomplishment of the turning point and provide a memorable marker of it. Vacations also provide opportunities for people to face and overcome challenges, or to establish a sense of independence and self-sufficiency. For these reasons, some vacations can be perceived as life changing.

According to Seligman and Csikszentmihalyi (2000, p. 5), positive psychology focuses on 'positive subjective experience, positive individual traits, and positive institutions' in order to improve quality of life. There is ample evidence in participants' reflections on their meaningful vacation experiences for the contribution of tourism to each of these aspects. The words 'happy' or 'happiness', for example, were used 90 times in participants' responses; positive traits such as persistence, appreciation of diversity, aesthetic appreciation, open-mindedness and commitment were implied, if not explicitly named; and tourism as a positive institution (one that moves individuals toward better citizenship) might be argued from participants' accounts of their meaningful vacation experiences.

Pearce (2009, p. 46) proposed that tourism might be considered a positive institution that promotes 'personal growth and human flourishing'. The findings of this study confirm that at least for some people, some of the time, this is the case. Warnings from Moscardo (2009) would caution, however, that this is not always the case: some people report negative experiences of tourism; the costs of tourism may actually be harmful to quality of life (through risk of injury or disease, financial and opportunity costs and disruption to local social and community networks); and tourism's impact on host populations and environments can also be negative. Similarly, McKercher (in Moscardo *et al.*, 2014) argues that tourism is a self-indulgent behaviour that may not be sustainable for the planet as a whole. Such negative experiences would not have been detected in the current study because of its intentional focus on the things that make vacations meaningful. In this regard, however, the study accomplished what it set out to do: it has documented the many sources of meaning that are inherent in vacations, from strengthening bonds with family and friends through to life-changing readjustments and moments of insight. Perhaps the tourism industry, and individual tourists themselves, can benefit from reflection on these sources of meaning in order to create more meaningful tourism experiences whose benefits outweigh their costs.

# References

Andereck, K., Bricker, K. S., Kerstetter, D., & Nickerson, N. P. (2006). Connecting experiences to quality: Understanding the meanings behind visitors' experiences. In G. Jennings & N. P. Nickerson (Eds.), *Quality tourism experiences* (pp. 81–98). Burlington, MA: Elsevier Butterworth-Heinemann.

Belk, R., & Yeh, J. (2011). Tourist photographs: Signs of self. *International Journal of Culture, Tourism and Hospitality Research*, 5(4), 345–353.

Botterill, T. D., & Crompton, J. L. (1996). Two case studies: Exploring the nature of tourist's experience. *Journal of Leisure Research*, 28(1), 57–82.

Cederholm, E. A. (2004). The use of photo-elicitation in tourism research: Framing the backpacker experience. *Scandinavian Journal of Hospitality and Tourism*, 4(3), 225–241.

Darity, W. A. (Ed.). (2008). *International encyclopedia of the social sciences* (Vol. 8, 2nd ed.). Detroit: Macmillan Reference USA.

Delle Fave, A., Brdar, I., Wissing, M. P., & Vella-Brodrick, D. A. (2013). Sources and motives for personal meaning in adulthood. *Journal of Positive Psychology*, 8(6), 517–529.

Dolnicar, S., Yanamandram, V., & Cliff, K. (2012). The contribution of vacations to quality of life. *Annals of Tourism Research*, 39(1), 59–83.

Emmons, R. A. (2003). Personal goals, life meaning, and virtue: Wellsprings of a positive life. In C. L. M. Keyes & J. Haidt (Eds.), *Flourishing* (pp. 105–128). Washington, DC: APA.

Falassi, A. (1987). *Time out of time: Essays on the festival*. Albuquerque: University of New Mexico Press.

Gilbert, D., & Abdullah, J. (2004). Holidaytaking and the sense of well-being. *Annals of Tourism Research*, 31(1), 103–121.

Harper, D. (2002). Talking about pictures: A case for photo elicitation. *Visual Studies*, 17, 13–26.

Harrison, J. (2003). *Being a tourist: Finding meaning in pleasure travel*. Vancouver: UBC Press.

Kim, J.-H., Ritchie, J. R. B., & McCormick, B. M. (2012). Development of a scale to measure memorable tourism experiences. *Journal of Travel Research*, 51(1), 12–25.

Leiper, N. (2004). *Tourism management* (3rd ed.). Sydney: Pearson Education.

Little, D., & Schmidt, C. (2006). Self, wonder and God! The spiritual dimensions of travel experiences. *Tourism*, 54(2), 107–116.

Lo, I. S., & McKercher, B. (2015). Ideal image in process: Online tourist photography and impression management. *Annals of Tourism Research*, 52, 104–116.

Moscardo, G. (2009). Tourism and quality of life: Towards a more critical approach. *Tourism and Hospitality Research*, 9, 159–170.

Moscardo, G., Dann, G., & McKercher, B. (2014). Do tourists travel for the discovery of self or search for the 'other'? *Tourism Recreation Research*, 39(1), 81–106.

Packer, J., & Ballantyne, R. (in press). Conceptualising the visitor experience: A review of literature and development of a multifaceted model. *Visitor Studies*.

Pearce, P. (2009). The relationship between positive psychology and tourist behavior studies. *Tourism Analysis*, 14, 37–48.

Prentice, R. C., Witt, S. F., & Hamer, C. (1998). Tourism as experience: The case of heritage parks. *Annals of Tourism Research*, 25(1), 1–24.

Richards, G. (1999). Vacations and the quality of life: Patterns and structures. *Journal of Business Research*, 44, 189–198.

Seligman, M. E. P., & Csikszentmihalyi, M. (2000). Positive psychology: An introduction. *American Psychologist*, 55(1), 5–14.

Steger, M., Shim, Y., Rush, B., Brueske, L., Shin, J., & Merriman, L. (2013). The mind's eye: A photographic method for understanding meaning in people's lives. *Journal of Positive Psychology*, 8(6), 530–542.

Stein, K. (2011). Getting away from it all: The construction and management of temporary identities on vacation. *Symbolic Interaction*, 34(2), 290–308.

Stylianou-Lambert, T. (2012). Tourists with cameras: Reproducing or producing? *Annals of Tourism Research*, 39(4), 1817–1838.

Tussyadiah, I. P. (2014). Toward a theoretical foundation for experience design in tourism. *Journal of Travel Research*, 53(5), 543–564.

Wilson, E., & Harris, C. (2006). Meaningful travel: Women, independent travel and the search for self and meaning. *Tourism*, 54(2), 161–172.

# 3 Tourism and love

## How do tourist experiences affect romantic relationships?

*Jessica de Bloom, Sabine Geurts and Martin Lohmann*

### Introduction

The need to belong, that is the desire to form interpersonal bonds, is an inborn fundamental human need and essential to well-being (Baumeister & Leary, 1995; Ryan & Deci, 2000). In several empirical studies, the only factor that clearly discriminates happy people from unhappy people turned out to be the strength of people's social relationships (e.g. Maas *et al.*, 2009; Mitchell & Popham, 2008). Compared to unhappy people, happy people are highly social and have stronger, fulfilling social and romantic relationships (Hartig, Evans, Jamner, Davis & Gärling, 2003). An eight-year longitudinal study demonstrated that time spent with one's partner and marital satisfaction not only promote happiness but also long-term physical health (Waldinger & Schulz, 2010).

In order to build and strengthen positive social relationships with one's partner, free time spent together is essential to fulfil one's need for relatedness (Ryan, Bernstein & Brown, 2010). However, for most working people, free time is limited to a few hours at the end of the work day and during the weekends. Accordingly, vacation from work as a long and unbroken span of leisure time may constitute a prime opportunity for employees to reconnect with their loved ones, to engage in positive social interactions and to consolidate their bonds.

Several existing studies have shown that vacations have a positive impact on family functioning (e.g. Durko & Petrick, 2013; Lehto, Choi, Lin & MacDermid, 2009; Lehto, Lin, Chen & Choi, 2012; Shaw, Havitz & Delemere, 2008). Most of these studies have been qualitative, suggesting that touristic experiences generate shared memories, improve communication within the family and, subsequently, result in feelings of togetherness and cohesion. Quantitative studies are rare, however, and only a few of these studies have focused on tourism and its link with relationship dynamics in couples. A literature search using 'romantic relations', 'love', 'tourism', 'vacation' or 'holidays' as key terms renders predominantly studies on sex tourism (e.g. Herold, Garcia & DeMoya, 2001; Jeffreys, 2003; Takano, Nakamura & Watanabe, 2002) or reproductive tourism, i.e. travelling to foreign countries for fertility treatments (e.g. Inhorn & Patrizio, 2009; Voigt & Laing, 2010). A key publication in the area of sex and tourism edited by Bauer and McKercher (2003) explored the role of romance and sex as motivators for travel (e.g. honeymoon, romantic getaways for couples or commercial sex tours), the nature of the encounter (e.g. balanced, mutually rewarding or unbalanced exploitative relationships) and the role of tourism as a direct or indirect facilitator of romantic and sexual encounters. Whilst this work is important in its own regard, it does only address one aspect of love, and it also does not render an answer to the question whether and how existing romantic relationships change during vacations. Despite the fact that the quality of relationships between travellers is expected to determine how tourist destinations are perceived (Trauer & Ryan, 2005), 'the subject of love and tourism appears to have no place in the minds of social scientists'. (Singh, 2002, p. 1).

Thus, despite their potential as relationship boosters, shared holidays as a means to strengthen romantic relationships have rarely been put to the test in empirical research. In this chapter, we briefly review the existing literature to arrive at hypotheses for our current study.

## Literature review

According to the DRAMMA model (Newman, Tay & Diener, 2014), leisure time is thought to improve well-being because it enables people to mentally *D*isengage from their work and *R*elax, provides high levels of *A*utonomy, offers opportunities for *M*astery experiences, gives *M*eaning to life and increases levels of social *A*ffiliation (e.g. Csikszentmihalyi, 1991; Fritz & Sonnentag, 2006; Sonnentag & Fritz, 2015; Stebbins, 2001). In line with the Self-Determination Theory (Ryan & Deci, 2000), relatedness refers to the higher order need to belong. High levels of relatedness imply feeling closely connected to another person and can also describe the feeling of taking care of and being taken care of by a close other. Changes in relationship dynamics, especially with regard to increasing feelings of relatedness during free time, constitute exploratory mechanisms that connect leisure time and well-being. According to Davidson (1996), vacations can be assumed to affect romantic relationships positively in two ways. First, they enable couples to spend more time together than during working periods. Second, holidays remove everyday strain. During busy working weeks, employees may be so stressed and exhausted that they are less able to enjoy joint time with their partners. They may be less willing or able to invest time and effort into their relationships. At the end of a stressful workday, possibly after putting moody children to bed and taking care of household chores, a person may be unlikely to surprise her/his partner with a romantic candlelight dinner or a relaxing massage. Both time and energy may be lacking. By contrast, during a holiday, without everyday hassles and household tasks in the work and the home domain, romantic partners may find it easier to focus on each other and their relationships. In line with these assumptions, several studies within the field of leisure sciences have demonstrated that joint free-time activities increase marital satisfaction (e.g. Johnson, Zabriskie & Hill, 2006; Smith, Snyder, Trull & Monsma, 1988). This is especially true for novel, arousing shared activities (Aron, Norman, Aron, McKenna & Heyman, 2000).

During holidays and travelling to strange places, the chance to engage in new, offbeat or exciting activities is greater than during normal working days.

One of the first quantitative studies to focus on romantic couples' vacations and relationships investigated changes in the amount and quality of conversations before, during and after a short domestic holiday in 80 Dutch employees. Results showed that vacationers had more conversations with their partners during vacation than before and also rated the quality of these conversations more positively (De Bloom, Geurts & Kompier, 2012). Recently, Durko and Petrick (2015) published a paper in which they suggest that vacation satisfaction assists relationship commitment. They propose that vacations provide working couples with a break from their usual work and home obligations and offer them the chance to engage in pleasurable, joint leisure activities, both of which have been shown to positively affect relationship satisfaction (Lim & Chen, 2009; Lim & Teo, 2005; Sirgy, Kruger, Lee & Yu, 2011). Durko and Petrick (2015) tested their propositions in a cross-sectional sample of 472 participants who, retrospectively, evaluated their levels of satisfaction with their last holiday and current relationship satisfaction. Vacation satisfaction was linked to relationship satisfaction and commitment, suggesting that travel may serve as 'relationship therapy' (Durko & Petrick, 2015, p. 1) and that it could make sense to 'prescribe travel' for troubled couples in order to improve their relationships (Petrick & Huether, 2013, p. 705).

## Hypotheses and research aims

We hypothesize that during vacation, compared to regular working weeks, more time is spent together with the partner (H1), the quality of social interactions with the partner is rated more positively (H2), reported levels of relatedness are higher (H3) and relationship satisfaction is higher (H4). Relationship satisfaction is considered an essential component in remaining committed to a relationship – meaning staying together with a person. It refers to the overall quality of a relationship and the extent to which a partner fulfils a variety of individual needs (Christensen & Schunn, 2005; Dijksterhuis & Meurs, 2006). Together, the four relationship indicators are expected to be associated with higher levels of happiness during vacation (H5). Happiness is defined as an indicator of overall subjective well-being and refers to experiencing frequent joy and infrequent negative emotions (Csikszentmihalyi, 2013; Diener, 2000). In tourism research, happiness is considered a key outcome of beneficial touristic experiences (Filep, 2012; Filep & Deery, 2010). Accordingly, several studies have indeed shown that travelling increases happiness (e.g. De Bloom, Geurts & Kompier, 2013; Nawijn, 2010; Nawijn, Mitas, Lin & Kerstetter, 2013).

Summing up, this quantitative study explores the potential link between vacationing and romantic relationships. The contribution of this study is twofold. First, it generates empirical evidence on the relation between tourism and relationship dynamics. Second, it provides an answer to the question of whether fulfilment of the need to belong during a tourist experience may constitute an exploratory mechanism in the relation between tourism and happiness. This twofold contribution may yield some interesting implications for tourism marketing.

## Method

### *Procedure*

We conducted a longitudinal study. Data were collected on nine occasions: once before vacation, three or four times during vacation (depending on the individual vacation duration), twice in the first week after vacation (averaged into one occasion) and one time during the second, third and fourth week after work resumption (Table 3.1).

We defined a vacation as 'a prolonged period of absence from work granted to an employee, used for rest, recreation or travel and lasting more than two days' (De Bloom, 2012, p. 13). In this study, we were especially interested in long summer holidays. Therefore, a requirement to take part in this study was that the participants' holidays lasted at least two consecutive weeks and took place in the time period between 15 June and 22 August. There were no other restrictions concerning the travel destination or type of holiday. Accordingly, the summer vacations included in this study varied widely from a camping trip in Southern France to hiking in Austria, to a beach holiday in Italy, to sailing in the Netherlands.

Before and after vacation, participants were asked to fill in online questionnaires for which they received an individual log-in code via email. Each email message was accompanied by an SMS reminder around four o'clock in the afternoon on the participant's personal cell phone. The participants were requested to fill in the questionnaires at the same time of the day, preferably shortly before going to bed.

Three weeks before vacation, the participants filled in a general questionnaire assessing demographics (e.g. age, marital status, education), basic job information (e.g. weekly work hours) and vacation characteristics (e.g. length, destination). The pre-vacation baseline measurements of happiness and relationship indicators were scheduled to be taken on Tuesday, two weeks prior to vacation (Pre).

Before the vacation, each participant received a cell phone with a prepaid SIM card so that calling would be possible free of charge during a vacation abroad. During the vacation, we held individual telephone interviews on the fourth (Inter 1), eighth (Inter 2), twelfth (Inter 3) and sixteenth day (Inter 4) after the start of the holiday. Participants were called between 5:00 and 8:00 p.m., and the structured telephone interviews lasted about 10 to 15 minutes per person.

After returning home and resuming work, the participants again filled in online questionnaires on their first work day, on the next to last day of their first week of work resumption (averaged into Post 1) and on Tuesdays during the second (Post 2), third (Post 3) and fourth weeks after vacation (Post 4).

To reduce drop out and incomplete responses as much as possible, we applied several measures suggested by Newman (2009). For instance, the purpose and consequences of nonresponse were explained in detail and each participant was

Table 3.1 Research design

| Before vacation | | During vacation | | | | After vacation | | | | |
| --- | --- | --- | --- | --- | --- | --- | --- | --- | --- | --- |
| GQ | Pre | Inter 1 | Inter 2 | Inter 3 | Inter 4 | Post 1 | | Post 2 | Post 3 | Post 4 |
| | | | | | | Post1.1 | Post 1.2 | | | |
| Three weeks before | Two weeks before | 4th day | 8th day | 12th day | 16th day | 1st work week | | 2nd work week | 3rd work week | 4th work week |
| • Demographics<br>• Basic job information<br>• Vacation characteristics | • Happiness<br>• Time with partner<br>• Quality interactions<br>• Relatedness<br>• Relationship satisfaction | • Happiness<br>• Time with partner<br>• Quality interactions<br>• Relatedness<br>• Relationship satisfaction | • idem | • idem | • idem | • Happiness<br>• Time with partner<br>• Quality interactions<br>• Relatedness<br>• Relationship satisfaction | | • idem | • idem | • idem |

Note: GQ = General questionnaire; Post 1.1 = first work day after holiday; Post 1.2 = next to last day in first working week after holiday.

given a tailor-made time schedule with his/her individual measurement occasions. Participants were also addressed by name in each email message we sent and a lottery prize was announced with higher chances of winning for each fully completed questionnaire. These strategies were successful, as the response rates varied between 85 (Inter 4) and 97 per cent (Pre, Post 1 and Post 2). After the data collection, participants were thanked and the winners of the lottery prizes were announced.

## Sample

Participants were recruited with the help of leaflets handed out around the city of Nijmegen and several ads placed in local newspapers. Three lottery prizes served as an incentive: a week vacation in Austria, a long weekend in the Netherlands and a €100 cheque. Initially, 65 participants met the inclusion criteria of the study (i.e. active command of Dutch, at least 24-hours paid work per week, Internet and email access at home, no objections to being called during vacation). Of this sample, 54 persons completed the data collection phase until the end (response rate: 83 per cent). As we were interested in the effects of tourism on romantic partners, we excluded 19 singles who spent their vacations alone. This resulted in a final sample of 35 individual persons. The results reported on in this study therefore refer to relationship dynamics in 35 couples, as reported by 35 people independently. Mean age of the participants was 40.9 years (SD = 11.7) and 20 participants were female. Half of the participants (48.6 per cent) lived together with children (aged 7.9 years on average), while 37.1 per cent lived together without children. The remaining participants did not share a home.

Of the sample, 57.1 per cent held a college or university degree, 25.7 per cent were medium educated and 17.1 per cent were lower educated. About a fourth of the sample (25.7 per cent) described themselves as technicians or associated professionals (e.g. webmaster), 25.7 per cent were managers or senior officials, 22.9 per cent were professionals (e.g. doctors or consultants) and the remaining 25.8 per cent had other occupations (e.g. clerical support workers, service or sales workers). The majority had a permanent contract (65.7 per cent), 22.9 per cent had a temporary contract and 11.5 per cent worked freelance or were self-employed. Participants worked on average 33.7 hours per week (SD = 6.2) with a minimum of 24 hours and a maximum of 40 hours per week. Overtime work was on average 3.8 hours per week (SD = 5.2).

Mean duration of people´s holiday trips was 22.8 days (SD = 4.3), ranging from 15 to 30 days. Holiday destinations were mainly European countries. Top destinations were France (25.7 per cent), the Netherlands (14.3 per cent) and Austria (11.4 per cent). Only two persons travelled outside Europe (to the USA). Participants described their vacations as a 'relaxing holiday' (54 per cent), 'active holiday' (48 per cent), 'city trip' (24 per cent), 'round trip' (28 per cent), 'cultural trip' (22 per cent) and/or 'nature holiday' (17 per cent). About half of the participants (54 per cent) characterized their travel accommodations as middle class while the other half (42 per cent) described it as simple or low budget. Only 4 per cent stated that they did stay in luxury, upper-class accommodation.

## Measures

Due to the frequent repeated measurements before, during and after vacation, the data collection was very time-consuming for the participants. Hence we had to reduce the number of items in the questionnaires as much as possible. In addition, we had to bear in mind that the questions needed to be comprehensible when presented in oral form, as telephone interviews were used for data collection during vacation. Whenever possible, we used single-item indicators which were shown to be valid and user-friendly replacements for long, time-consuming scales which often contain a large number of very similar items (Elo, Leppänen & Jahkola, 2003; Uysal, Sirgy, Woo & Kim, 2016; Van Hooff, Geurts, Taris & Kompier, 2007). This approach is common in psychological research using diary design with repeated measures across several hours, days or weeks (for examples, see Demerouti, Bakker, Sonnentag & Fullagar, 2012; Sonnentag, 2001; Van Hooff, Geurts, Kompier & Taris, 2007). For most items, the basic Dutch grade notation system ranging from 1 (extremely low/negative) to 10 (extremely high/positive) was adopted and the first and the last grades were anchored. As the participants were all familiar with this grading system, the answering format was straightforward and very easy to understand.

We assessed *happiness* with the question, 'How happy do you feel today?' This item was based on the general measure presented and validated by Abdel-Khalek (2006). Options for answers ranged from 1 = very unhappy to 10 = very happy. *Time spent with partner* was measured with the question, 'How much time have you spent with your partner today (e.g. talking, playing games, undertaking common activities etc.)?' Participants could choose from the following answering categories: 1 = less than 1 hour, 2 = 1–2 hours, 3 = 2–4 hours, 4 = 4–6 hours, 5 = 6–8 hours, 6 = more than 8 hours. The *quality of social interactions with the partner* was rated with the question, 'How would you rate the interactions you had with your partner today?' Participants replied on a scale from 1 = very bad to 10 = very good. Feelings of *relatedness* were measured with the question, 'How close do you feel to your partner today?' Possible answers ranged from 1 = not close at all to 10 = very close. This item was based on Ryan and Deci's self-determination theory (2000) and highly similar to the item Ryan *et al.* (2010) used to measure relatedness during weekends in another study. The question 'How satisfied do you feel about the relationship with your partner today?' was used to assess *relationship satisfaction*. The wording of this item is based on studies measuring general life satisfaction with a single-item scale (Uysal *et al.*, 2016). Participants could reply on a scale from 1 = very dissatisfied to 10 = very satisfied.

*Statistical analyses*

After inspecting zero-order correlations between the variables, we analysed the changes in relationship dynamics and happiness with repeated measures analysis of variance (RM ANOVA) for each of the variables. This analysis demonstrates whether means differ across time. Pairwise post-hoc tests were applied to test which moments in time differed from each other. We focused especially on the comparison between the vacation period compared to baseline (pre-vacation level) and the levels after the vacation (post-vacation levels). Bonferroni correction was applied to counteract the risk of incorrectly rejecting the null hypothesis arising from multiple comparisons (Dunn, 1961). We conducted RM ANOVAs, including all nine measurement occasions separately for fine-grained analyses over time. To get a better general overview, we combined the measurement occasions during (Inter) and after vacation (Post).

We additionally calculated effect size Cohen $d$ for the difference between baseline and vacation values (Pre vs. Inter) because they render important additional information about the magnitude of the effects found. This is especially true for studies with rather small sample sizes like ours (Cohen, 1990; Sullivan & Feinn, 2012). In line with Cohen (1990), effect sizes smaller than 0.5 were considered small, $d$s between 0.5 and 0.8 were considered medium and $d$s greater than 0.8 were defined as large effect sizes.

In order to investigate the link between people's romantic relationship dynamics and potential changes in happiness, we calculated partial correlations. We averaged happiness during vacation (Inter 1–4) and controlled for baseline levels of happiness (i.e. before vacation, Pre) to investigate the variables which possibly affect the *change* in happiness from before to during vacation.

We conducted a regression analysis to test the relative weight of the four relationship indicators (time with partner, quality of interactions, relatedness, relationship satisfaction) for changes in happiness during vacation. In other words, we tested which relationship indicators were most important for changes in happiness during vacation.

## Results

Means before, during and after vacation for happiness, time spent with the partner, quality of interactions, relatedness and relationship satisfaction are displayed in Table 3.1 and Figure 3.1.

Before proceeding with the analyses to test our hypotheses, we conducted correlation analyses. Intercorrelations for the studied variables across the different measurement occasions were relatively high and ranged between $r = -0.10$, $p > 0.57$ (time spent with partner at Inter 1 and at Post 2) and $r = 0.89$, $p < .01$ (relatedness at Post 3 and at Post 4). At the same measurement occasion, correlations between the five different variables varied between $r = -0.02$, $p = 0.92$ (time spent with partner and happiness during vacation) and $r = 0.90$, $p < 0.01$ (relatedness and relationship satisfaction after vacation).

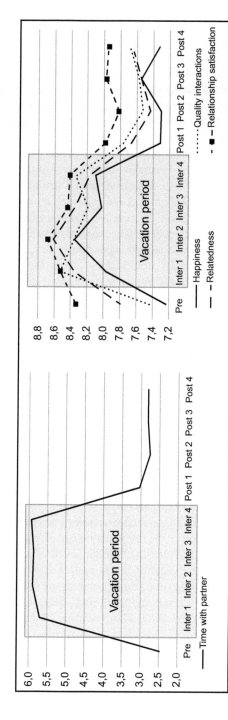

*Figure 3.1* Time with partner, happiness and relationship indicators across a summer vacation period

## *Changes in relationship indicators*

Repeated measures ANOVAs demonstrated that the time couples spent together varied significantly across time. Pairwise post-hoc tests demonstrated that vacationers spent significantly more time with their partners during holidays than before and after (Table 3.2). Before vacation, mean score was 2.5 and during vacation, mean score was 5.8. So during regular working weeks, couples actively interacted for two to three hours per day. During vacation, this time increased to about eight hours per day. Effect size Cohen $d$ was large ($d = 3.62$) for this change. Hypothesis 1 was supported.

The quality of interactions also varied across time (Table 3.2).

The quality of interactions during vacation (Inter) was significantly higher than before and after vacation. The change from baseline to vacation in terms of effect size was medium ($d = 0.79$). A fine-grained analysis, including all nine measurement occasions, showed that during the first and last vacation occasion (Inter 1 and Inter 4), the quality of interactions was more positive than after vacation (Post 2 to Post 4). Hypothesis 2 was mainly supported.

Feelings of relatedness changed significantly across time as well. Overall, relatedness during vacation was higher than after vacation. However, the change from Pre to Inter was non-significant and relatively small ($d = 0.45$). When all nine measurement occasions were incorporated in the analyses, Bonferroni comparisons indicated that relatedness on the first vacation occasion (Inter 1) was higher than after vacation (Post 1). Levels on the second vacation occasion were significantly higher than before (Pre) and after vacation (Post 1 to Post 4). Relatedness was also significantly higher on the third vacation occasion (Inter 3) than after vacation (Post 1 to Post 4). On the fourth vacation occasion, relatedness did not differ from pre- and post-levels. Hypothesis 3 was partly supported.

Relationship satisfaction also varied across time (Table 3.2). Satisfaction during vacation (Inter) was higher than after (Post). Effect size Cohen $d$ for the difference between Pre and Inter was 0.17, representing a small effect. A fine-grained analysis, including nine measurement occasions, demonstrated that relationship satisfaction on the first, second and third vacation occasion was significantly higher than satisfaction on most occasions after vacation (Post 1, 2 and 4). Relationship satisfaction on the last vacation occasion did not differ from baseline or post-vacation levels. Note that baseline levels of satisfaction did not differ from values reported after vacation, meaning that satisfaction did not significantly decrease after vacation (even though the means seem to suggest so). Overall, relationship satisfaction was higher during vacation than during most other occasions, especially the occasions after vacation, which partly confirmed Hypothesis 4.

Summing up, employees spent significantly more time with their partners during holidays than during working weeks. The quality of these interactions greatly improved and levels of relatedness as well as relationship satisfaction were perceived slightly higher during the holiday.

Table 3.2 Means, standard deviations and results from repeated measures ANOVAs

| | Means (SD) | | | | | | | | | | | RM ANOVAs for 9 and 3 occasions | Significant post-hoc tests |
|---|---|---|---|---|---|---|---|---|---|---|---|---|---|
| | Range | Pre | Inter 1 | Inter 2 | Inter 3 | Inter 4 | Inter | Post 1 | Post 2 | Post 3 | Post 4 | Post | | |
| Happiness | 1–10 | 7.2 (1.1) | 8.0 (1.3) | 8.4 (1.0) | 8.0 (1.2) | 8.1 (1.1) | 8.1 (0.9) | 7.3 (1.3) | 7.3 (1.2) | 7.6 (1.2) | 7.3 (1.4) | 7.4 (1.0) | $F_{(8, 16)} = 4.1, p < 0.01$<br>$F_{(3, 30)} = 12.9, p < 0.01$ | Inter 2 > Post 1 & 2;<br>Inter 3 & 4 > Pre<br>Inter > Pre & Post |
| Time with partner | 1–6 | 2.5 (1.2) | 5.7 (0.7) | 5.9 (0.4) | 5.9 (0.4) | 5.9 (0.3) | 5.8 (0.3) | 3.0 (1.2) | 2.8 (1.2) | 2.8 (1.0) | 2.8 (1.1) | 2.9 (0.9) | $F_{(8, 16)} = 36.9, p < 0.01$<br>$F_{(2, 28)} = 187.5, p < 0.01$ | Inter 1–4 > Pre,<br>Post 1–4<br>Inter > Pre & Post |
| Quality interactions | 1–10 | 7.5 (1.3) | 8.5 (1.0) | 8.4 (1.1) | 8.2 (1.2) | 8.3 (0.9) | 8.4 (0.9) | 7.8 (1.1) | 7.5 (1.4) | 7.6 (1.3) | 7.7 (1.2) | 7.6 (1.1) | $F_{(8, 16)} = 3.9, p = .01$;<br>$F_{(2, 28)} = 21.2, p = <.01$ | Inter 1 > Post 1–4;<br>Inter 4 > Post 2–4<br>Inter > Pre & Post |
| Relatedness | 1–10 | 7.8 (1.2) | 8.4 (1.2) | 8.6 (1.1) | 8.3 (1.5) | 8.2 (1.3) | 8.4 (1.0) | 7.7 (1.1) | 7.4 (1.4) | 7.6 (1.6) | 7.7 (1.3) | 7.6 (1.2) | $F_{(8, 16)} = 5.1, p < .01$<br>$F_{(2, 28)} = 17.6, p < .01$ | Inter 1 > Post1;<br>Inter 2 > Pre,<br>Post 1–4;<br>Inter 3 > Post 1–4<br>Inter > Post |
| Relationship satisfaction | 1–10 | 8.3 (1.2) | 8.5 (1.3) | 8.7 (1.0) | 8.4 (1.5) | 8.4 (1.0) | 8.5 (1.0) | 8.0 (1.0) | 7.8 (1.0) | 8.0 (1.3) | 7.9 (1.2) | 7.9 (1.0) | $F_{(8, 16)} = 3.6, p = 0.01$<br>$F_{(2, 27)} = 15.9, p < 0.01$ | Inter 1 > Post 2,<br>Inter 2 > Post 1 & 2;<br>Inter 3 > Post 2 & 4<br>Inter > Post |

Note: Post-hoc tests with Bonferroni correction for multiple comparisons. Only post-hoc tests for comparisons Inter versus Pre and Post reported.

*Relationship dynamics and happiness*

Levels of self-reported happiness changed significantly across time. Happiness was generally higher during than before and after vacation. Effect size for the change from Pre to Inter was $d = 0.72$, representing a medium effect (see Table 3.2).

Partial correlation analyses demonstrated that changes in happiness during vacation were significantly and strongly associated with quality of interactions with the partner ($pr = 0.64$, $p < 0.001$), feelings of relatedness ($pr = 0.77$, $p < 0.001$) and relationship satisfaction ($pr = 0.83$, $p < 0.001$). Happiness change was not related to the time spent with the partner during holidays ($pr = 0.03$, $p = 0.86$).

In the next step of the analysis, we conducted a regression analysis. Happiness during vacation constituted the dependent variable in this analysis. In the first step, we entered baseline happiness as the first independent variable, because we wanted to predict the *change* in happiness during vacation with the help of the relationship indicators. Happiness before vacation explained 4 per cent of the total variance in happiness during vacation ($\Delta R^2 = 0.04$, $\beta = 0.20$, $p = 0.29$). In the next step, we simultaneously entered the four variables related to people's romantic relationships: 1) time spent with the partner, 2) quality of interactions, 3) relatedness and 4) relationship satisfaction. Together, these variables explained 69 per cent of the variance of happiness during vacation. Inspection of the beta weights demonstrated that these were non-significant for time spent with partner ($\beta = -0.04$, $p = 0.72$), quality of interactions $\beta = -0.37$, $p = 0.11$) and relatedness ($\beta = 0.23$, $p = 0.40$). Relationship satisfaction was the only highly significant predictor for happiness during vacation ($\beta = 0.94$, $p = 0.005$). In total, the model including baseline happiness explained 73 per cent of the variance in happiness during holidays ($F(4, 25) = 13.45$, $p = < 0.001$). Hypothesis 5 was supported for relationship satisfaction only. From all the relationship variables we investigated, relationship satisfaction most strongly affected changes in happiness during vacation compared to before vacation.

## Discussion

For romantic couples, a period of travelling may constitute an opportunity par excellence to focus on their relationships and renew their love for each other. During vacations, partners have more time at their disposal to engage in joint activities and communicate with each other. In combination with the relaxed atmosphere and the absence of job stress and everyday hassles at home (e.g. household chores, childcare), this extra time may lead to feelings of belongingness and relationship satisfaction. It is possible that these potential changes in relationship dynamics can explain why working people's well-being increases during vacations.

To test these assumptions, we set up a longitudinal field study to track happiness, time spent with one's partner, quality of interactions with one's partner, feelings of relatedness and relationship satisfaction before, during and after a long summer vacation in a sample of 35 Dutch employees. In line with our hypotheses, vacationing was indeed associated with higher time investment in relationships as well as substantial improvements in social interactions between romantic couples, feelings of relatedness and relationship satisfaction. Further analyses revealed that from these variables, relationship satisfaction was most accountable for the increase in happiness during compared to before vacation.

Our findings underscore the importance of touristic experiences for romantic partners and their potential for repairing troubled relationships (Durko & Petrick, 2015). Interestingly, the Malaysian government introduced a state-funded holiday programme for couples with marital problems called the 'Second Honeymoon Program', and the Catholic Church has taken similar initiatives by offering 'marriage enrichment retreats' for couples married for five years or more (Chida & Steptoe, 2010). These programmes faced criticism in the public media, but research seems to confirm that they may provide benefits for couples. It is somewhat surprising and curious that the effects of these interventions have not yet been scientifically examined and reported.

The people taking part in this study were quite happy people with already satisfying relationships (see descriptives at baseline in Table 3.2). As this sample reported spontaneous improvements in their relationships, touristic experiences seem a promising approach to strengthen relationships. However, it may also be that a vacation either 'makes or breaks' a relationship. For a couple which already has serious problems, travel and the associated pitfalls such as sleep deprivation, culture shock or health problems (e.g. due to food poisoning or sunburn) may add additional stress which could lead to an escalation of a strained situation. More time being exposed to each other may also increase the risk of latent irritating characteristics becoming more manifest. More research is needed in order to understand which persons under which circumstances profit most from a period of travel with their partners.

It is also interesting to note that improvements in relationship satisfaction lasted only for a brief period. Upon returning home after vacation, the positive effects disappeared very rapidly. This finding is in line with results from earlier studies, demonstrating that beneficial vacation effects on life satisfaction, satisfaction with different aspects of life and happiness vanish within the first week of work resumption (e.g. De Bloom *et al.*, 2010; Hoopes & Lounsbury, 1989; Lohmann, 1996; Nawijn, Marchand, Veenhoven & Vingerhoets, 2010). After a period of quality time, full of attention from and for the partner, joyful activities together and free of hassles, returning to everyday working life and routines may be difficult. The sharp contrast between vacationing and working life which prevents partners from spending much time together could make couples feel slightly dissatisfied about their relationships initially. Still, happy holiday memories last, and they may act as a buffer in difficult times (Shaw *et al.*, 2008). Future research could investigate the potential of holiday memories as a relationship resource and stress buffer.

Theoretically, our study indicates that positive changes in social relationships constitute an important mechanism linking vacationing and well-being. This link has been suggested earlier (e.g. Newman *et al.*, 2014; Ryan & Deci, 2000), but so far only a few studies have empirically examined the role of social relationships and relatedness in connecting leisure and well-being, especially in regard to vacations.

This study indicates that holidays enable working people to spend quality time with their partners. More importantly, tourist experiences seem to temporarily boost people's romantic relationships and enable couples to revive their love, which may also explain why tourism can foster human well-being and happiness.

### *Limitations and suggestions for future research*

The sample size of the current study was rather small, and the participants were fairly well-educated, limiting this study's external validity to certain populations. However, our research design with repeated weekly measurements taken from the same persons across a long time period (nine weeks on average) makes causal inferences more likely. Moreover, as we were able to find significant links between vacations, relationship changes and happiness in a small sample and the accompanying low statistical power, we are confident that studies with larger samples would find similar results. We also have no reason to assume that romantic relationships would develop differently in persons with different socio-economic status or educational level. However, research on this topic is scarce, and the findings should be replicated in more diverse and larger samples.

Correspondingly, it would be interesting to investigate whether 'staycations' affect romantic relationships and happiness in a similar way as holidays spent outside the home environment. It can be speculated that romantic couples who spend their holidays within their usual domiciles engage in different types of activities than couples who undertake a trip. Due to the proximity of one's usual surroundings, it may, for example, be more difficult to refrain from work-related tasks and domestic chores at home. This may be especially true for women who generally have less free time and are burdened with more domestic tasks at home than men (Mattingly & Blanchi, 2003). For women with small children, holidays are often work-filled and full of obligations (Davidson, 1996). 'Staycations' may be more risky for them, because they may end up working for a great deal of their time. It may also be that couples engage in fewer joint activities during staycations, because they may meet friends or family separately or spend time on their own hobbies. Future research needs to address if and how vacations differ from 'staycations' in general and in relation to relationship dynamics in particular.

Another shortcoming of this study is our reliance on single-item questionnaires. As the available body of knowledge on relationship changes across a holiday period is limited, our aim was to get a first overview on the possible changes that may occur. Therefore, we assessed various different concepts and, consequently, had to limit the amount of items measuring each concept. We kept in mind that the questionnaires had to be filled out shortly before going to bed and should not interfere with bedtime activities. In future studies, it could be useful to focus on fewer concepts and measure these concepts with more items. Assessment at other time points of the day could also be useful to make sure that our measurement time did not affect the reports of relationship quality. In addition to self-report questionnaires, future studies could also utilise different sources of information. The most obvious addition would be ratings of relationship satisfaction and relatedness of both partners, which would also require advanced multilevel modelling of the data. As the main purpose of the initial data collection was to investigate the effect of vacation in general, we do, unfortunately, only have data from one partner. Future studies could aim to recruit dyads who travel together and follow these dyads before, during and after their holidays. This information could be complemented with analyses of videotaped conversations or physiological data. With regard to social relationships, changes in oxytocin, also called the 'bonding hormone' (Grewen, Girdler, Amico & Light, 2005) may be highly interesting to study across vacations.

An additional shortcoming concerns the interconnectedness between the studied variables. For instance, happiness and relationship satisfaction correlated quite highly during vacation ($r = 0.81$, $p < 0.01$). This may have masked other potential relationships, especially when these variables were entered simultaneously in the regression analysis. Spending time together is, for example, a precondition for positive interactions to happen and for the experience of benefits in a healthy, fulfilling relationship. Relationship satisfaction may actually represent a combination of the other factors. So only if couples spend time together, engage in high-quality interactions and feel closely related will they report high levels of relationship satisfaction.

Last but not least, the study focused on rather long holiday trips. Three-week holiday trips are a European phenomenon and much less common in other countries (Ray, Sanes & Schmitt, 2013). It is possible that these long trips affect relationships differently than shorter trips. However, the non-significant correlations between vacation duration and relationship indicators do not point in this direction (correlation coefficients varied between -0.29 for time spent with partner and 0.06 for quality of interactions). Still more research in shorter and different types of vacations (e.g. domestic holidays, holidays spent at home, sports holidays) may render interesting new insights.

Overall, we agree with Petrick and Huether (2013, p. 707) that it is 'difficult to understand how a field of study as diverse as tourism, with over 40 years of strong inquiry, has barely started to examine potential benefits for tourists'.

# References

Abdel-Khalek, A. M. (2006). Measuring happiness with a single-item scale. *Social Behavior and Personality*, 34(2), 139–150.

Aron, A., Norman, C. C., Aron, E. N., McKenna, C., & Heyman, R. E. (2000). Couples' shared participation in novel and arousing activities and experienced relationship quality. *Journal of Personality and Social Psychology*, 78(2), 273–284.

Bauer, T. G., & McKercher, B. (2003). *Sex and tourism: Journeys of romance, love, and lust*. Binghamton: The Haworth Hospitality Press.

Baumeister, R. F., & Leary, M. R. (1995). The need to belong: Desire for interpersonal attachments as a fundamental human motivation. *Psychological Bulletin*, 117(3), 497–529.

50   *Jessica de Bloom et al.*

Chida, Y., & Steptoe, A. (2010). Greater cardiovascular responses to laboratory mental stress are associated with poor subsequent cardiovascular risk status: A meta-analysis of prospective evidence. *Hypertension*, 55(4), 1026–1032. doi: 10.1161/hypertensionaha. 109.146621

Christensen, Bo T., & Schunn, Christian D. (2005). Spontaneous access and analogical incubation effects. *Creativity Research Journal*, 17(2–3), 207–220. doi: 10.1080/ 10400419.2005.9651480

Cohen, J. (1990). Things I have learned (so far). *American Psychologist*, 45(12), 1304. doi: 10.1037/0003–066X.45.12.1304

Csikszentmihalyi, M. (1991). *Flow: The psychology of optimal experience* (Vol. 41). New York: Harper Perennial.

Csikszentmihalyi, M. (2013). *Flow: The psychology of happiness*. New York: Random House.

Davidson, P. (1996). The holiday and work experiences of women with young children. *Leisure Studies*, 15(2), 89–103. doi: 10.1080/026143696375648

De Bloom, J. (2012). *How do vacations affect workers' health and well-being? Vacation (after-) effects and the role of vacation activities and experiences* (PhD), Radboud University Nijmegen, 's Hertogenbosch: BoxPress.

De Bloom, J., Geurts, S. A. E., & Kompier, M. A. J. (2012). Effects of short vacations, vacation activities and experiences on employee health and well-being. *Stress and Health*, 28(4), 305–318.

De Bloom, J., Geurts, S. A. E., & Kompier, M. A. J. (2013). Vacation (after-) effects on employee health and well-being, and the role of vacation activities, experiences and sleep. *Journal of Happiness Studies*, 14(2), 613–633. doi: 10.1007/s10902–012–9345–3

De Bloom, J., Geurts, S. A. E., Taris, T. W., Sonnentag, S., De Weerth, C., & Kompier, M. A. J. (2010). Effects of vacation from work on health and well-being: Lots of fun, quickly gone. *Work & Stress*, 24, 196–216.

Demerouti, E., Bakker, A. B., Sonnentag, S., & Fullagar, C. J. (2012). Work-related flow and energy at work and at home: A study on the role of daily recovery. *Journal of Organizational Behavior*, 33(2), 276–295. doi: 10.1002/job.760

Diener, Ed. (2000). Subjective well-being: The science of happiness and a proposal for a national index. *American Psychologist*, 55(1), 34–43. doi: 10.1037/0003–066x.55.1.34

Dijksterhuis, Ap, & Meurs, Teun. (2006). Where creativity resides: The generative power of unconscious thought. *Consciousness and Cognition*, 15(1), 135–146. doi: 10.1016/j. concog.2005.04.007

Dunn, O. J. (1961). Multiple comparisons among means. *Journal of the American Statistical Association*, 56(293), 52–64.

Durko, A. M., & Petrick, J. F. (2013). Family and relationship benefits of travel experiences: A literature review. *Journal of Travel Research*, 52(6), 720–730. doi: 10.1177/ 0047287513496478

Durko, Angela M., & Petrick, James F. (2015). Travel as relationship therapy: Examining the effect of vacation satisfaction applied to the investment model. *Journal of Travel Research*. doi: 10.1177/0047287515592970

Elo, A., Leppänen, A., & Jahkola, A. (2003). Validity of a single-item measure of stress symptoms. *Scandinavian Journal of Work, Environment & Health*, 29, 444–451.

Filep, S. (2012). Positive psychology and tourism. In M. Uysal, R. Perdue & J. Sirgy (Eds.), *The handbook of tourism and quality-of-life: The missing links* (pp. 31–50). Dordrecht: Springer.

Filep, S., & Deery, M. (2010). Towards a picture of tourists' happiness. *Tourism Analysis*, 15(4), 399–410. doi: 10.3727/108354210X12864727453061

Fritz, C., & Sonnentag, S. (2006). Recovery, well-being, and performance-related outcomes: The role of workload and vacation experiences. *Journal of Applied Psychology*, 91, 936–945.

Grewen, K. M., Girdler, S. S., Amico, J., & Light, K. C. (2005). Effects of partner support on resting oxytocin, cortisol, norepinephrine, and blood pressure before and after warm partner contact. *Psychosomatic Medicine*, 67(4), 531–538.

Hartig, T., Evans, G. W., Jamner, L. D., Davis, D. S., & Gärling, T. (2003). Tracking restoration in natural and urban field settings. *Journal of Environmental Psychology*, 23(2), 109–123.

Herold, E., Garcia, R., & DeMoya, T. (2001). Female tourists and beach boys: Romance or sex tourism? *Annals of Tourism Research*, 28(4), 978–997.

Hoopes, L. L., & Lounsbury, J. W. (1989). An investigation of life satisfaction following a vacation: A domain specific approach. *Journal of Community Psychology*, 17, 129–140.

Inhorn, M. C., & Patrizio, P. (2009). Rethinking reproductive 'tourism' as reproductive 'exile'. *Fertility and Sterility*, 92(3), 904–906.

Jeffreys, Sheila. (2003). Sex tourism: Do women do it too? *Leisure Studies*, 22(3), 223–238. doi: 10.1080/026143603200075452

Johnson, H. A., Zabriskie, R. B., & Hill, B. (2006). The contribution of couple leisure involvement, leisure time, and leisure satisfaction to marital satisfaction. *Marriage & Family Review*, 40(1), 69–91.

Lehto, X. Y., Choi, S., Lin, Y.-C., & MacDermid, S. M. (2009). Vacation and family functioning. *Annals of Tourism Research*, 36(3), 459–479.

Lehto, X. Y., Lin, Y.-C., Chen, Y., & Choi, S. (2012). Family vacation activities and family cohesion. *Journal of Travel & Tourism Marketing*, 29(8), 835–850.

Lim, Vivien K. G., & Chen, Don J. Q. (2009). Cyberloafing at the workplace: Gain or drain on work? *Behaviour & Information Technology*, 31(4), 343–353. doi: 10.1080/01449290903353054

Lim, Vivien K. G., & Teo, Thompson S. H. (2005). Prevalence, perceived seriousness, justification and regulation of cyberloafing in Singapore: An exploratory study. *Information & Management*, 42(8), 1081–1093. doi: 10.1016/j.im.2004.12.002

Lohmann, Martin. (1996). You'll better stay at home? – Studies on the recreational effects of holidays and holiday tourism. *Revue de Tourisme*, 3, 39–44.

Maas, Jolanda, Verheij, Robert A., de Vries, Sjerp, Spreeuwenberg, Peter, Schellevis, Francois G., & Groenewegen, Peter P. (2009). Morbidity is related to a green living environment. *Journal of Epidemiology and Community Health*, 63(12), 967–973.

Mattingly, M. J., & Blanchi, S. M. (2003). Gender differences in the quantity and quality of free time: The U.S. experience. *Social Forces*, 81(3), 999–1030. doi: 10.1353/sof.2003.0036

Mitchell, Richard, & Popham, Frank. (2008). Effect of exposure to natural environment on health inequalities: An observational population study. *The Lancet*, 372(9650), 1655–1660.

Nawijn, J. (2010). The holiday happiness curve: A preliminary investigation into mood during a holiday abroad. *International Journal of Tourism Research*, 12, 281–290. doi: 10.1002/jtr.1756

Nawijn, J., Marchand, M., Veenhoven, R., & Vingerhoets, A. (2010). Vacationers happier, but most not happier after a holiday. *Applied Research in Quality of Life*, 5, 35–47.

Nawijn, J., Mitas, O., Lin, Y., & Kerstetter, D. (2013). How do we feel on vacation? A closer look at how emotions change over the course of a trip. *Journal of Travel Research*, 52(2), 265–274.

Newman, D. A. (2009). Missing data techniques and low response rates: The role of systematic nonresponse parameters. In C. E. Lance & R. J. Vandenberg (Eds.), *Statistical and methodological myths and urban legends: Doctrine, verity and fable in the organizational and social sciences* (pp. 7–36). London: Routledge.

Newman, D. B., Tay, L., & Diener, E. (2014). Leisure and subjective well-being: A model of psychological mechanisms as mediating factors. *Journal of Happiness Studies*, 15, 555–578. doi: 10.1007/s10902–013–9435-x

Petrick, J. F., & Huether, D. (2013). Is travel better than chocolate and wine? The benefits of travel: A special series. *Journal of Travel Research*, 52(6), 705–708.

Ray, R., Sanes, M., & Schmitt, J. (2013). *No-vacation nation revisited*. Washington, DC: Center for Economic and Policy Research.

Ryan, R. M., Bernstein, J. H., & Brown, K. W. (2010). Weekends, work, and well-being: Psychological need satisfactions and day of the week effects on mood, vitality, and physical symptoms. *Journal of Social and Clinical Psychology*, 29(1), 95–122.

Ryan, R. M., & Deci, E. L. (2000). Self-determination theory and the facilitation of intrinsic motivation, social development, and well-being. *American Psychologist*, 55, 68–78.

Shaw, S. M., Havitz, M. E., & Delemere, F. M. (2008). I decided to invest in my kids' memories: Family vacations, memories, and the social construction of the family. *Tourism Culture & Communication*, 8(1), 13–26.

Singh, S. (2002). Love, anthropology and tourism. *Annals of Tourism Research*, 29(1), 261–264. doi: 10.1016/S0160–7383(01)00044–5

Sirgy, M. J., Kruger, P. S., Lee, D.-J., & Yu, G. B. (2011). How does a travel trip affect tourists' life satisfaction? *Journal of Travel Research*, 50(3), 261–275. doi: 10.1177/0047287510362784

Smith, Gregory T., Snyder, Douglas K., Trull, Timothy J., & Monsma, Brian R. (1988). Predicting relationship satisfaction from couples' use of leisure time. *The American Journal of Family Therapy*, 16(1), 3–13. doi: 10.1080/01926188808250702

Sonnentag, S. (2001). Work, recovery activities, and individual well-being: A diary study. *Journal of Occupational Health Psychology*, 6, 196–210.

Sonnentag, S., & Fritz, C. (2015). Recovery from job stress: The stressor-detachment model as an integrative framework. *Journal of Organizational Behavior*, 36(1), 72–103. doi: 10.1002/job.1924

Stebbins, Robert A. (2001). Serious leisure. *Society*, 38(4), 53–57.

Sullivan, G. M., & Feinn, R. (2012). Using effect sizes-or why the p value is not enough. *Journal of Graduate Medical Education*, 4(3), 279–282. doi: 10.4300/JGME-D-12–00156.1

Takano, Takehito, Nakamura, Keiko, & Watanabe, Masafumi. (2002). Urban residential environments and senior citizens' longevity in megacity areas: The importance of walkable green spaces. *Journal of Epidemiology and Community Health*, 56(12), 913–918.

Trauer, B., & Ryan, C. (2005). Destination image, romance and place experience: An application of intimacy theory in tourism. *Tourism Management*, 26(4), 481–491. doi: 10.1016/j.tourman.2004.02.014

Uysal, M., Sirgy, M. J., Woo, E., & Kim, H. (2016). Quality of life (QOL) and well-being research in tourism. *Tourism Management*, 53, 244–261. doi: 10.1016/j.tourman.2015.07.013

Van Hooff, M. L. M., Geurts, S. A. E., Kompier, M. A. J., & Taris, T. W. (2007). Workdays, in-between workdays and the weekend: A diary study on effort and recovery. *International Archives of Occupational and Environmental Health*, 80, 599–613.

Van Hooff, M. L. M., Geurts, S. A. E., Taris, T. W., & Kompier, M. A. J. (2007). How fatigued do you currently feel? Convergent and discriminant validity of a single-item fatigue measure. *Journal of Occupational Health*, 49, 224–234.

Voigt, C., & Laing, J. H. (2010). Journey into parenthood: Commodification of reproduction as a new tourism niche market. *Journal of Travel & Tourism Marketing*, 27(3), 252–268.

Waldinger, R. J., & Schulz, M. S. (2010). What's love got to do with it? Social functioning, perceived health, and daily happiness in married octogenarians. *Psychology and Aging*, 25(2), 422–431.

# 4 Tourists' accounts of learning and positive emotions through sensory experiences

*Xavier Matteucci*

## Introduction

Research in cognitive sciences shows that emotions are often more powerful determinants of human behaviour than rational thinking is (Sylwester, 1994). In the social and management sciences, many have argued that it is important to understand consumers' emotional responses because emotions strongly influence motivation, satisfaction and behavioural intentions (Dubé & Menon, 2000; Gnoth, 1997; Prayag, Hosany & Odeh, 2013). Further, in the travel and tourism context, satisfactory experiences are deemed to positively contribute to tourists' overall quality of life (Sirgy, 2002). There is also a clear link between positive emotions experienced at a destination and memorable tourism experiences (Tung & Ritchie, 2011). A memorable or rewarding experience is not strictly characterised by positive emotions felt at the destination, but it also involves a number of personal benefits such as social, intellectual, self and physical development (ibid). Positive personal outcomes such as knowledge acquisition and self-discovery on holiday are therefore closely bound to emotional tourism experiences. Since we experience the world through our whole body, tourists' experiences (hence emotions) are intricately linked to sensory impulses registered at the destination. By giving the example of the act of strolling 'the alleys of an Arab city with its unique sights, sounds, smells; and to look the inhabitants in the eye, see their frowns and their smiles', Csikszentmihalyi (2012) himself recognises the crucial importance of the senses in tourism experiences. Tourists' sensory experiences, therefore, partly explain the positive emotions and the learning outcomes associated with travel and tourism. Despite the central role of the sentient body in tourism, few researchers have paid attention to tourists' sensory experiences in their multi-dimensions (Crouch & Desforges, 2003; Matteucci, 2014).

Alongside the experience of flow (Csikszentmihalyi, 1990) and eudaimonia (Waterman, 1993), the experience of pleasure through sensory gratification is conducive to feelings of happiness (Peterson, Ruch, Beermann, Park & Seligman, 2007). Surprisingly, despite the relevance of the sensorial realm to understanding human positive emotions, investigations of sensation and pleasures have also received very little attention in positive psychology (Biswas-Diener *et al.*, 2015). In a similar vein, Bryant, Chadwick and Kluwe (2011) also contend that much research in psychology has primarily focused on affective states and outcomes, thus leaving the twists and turns of positive experiences little explored through other modalities. This chapter seeks to address these gaps by exploring tourists' sensory experiences through various activities in Seville, Spain. Before the methodology and the research findings are presented, a brief review of literature around the senses highlights the connection between the sensory information we perceive and the emotions we feel as a consequence of our perceptions. Some past studies concerned with tourist sensory experiences are also presented.

## The emotional and perceptual systems

The term sense, as a verb, generally refers to either the ability to feel/perceive, or the ability to understand as in *sense-making*. Sense, as feeling or perception, is broadly triggered through the sense organs of touch, smell, sight, hearing and taste. For example, we talk about 'feeling cold' or 'hearing the sound of music'. Rodaway (1994) believes that these two aspects (sense as perception and meaning) are closely related and are both dependent on the environment. He explains that the 'sensuous experience and understanding is grounded in previous experience and expectation, each dependent on sensual and sensory capacities and educational training and cultural conditioning' (p. 5). While in everyday language the terms *sensation* and *perception* are used interchangeably, in reality, sensation and perception are distinct. Sensation is the process of picking up information from the outside world and sending it to the brain (Goldstein, 2009). Unlike perception, that Goldstein (2009, p. 8) defines as a 'conscious sensory experience' and which entails the selection, organisation and interpretation of information, sensation bluntly corresponds to a raw unsettled feeling. What these definitions tell us is that both sensation and perception are profoundly corporeal and that since perception emerges out of a body-mind exercise, there are no experiences without bodies, hence the importance of attending to the sensuous for any complete examination of emotional experiences.

Gibson (1966) provides an alternative classification to the traditional unbound five senses in which the senses are categorised as five perceptual systems: (1) the basic orienting system, (2) the auditory system, (3) the haptic system, (4) the taste-smell system and (5) the visual system. For Gibson, the senses are active and interrelated rather than being passive and mutually exclusive; in this way, Gibson recognises the complex multi-sensuality of human perception. Moreover, by considering the body as a sense organ, Gibson includes body movements amongst the human sensorium. Body orientation and the sense of touch (haptic) strongly overlap since balance and orientation can be reached while in locomotion, for which muscles and joints are necessary, not to mention the permanent contact of the skin with the earth. The sensory sensation of movements is usually referred to as kinaesthesia. The creative process of perception in which corporeal sensations and meaning are enmeshed is acknowledged by French existential phenomenologist Maurice Merleau-Ponty (2005), who posits that human agency and the world are inseparable. The relationship between the human body and its environment forms the basis of a number of concepts such as *embodiment, emplacement, perfor-mance* and Deleuzian *becoming* that are useful in researching tourist experiences (Andrews, 2005; Crouch, 2009; Matteucci, 2014).

Like Merleau-Ponty and Rodaway, scientists have long dismissed the idea that the body and the brain are two separate entities; instead, neuroscientists have demonstrated the close connections between the brain (where our emotional system is located) and peripheral body parts, as well as other organs such as the skin in the processing of emotional information (Niedenthal, Wood & Rychlowska, 2014). Sylwester (1994) explains that emotions are regulated by the limbic system and the cerebral cortex. He also explains how sensory information is processed through these two regulators. In the limbic system, the amygdala filters and decodes complex sensory inputs which are then sent to the brain by the thalamus, which therefore acts as a connector between the amygdala and the rest of the brain. In addition to the amygdala, chemical molecules called pheromones are released from the skin of a secreting individual to trigger neural responses in a receiving other. Pheromones are said to regulate sexual behaviour and alter our level of comfort in a social context. The cerebral cortex receives, organises and gives meaning to sensory information before it makes decisions and triggers behavioural responses. While the whole emotional process is a more complex one, this brief description serves to indicate the crucial role played by sensory information in delivering emotional experiences.

Whereas a detailed review of literature around the body and senses across disciplines is beyond the scope of this chapter (see Agapito, Mendes & Valle, 2013; Onfrey, 2006), it is worth pointing to a number of studies which have explored tourists' sensory experiences. First, it should be mentioned that some commentators (e.g. Edensor & Falconer, 2011; Scarles, 2009) have questioned the privileged status of the sense of vision in tourism, as epitomised through tourists' practices such as sightseeing and photography, by arguing that some tourism experiences may be dominated by other senses and that vision is never isolated from olfactory, aural or kinaesthetic experiences. Some research on non-visual sensualities includes Dann and Jacobsen's (2002) work on olfactory descriptions in literary travel accounts. In an ethnographic study, Andrews (2005) examines the role of smell and hearing in tourists' experiences of a resort setting in Mallorca. Andrews illustrates how the senses of smell and hearing are powerful conduits through which one becomes aware of her/his own identity. Pilcher, Newman and Manning (2009) focused on the sense of hearing in an attempt at evaluating quality experiences in a North American national park. In Menorca, Obrador Pons (2007) explores haptic experiences on the beach and argues that by attending to naked bodies and the sense of touch, we rediscover the beach as a site of enchantment and relationships that can inspire deep attachment to our world. Everett (2009) and Falconer (2013) attend to food experiences. For instance, Everett (2009, p. 353) reveals that 'tourists only felt they had experienced the place when they undertook multi-sensory activities such as eating fish by the sea; and a sense of temporal escape was only truly realised once the body was sensorially immersed'. Others have more holistically examined embodied experiences in tourist settings (e.g. Saldanha, 2002 in Goa, India). Additionally, Edensor (2006) discusses the politics of tourist spatial configurations, which he argues, either render the experience of 'otherness' as comfortable and familiar (thus perpetrating social order through commodification), or instead confront tourists' sensuous encounters with unfamiliar environments, which have the potential to disturb, thwart and unsettle embodied identities.

## Methodology

The data that follows stems from research conducted with 20 tourists (16 females and 4 males) who were primarily interested in the practice of flamenco in Seville; however, the sensory experiences they report far exceed the boundaries of flamenco settings. The research participants who came from various French- and English-speaking countries, such as France, Switzerland, Canada, the United Kingdom and the United States, spent between one week and a few months in the southern region of Andalusia. In the Andalusian capital, they partook in flamenco dance or guitar courses, but also participated in traditional tourist activities such as visiting cultural attractions, rambling the narrow city streets and squares and eating local food on bar terraces. Seville, Andalusia's largest city with about 703,261 inhabitants (Ayuntamiento de Sevilla, 2014), spreads along both sides of the river Guadalquivir and boasts a rich flamenco tradition. Every year thousands of tourists congregate in Seville to experience flamenco in its diverse forms such as concerts, festivals or flamenco dance, music or singing classes.

Data were collected between September 2009 and May 2010. Research participants were purposively recruited at flamenco schools in the picturesque districts of Triana and Macarena. The central research question which guided this research was 'what is the role of the body and senses in the tourist experience of flamenco?' To research tourists' sensual experiences in Seville, I employed a constructivist grounded theory (Charmaz, 2006) research strategy in which data was collected through informal in-depth interviews and participant observation. Furthermore, during the interviews, I used a set of 18 flamenco-related images in an attempt to flesh out the more intimate aspects of the tourists' embodied experiences (see Matteucci, 2013, for a detailed account on the use of images in this project). The interview data was recorded and transcribed verbatim. The interview audio files provide sensory evidence for Seville's heartbeat. The vast majority of the interview recordings is filled with the sound of music in some ways: flamenco guitar and feet stamping punctuated my interview with Pauline and her daughter Patricia, the sound of fanfare intruded the relatively peaceful atmosphere of Plaza San Lorenzo while talking to James, the sound of Arabian darburka pleasantly livened up my interview with Alice, and the sound of pop, rock and sevillanas played on the radio supplemented the many loud voices in and outside bars throughout other interviews. The audio files provide some evidence for the indeterminacy of non-tourist places where the interviews were conducted and in which rich local sounds and other textures inflated the tourists' senses. Moreover, the distractions that the sounds of Seville afford facilitated the data collection in that those phonic disruptions naturally opened new streams of discussions, thus enabling tourists to recall sensations and events and tell new anecdotes. Field notes were taken, and the interview textual data was analysed following Charmaz's (2006) three-step coding process (initial, focused and theoretical coding).

## Findings

The tourists' accounts of their experiences in Seville are replete with sensory descriptions. The kinaesthetic, haptic, auditory, gustatory, olfactory or visual experiences articulated by the research participants resulted in a wide range of learning outcomes such as enhanced physical skills and increased body awareness. In an attempt to produce a clear account of the role played by the body and senses in the respondents' experiences, the findings have been categorised following Gibson's (1966) classification of the senses as five perceptual systems: (1) the basic orientation system, (2) the haptic system, (3) the auditory system, (4) the taste-smell system and (5) the visual system.

### *Orientation and haptic systems*

Many female informants made mention of the strenuous work of their bodies in the learning process of flamenco dance. To achieve dexterity, speed and equilibrium, hard physical work is required. Some research participants talked about experiencing their bodies in terms of new bodily sensations. As in the case of Juliette, some informants have discovered new bodily sensations through their many hours of practice. Although heightened bodily feelings may be confined to specific settings and performances, these feelings seem to contribute to an overall appreciation of the potentialities of one's own body:

> Physically, I've discovered sensations that I didn't know before. I've learned that I could do certain things with my body that not even [I had thought I could do before] . . . It's like when you see someone dancing Capoeira – I'm like 'wow'! It's amazing! Well, when you manage to do it with your own body, you . . . So, physically, I've discovered amazing sensations.

The latter quote provides some insight into the sensuous nature of leisure experiences and in this way emphasises the importance of bodily feelings in learning experiences. Here, although Juliette does not manage to explicitly articulate the types of sensations that she feels while dancing, her description still informs us of the interrelations that exist between physical skills acquisition, cognitive awareness and feelings of a transforming body. She uses the adjective 'amazing', which points to positive emotions and highly pleasurable sensations.

Outside the boundaries of the flamenco class, respondents have experienced their bodies in other distinctive activities such as walking and cycling around town, but also dancing in bars and at the local *feria* and just being in various places in the presence of friends and members of the host community. Seville enjoys many cycling lanes, pedestrian areas and an extensive public transportation system, including buses, trams, trains and metro lines. While most informants chose to walk, others such as Catherine preferred to cycle. Catherine clearly pointed out that, for her, the choice of cycling was because of her previous experience of being in Seville. She had known Seville enough to now commute on two wheels. For her, cycling not only proved her level of self-confidence in riding a bike in a foreign city and ascertained her geographical knowledge, it also most certainly made her feel like a local. For Catherine, cycling may have contributed to giving her a sense of local identity, which in turn may have boosted her self-esteem. Thus acting like a resident confers Catherine with what may be seen as an elevated status. Alternatively, for Aglaé, walking enabled her to explore and experience places:

> I love strolling around when I have time for myself. I look at all the street names; I take pictures . . . I behave like a tourist. Yeah, I love walking along the river, along the Guadalquivir; especially the first days I was here, I would walk along the river; some people would play the guitar and stuff. So, yeah, I like sitting by the river and listening to people playing the guitar.

Pink (2008, p. 3) cites the work of De Certeau (1984) on the practice of everyday life, which she argues provides 'a starting point for understanding movement as a form of place-making'. According to De Certeau, walking is 'a process of *appropriation* of the topographical system on the part of the pedestrian'. Although walking may be taken for granted by the informants, it gave Aglaé and others a measure and an appreciation of the city. A stroll along the river may open to serendipitous encounters with people playing the flamenco guitar and allow the self to focus on being in the here (on the river banks) and now, as opposed to situating the focus on going to a particular destination. The experience of idiosyncratic textures along the Guadalquivir engages Aglaé's senses to the full; it awakens her sense of geography. Besides, her experience is enjoyable. For Céline, who follows the same route every day to go to her flamenco school, walking along *calle feria* offers time and space for daydreaming. She says that if she lived in Seville, she would not like to live close to the cathedral but in the beautiful urban area of *La Macarena*. The walk gives rise to a reverie – a reverie in which she sees herself living in Seville, as in a staged performance, or as Edensor (2006, p. 42) puts it, the stroll provides 'a host of stimulating sensations and material for imaginative speculation'. Céline and Aglaé seek sensual immersion in the flux of the crowds and through urban dwellings. Like the figure of the flaneur (Edensor, 2006), the two females are sensually alert, contemplative, open to unpredictable events and enjoy roaming and discovering spaces.

### Auditory system

The respondents' references to the sense of hearing were abundant and diverse. While most respondents referred to the sound of flamenco in its different forms (flamenco music, guitar, feet stamping, percussion, *jaleo*,[1] voices), a variety of other sounds were reported – most notably the sound of street life. Particularly meaningful were the informants' serendipitous experiences of flamenco in public places. Not only does one hear flamenco or sevillanas coming out of cars and house windows, but it is also common to hear people sing or play the guitar on plazas, promenades and construction sites. In the next two excerpts, the serendipitous encounters underscore the prominence of the senses in producing memorable experiences. First, Celina refers to her experience of the *Semana Santa* (Easter) festival in Seville:

> Watching a parade and seeing somebody belt out a Saeta[2] is like absolutely – you know – on the spur of the moment that was amazing. Going into a bar, and seeing all of a sudden [someone] start[s] singing. You know, when you are walking down the street and these young kids have their boom busters going on really loud in their cars . . . the flamenco rhythm, you know . . .

In Celina's account, serendipity, which entails the dimensions of contingency and discovery, is revealed by the key phrase 'all of a sudden'. The other phrase 'on the spur of the moment that was amazing' suggests a brief loss of awareness. By loss of awareness it is meant that Celina is spontaneously and profoundly involved in the event, which, in turn, may indicate that she forgets everything but this particular event. At least, she seems to forget about herself as a visitor during a short lapse of time as she merges with the event itself. In addition, Celina uses the verb 'belt out', thus suggesting that the plaintive song was loud and emotional. Baffling habitual sensual modalities and inspiring awe, the *saeta* experience is a very sensuous one. The experience appears to be rewarding in such a way that it seems reasonable to suggest that it resembles Csikszentmihalyi's (1990) concept of *flow* and Hom Cary's (2004) concept of the *tourist moment,* both of which encompass the dimensions of loss of self-consciousness and intrinsic reward.

Second, Aron's experience of a small guitar performance in a corner bar which he had accidentally discovered provides another example for the role of the sense of hearing in delivering positive emotions:

> The comfort of the sound . . . The comfort of the sound 'cause that's what made me . . . and I can't explain that 'cause that's one of the true . . . one of the mysterious things anyway.

Aron's description is somehow contemplative. The use of the word 'comfort' suggests a wholesome feeling where the body and mind are at rest. The term 'comfort' also describes a desirable state whereby a very enjoyable experience is characterised by relaxation and a floating feeling of well-being. Although, and like for most extraordinary experiences, Aron finds his experience hard to put into words, he nevertheless reports the mysterious effect of the sound on him. The magic or divine character of the adjective 'mysterious' even elevates Aron's experience to a spiritual level.

## *Taste-smell system*

Accounts of gustatory and olfactory experiences were scarce. This scarcity may be explained by a number of reasons. For example, people may find it difficult to articulate olfactory sensations (Porteous, 1985). With smell and taste being considered intimate senses (Rodaway, 1994) – at least in the Western world – their reporting may be perceived problematic. Furthermore, in the informants' experiences, other senses may have been dominant, thus giving the senses of smell and taste minor roles. Although a few tourists talked about the local food and coffee in positive terms, their descriptions remained poor. Therefore, the focus here is set on olfaction. Interestingly, while positive experiences were expressed in relation to the local vegetation such as flowers, plants and trees, negative evaluations were associated with urban environments:

> Actually, well I have to say that one of the top experiences that I've had – my partner was here during Easter, we went to Barrio Santa Cruz, and there is a little square, there're a few little squares, but one of them, Doña Elvira, it's a little square with restaurants and I think one or two peñas. And, orange trees blooming, and the fragrance just sitting there. Just so you know, we spent the afternoon, kind of drinking a bottle of wine [laugh] and having a conversation. But in an environment so . . . [it] was so amazing because of orange trees. I mean, the time when the orange trees were blooming here. It was absolutely amazing.
>
> (Irene)

> What blew my mind the other day was that we walked past [a garden] . . . not far from Plaza de España, actually towards the university, towards the old tobacco plant, and there, the fragrances are amazing. You have everything. You have the plane trees that you see along the roads in the South of France, but you also have ficus trees – I don't know how many times centenary – trees that could come from the desert, you know those weird sort of kaki trees, then orange trees . . . yeah and the stone pines. There're many aromas – It's so beautiful!'
>
> (Céline)

These two lengthy quotes call for at least three observations. First, the enchantment experienced by Irene and Céline is conveyed via a number of key phrases ('top experiences', 'what blew my mind'), nouns ('fragrance', 'aromas') and adjectives ('amazing', 'absolutely amazing', beautiful'). Second, both women embed their olfactory sensations within a particular environment which may be seen as romantic for Irene ('little square') or exotic for Céline ('South of France', 'desert'). This underscores Gibson's idea that the environment adds dimensions to sensory information. Third, it is difficult to disassociate the olfactory from the visual sensations as the smell is intricately linked to the sight of flowers and plants ('[it] was so amazing because of orange trees', 'there're many aromas – it's so beautiful'). These two excerpts suggest that looking and smelling may pertain to only one, yet multifaceted, activity which involves one experiencing body in one environment (Ingold, 2000). This view therefore blurs the boundaries which separate the human body from its distinctive sense organs, and it further dissolves the body/environment dichotomy. The following quote shows that a negative olfactory evaluation does not necessarily translate into a negative experience; rather it can illuminate the personal meanings ascribed to places and have the potential to make people become aware of their own cultures:

> The things you notice . . . the smell of horse shit. This is strange. You know, especially coming from the US where everything is very sanitised – you know – nobody don't, people don't like when things don't smell good . . . or smell unpleasant, and you know, when you come here it just seems more authentic and real and not sanitised – you know – 'god! There is a big pile of horse shit here'. You don't have people constantly coming up cleaning it up so people don't have to smell horse, horse shit . . . what I'm saying like Americans we are so sensitive, we don't want to smell unpleasant things, you know.
> (James)

The smell of horse manure gave James a sense of experiencing the real Seville – a Seville as it is experienced everyday by its residents and therefore not commodified to cater to its visitors. This more authentic sensual experience of Seville is constituent of self-knowledge processes. James's olfactory experience of Seville enabled him to become aware of his own and more generally American sensitivity towards unpleasant smells and the sight of unpleasant objects.

### Visual system

For many research participants, and particularly in the flamenco course context, the act of watching was associated with learning. Many informants linked learning to their active and focused observation of people in distinctive places, as in the case of Anna who refers to her avid gaze at the flamenco dancers:

> You want to discover more; you want to see more; you want to hear more; always more; see concerts; see real people. Of course, you see them on television or on Internet but it's not the same as seeing them on site. You can really see them fully into their own thing, so you discover even more. It's amazing, like by only watching . . . sometimes, I tell myself to watch and watch and watch as to feed my eyes for later being able to enjoy from it like when I am back home, until a few months after.

Anna may feel the urge to inscribe her memory with a flow of images derived from her active gaze. The repetition of verbs ('discover', 'see', 'watch') and the use of adjectives ('more', 'always more', 'even more') both reveal the tourist experience as an opportunity to indulge the senses in an excessive manner. Anna wants to see more or more intensely. For Anna, being in Seville provides an opportunity to feel and inflate her sensorial boundaries. The phrase 'to feed my eyes' also indicates that she uses her sense of sight as a conscious way of recording meaningful events which will accompany her long after her return home. By absorbing so many sensory cues, Anna may be looking for the few cardinal points that will remain stable and vivid long after the journey. Anna's experience is akin to what Bryant *et al.* (2011, p. 108) call a *world-focused* savouring experience which is characterised by the experiential absorption of external stimuli (watching dancers). Anna's description of feeding her eyes here and now for a longer lasting recollection also echoes the argument that people who savour events through anticipation are feeling positive emotions in the present (Bryant et al., 2011). In other words, Anna's positive feelings in the present are derived from her imagination of her future recollection of events of the time when she was in Seville.

A second example comes from Robert, who enjoys observing people in public places:

> I would go to a bar and sit there. Sometimes people talk, so I listen to them; I look [at them]; I look at what they eat. So I learn a lot. They are different, like they walk in here in the morning and they talk to each other. I don't feel they always know each other. It's more social here. I like that.

The way Robert gazes at people in bars reminds us of the setting of an experiment where he plays the role of the research observer and through which he may be anticipating surprise, enchantment, emotions and unanswered questions yet to arise. Robert's description indicates his appreciation of cultural difference and of the pleasurable feeling of immersion in an exotic environment. Although learning may set in here too, his gaze is more aesthetic as it is not driven by determined goals. Robert's gaze upon the world around him reveals that he is open to serendipity and a bundle of information signals which are not necessarily connected and precise. By making himself available to the world, Robert may simply be looking for an experience which will foster or illuminate his understanding of this world. He shows interest in the locals, he is alert and enjoys the experience of being in an exotic place. Robert's modes of being approximate what Onfray (2006) calls a *nomade-artiste* (nomadic artist) as one who 'understands without explanations, by natural impulses'. The *nomade-artiste* nourishes himself with 'intuitions and the immediate penetration of the essence of things' (p. 65).[3] Indeed, Robert captures the sociability of the Sevillians well when he remarks that although people do not necessarily know each other, they still naturally engage in conversations. James makes a similar comment based on his observation of bar visitation as he realises that everyone in Seville goes to bars, even 'little ladies' as he put it. Robert is mindful (Langer, 2002) in that he is alert and receptive to new situations while being situated in the present; at the same time, he is also clearly savouring the contingent experience of otherness. What is worth pointing out here is that there is not a single gaze but rather a multitude of gazes. Indeed, the previous quotes have revealed that while Anna's gaze is much more self-centred, Robert's eyes are more concerned with capturing a sense of place. While the data shows that the sense of sight is consciously used in the form of observation, as in the case of Anna and Robert, the sense of sight can be fortuitously activated by particular events:

> Here, I mean just coming to Seville where the colour of the light is different. And there are so many colours here, the building, the light, the sun, the colours, what people wear. I was wearing all black the other day and I really felt out of place. You know [laugh], 'cause like everyone wears red and different colours all the time. It's very colourful here.
>
> (Alice)

Although accidentally activated, a less focused-oriented vision can be equally powerful in delivering meaningful experiences. Alice came to feel 'out of place' as she realised that in her entirely black attire, she was standing in sharp contrast to the local, colourful environment. At this point in time, Alice becomes aware of herself and of the others. James also points out the many taboos present in US society. For example, he notices the way Spanish children are involved in the many facets of their parents' lives:

> Kids, that's the other thing – the children here. I mean – they bring their children here to the bars. I mean – bar is not the healthiest thing. But I think it's great because over there [in the US], we just have so many taboos. There are just things you don't do. You don't bring kids to bars. For feria, just kids, little children out until 4 in the morning. And you don't ever see that in the States, and it's things like that that make you know that this [Spain] is a different place. Hey look! The children are not fallen over dead; they are not getting kidnapped; they're not getting hit by cars . . . They grow up just fine and probably better for it, instead of being sheltered.

By observing how all generations of Spaniards alike gather in bars, mingle and talk to each other, James becomes aware of the north-western way of life with respect to sociocultural practices. Robert similarly remarks that Canadians work hard to save money with the idea in mind to retire one day. 'It's not like that here', he says about Spain. Knowing that Spain, and particularly the southern regions, had been severely hit by the recent economic crisis, both Maya and Natalie relatedly express their puzzlement as they see a constant buzz of people enjoying themselves around them. Whilst Natalie wishes 'it was like this at home' – Alberta, Canada – Maya even describes the Spaniards as epicureans and admits that she fully identifies with their way of being and living. As in the case of Maya, who adjusted well to her new environment, the idea of returning to her home country may appear as a burden. Here it becomes evident that the heightened awareness of home in conjunction with the recently borrowed modes of being and doing which pertain to a foreign destination both play a role in shaping new identities and in establishing a personal bond with the destination.

## Conclusion

The dearth of studies that have looked into tourist multi-sensory experiences informed the work presented in this chapter. The conceptual contribution of this study, therefore, lies in its focus on the sensorial realm to explore tourists' positive experiences. Constructivist grounded theory, as a performative and collaborative research method, provided useful heuristic tools to sensually engage with, and interpret, tourism phenomena. The tourists' experiences depicted here demonstrate the intricate entanglement of sensations with the experience of positive emotions (Biswas-Diener *et al.*, 2015). This study shows that the body, whether kinaesthetic, haptic, auditory, gustatory, olfactory or visual, is a powerful facilitator of learning in a broad sense. Tourists' sensual practices such as walking or cycling through Seville's heterogeneous spaces constitute modes of appropriation of urban spaces which mobilise tourists' fantasies and identities. It is argued that such practices are constituent of tourists' sense of place as well as their sense of being in their own bodies. Such embodied practices are likely to boost self-esteem (Matteucci, 2014) and foster feelings of living in accord with one's true nature. Learning was also expressed in terms of greater awareness of the tourist's own culture and of the full potential of the tourist's own body. These findings are congruent with the work of early developmental psychologists (e.g. Winnicott, 1960) who report that personal growth and, in particular, authentic behaviour are derived by greater body aware-ness and greater sensitivity of the emotional self. Tsur, Berkovitz and Ginzburg (2015) also found that both body awareness and emotional clarity are two essential components of self-knowledge processes which are necessary for the self to thrive. The sensory descriptions articulated by the informants also revealed the experience of positive emotions such as joy, interest and contentment. This way the tourists' sensory accounts conflate in memorable or peak experiences, which indicates that the more senses are aroused the more rewarding experiences are. Consequently, tourism activities which engage the whole body and provide social interactions are likely to trigger stronger emotional responses. Finally, this study allows for three main observations. First, the body and senses are not strictly a source of pleasure (or pain) but also powerful signifiers of meaning (Howes, 2008). Second, the tourists' sensory experiences trigger positive emotions which, in turn, are conducive to feelings of personal growth and improve well-being over time (Fredrickson, 2001). Third, tourism experiences are fluid, contingent and contextual (Edensor & Falconer, 2011); thus a full understanding of tourists' emotions requires researchers not only to go beyond the well-rehearsed and pre-scribed scales and tools of inquiry but also to immerse themselves in the lives of the people they study.

## Notes

1 *Jaleo* is a flamenco term referring to utterances or shouts of encouragement such as *Olé*!
2 *Saeta* is a religious and emotional song which is sung most often during public proces-sions such as during Semana Santa. It is said to belong to the flamenco repertoire.
3 Translated from the French language by the author.

# References

Agapito, D., Mendes, J., & Valle, P. (2013). Conceptualizing the sensory dimension of tourist experiences. *Journal of Destination Marketing & Management*, 2(2), 62–73.

Andrews, H. (2005). Feeling at home: Embodying Britishness in a Spanish charter tourist resort. *Tourist Studies*, 5(3), 247–266.

Ayuntamiento de Sevilla. (2014). *Padrón municipal de habitantes*. Servicio de Estadísticas. Retrieved 7 December 2014 from: http://www.sevilla.org/ayuntamiento/areas/area-de-hacienda-y-administracion-publica/servicio-estadistica/servicio-de-estadistica/consulta-y-descarga/numero-habitantes

Biswas-Diener, R., Linley, A., Dovey, H., Maltby, J., Hurling, R., Wilkinson, J., & Lyubchik, N. (2015). Pleasure: An initial exploration. *Journal of Happiness Studies*, 16, 313–332.

Bryant, F. B., Chadwick, E. D., & Kluwe, K. (2011). Understanding the process that regulate positive emotional experience: Unsolved problems and future directions for theory and research on savouring. *International Journal of Wellbeing*, 1(1), 107–126.

Charmaz, K. (2006). *Constructing grounded theory, a practical guide through qualitative analysis*. London: Sage.

Crouch, D. (2009). The diverse dynamics of cultural studies and tourism. In M. Robinson & T. Jamal (Eds.), *The Sage handbook of tourism studies* (p. 82–97). London: Sage.

Crouch, D., & Desforges, L. (2003). The sensuous in the tourist encounter. *Tourist Studies*, 3(1), 5–22.

Csikszentmihalyi, M. (1990). *Flow: The psychology of optimal experience*. New York: Harper & Row.

Csikszentmihalyi, M. (2012). Foreword. In S. Filep & P. Pearce (Eds.), *Tourist experience and fulfilment: Insights from positive psychology* (p. xii). London: Routledge.

Dann, G. M., & Jacobsen, J. K. (2002). Leading the tourist by the nose. In G. M. S. Dann (Ed.), *The tourist as a metaphor of the social world* (pp. 209–236). Wallingford: CABI Publishing.

De Certeau, M. (1984). *The practice of everyday life*. Berkeley: University of California Press.

Dubé, L., & Menon, K. (2000). Multiple roles of consumption emotions in port-purchase satisfaction with extended service transactions. *International Journal of Service Industry Management*, 11(3), 287–304.

Edensor, T. (2006). Sensing tourist spaces. In C. Minca & T. Oakes (Eds.), *Travels in paradox: Remapping tourism* (pp. 23–45). London: Rowman and Littlefield.

Edensor, T., & Falconer, E. (2011). Sensual geographies of tourism. In J. Wilson (Ed.), *The Routledge handbook of tourism geographies* (pp. 74–81). London: Routledge.

Everett, S. (2009). Beyond the visual gaze? The pursuit of an embodied experience through food tourism. *Tourist Studies*, 8(3), 337–358.

Falconer, E. (2013). Transformations of the backpacking food tourist: Emotions and conflicts. *Tourist Studies*, 13(1), 21–35.

Fredrickson, B. L. (2001). The role of positive emotions in positive psychology: The broaden-and-build theory of positive emotions. *American Psychologist*, 56(3), 218–226.

Gibson, J. J. (1966). *The senses considered as perceptual systems*. Boston: Houghton Mifflin.

Gnoth, J. (1997). Tourism motivation and expectation formation. *Annals of Tourism Research*, 24(2), 283–304.

Goldstein, E. B. (2009). *Sensation and perception* (8th ed.). Belmont: Wadsworth Cengage Learning.

Hom Cary, S. (2004). The tourist moment. *Annals of Tourism Research*, 31(1), 61–77.

Howes, D. (2008). Multi-sensory marketing in cross-cultural perspective (part 2): Making sense of the senses. *Perceptnet*. Retrieved 10 August 2014 from: http://www.percepnet.com/cien04_08_ang.htm

Ingold, T. (2000). *The perception of the environment*. London: Routledge.

Langer, E. (2002). Well-being: Mindfulness versus positive evaluation. In C. R. Snyder & S. J. Lopez (Eds.), *The handbook of positive psychology* (pp. 214–230). Oxford: Oxford University Press.

Matteucci, X. (2013). Photo elicitation: Exploring tourist experiences with researcher-found images. *Tourism Management*, 35, 190–197.

Matteucci, X. (2014). Forms of body usage in tourists' experiences of flamenco. *Annals of Tourism Research*, 46, 29–43.

Merleau-Ponty, M. (2005). *Phenomenology of perception*. London: Routledge.

Niedenthal, P., Wood, A., & Rychlowska, M. (2014). Embodied emotion concepts. In L. Shapiro (Ed.), *The Routledge handbook of embodied cognition* (pp. 240–249). London: Routledge.

Obrador Pons, P. (2007). A haptic geography of the beach: Naked bodies, vision and touch. *Social & Cultural Geography*, 8(1), 123–141.

Onfray, M. (2006). *Théorie du voyage: Poétique de la géographie*. Le livre de poche biblio essays.

Peterson, C., Ruch, W., Beermann, U., Park, N., & Seligman, M. P. (2007). Strengths of character, orientations to happiness, and life satisfaction. *The Journal of Positive Psychology*, 2(3), 149–156.

Pilcher, E. J., Newman, P., & Manning, R. E. (2009). Understanding and managing experiential aspects of soundscapes at Muir Woods National Monument. *Environmental Management*, 43, 425–435.

Pink, S. (2008). Mobilising visual ethnography: Making routes, making place and making images. *Forum Qualitative Sozialforschung/Forum: Qualitative Social Research*, 9(3), Art. 36.

Porteous, J. (1985). Smellscape. *Progress in Human Geography*, 9, 356–378.

Prayag, G., Hosany, S., & Odeh, K. (2013). The role of tourists' emotional experiences and satisfaction in understanding behavioural intentions. *Journal of Destination Marketing & Management*, 2, 118–127.

Rodaway, P. (1994). *Sensuous geographies: Body, sense and place*. London: Routledge.

Saldanha, A. (2002). Music tourism and factions of bodies in Goa. *Tourist Studies*, 2(1), 43–62.

Scarles, C. (2009). Becoming tourist: Renegotiating the visual in the tourist experience. *Environment and Planning D: Society and Space*, 27, 465–488.

Sirgy, M. J. (2002). *The psychology of quality of life*. Dordrecht: Kluwer Academic.

Sylwester, R. (1994). How emotions affect learning. *Educational Leadership*, 52(2), 60–65.

Tsur, N., Berkovitz, N., & Ginzburg, K. (2015). Body awareness, emotional clarity, and authentic behaviour: The moderating role of mindfulness. *Journal of Happiness Studies*. doi: 10.1007/s10902–015–9652–6

Tung, V. W. S., & Ritchie, J. R. B. (2011). Exploring the essence of memorable tourism experiences. *Annals of Tourism Research*, 38(4), 1367–1386.

Waterman, A. S. (1993). Two conceptions of happiness: Contrasts of personal expressiveness (eudaimonia) and hedonic enjoyment. *Journal of Personality and Social Psychology*, 64(4), 678–691.

Winnicott, D. W. (1960). The theory of the parent-infant relationship. *The International Journal of Psycho-Analysis*, 41, 585.

# 5 Dark tourism and dark events

## A journey to positive resolution and well-being

*Jennifer Laing and Warwick Frost*

## Introduction

In 2014, large crowds of visitors were attracted to an art installation in the moat of the Tower of London, *Blood Swept Lands and Seas of Red*, which commemorated the centenary of the outbreak of World War One. It comprised 888,246 ceramic poppies – one for each British or Imperial military fatality during the Great War. The sea of poppies was intended to be a place for reflection with respect to the lives that were lost. Part of the installation subsequently travelled around Britain in a roadshow as a prelude to being placed on permanent display at the Imperial War Museums in London and Manchester in 2018. The then British Prime Minister David Cameron explained the rationale for this decision (14–18 NOW, 2014):

> The whole country has been struck by the power of this work. Its scale and impact is breath-taking, and it has captured the public's imagination in a way that few things have done before. Although millions have made the journey to the Tower, many more have wanted to do so but have not been able to get there. The whole country suffered terribly from the loss of loved ones a hundred years ago so it is only right that everyone should have the opportunity to see this moving tribute closer to home.

The centenary, and the events which took place within its auspices, such as *Blood Swept Lands and Seas of Red*, could be conceptualised as a form of dark tourism. Defined as 'the packaging and consumption of death or distress as a tourist experience' (Strange & Kempa, 2003, p. 387), dark tourism has been examined from a variety of perspectives. These include motivations for engaging in dark tourism (Slade, 2003), the creation of a typology of dark sites, attractions and exhibitions (Stone, 2006) and the dark tourism visitor experience (Hall, Basarin & Lockstone-Binney, 2011; Stone & Sharpley, 2008). More recent work has recognised the existence of dark events, including dark commemorative events (Frost & Laing, 2013), as a focus for research.

It appears that one-off *dark commemorative events* have increased in size, scope, cost and influence in recent times, although they remain under-researched, as do commemorations in general (Frost & Laing, 2013). Recent examples are the one hundred and fiftieth anniversary of the Battle of Gettysburg (July 2013) and the seventieth anniversary of the D Day Landings in World War Two (June 2014), which both attracted widespread international news media coverage. The most high-profile example at the moment is the commemorative program for the Centenary of World War One. Yet we lack understanding as to why so much emphasis is placed on them by various governments and what their appeal is to other stakeholders, notably participants. This echoes calls by Stone (2011, p. 11) for more research on the 'implications and meanings [of dark tourism] for the broader cultural condition of society'.

The earlier quote by David Cameron suggests that these events can stir emotions and engage attendees in a thoughtful and positive way, even though the subject matter is tragic. One potentially fruitful area for research is to explore whether there are *social* or *psychological* benefits inherent in attending or participating in dark commemorative events, such as improvements in well-being. This would complement recent research on the design of charity challenge events that might shape well-being outcomes (Coghlan, 2015). It might form part of a broader body of research that examines the intersection between events and positive psychology and enhances our knowledge about the pivotal role of events in human lives.

## Dark commemorative events

*Dark commemorative events*, held on anniversary dates of incidents that are distressing, macabre or involve death or suffering, are 'specifically staged so that society may remember and reflect upon past occurrences and their relationship to today' (Frost & Laing, 2013, p. 1). They have a long history, reaching back at least to the sixteenth century (Cressy, 1989, 1994; Sharpe, 2005). One famous example of a recurrent dark commemorative event is Guy Fawkes Night or Bonfire Night, a commemoration of the failed plot on 5 November 1605 to blow up the Houses of Parliament in London. These types of events have become so ingrained in the cultural life of the countries that stage them that many of their original meanings have been lost or transformed over time. The element of protest in Bonfire Night, rooted in sectarian divisions, is now manifested in anger over contemporary scapegoats such as banks and international finance (Frost & Laing, 2013).

Frost and Laing (2013) have developed a typology to assist with understanding these events in more depth. The seven basic categories of dark commemorative events are: dark exhibitions; dark re-enactments; national days of mourning or remembrance; memorial services and concerts; significant anniversaries (generally one-off commemorations); dark parades, marches and processions; and dark festivals. Table 5.1 gives an example of each of these events.

Much of the academic research to date on dark commemorative events has focused on *dark exhibitions*, which Seaton (1999) characterises as the viewing of material evidence or symbolic representations of dark subject matter, usually within museums or art galleries. These exhibitions often attract dissonance, in terms of what is shown and how it is interpreted to visitors, which makes them a fertile subject for academic study. For example, plans by the Imperial War Museum

*Table 5.1* Typology of dark commemorative events

| Type | Example of event |
| --- | --- |
| 1. Dark exhibitions | 50th anniversary of the *Enola Gay* dropping the atomic bomb on Japan |
| 2. Dark re-enactments | Annual re-enactments of the Battle of Little Bighorn, USA |
| 3. National days of mourning or remembrance | Hiroshima Day, Japan |
| 4. Memorial services, openings of memorials, concerts, performances | Anzac Day at Gallipoli, Turkey |
| 5. Significant anniversaries (e.g. centenaries) | Bicentenary of the French Revolution |
| 6. Parades, marches, processions | Bloody Sunday March, Northern Ireland |
| 7. Festivals | Mt Kembla Mining Heritage Festival, Australia |

in London to create a permanent exhibition on the Holocaust were controversial, with some voicing concerns that the subject matter was either too painful or could only ever be 'partial and inadequate, and therefore positively harmful' (Cesarani, 2000, p. 61). Other exhibitions have been criticised for sanitisation, with an exhibition at the Smithsonian Museum of American History connected to the September 11, 2001, terrorist attacks being deliberately stripped of emotional content, which the curators argued would allow visitors to bring their *own* emotions to the story of September 11 (Stone, 2006). The *Enola Gay* Exhibition staged in 1995 to commemorate the fiftieth anniversary of the dropping of the atomic bomb on Japan was eventually cancelled because of a strong public backlash, primarily from veterans, who felt that history was being distorted, with the Japanese war record treated too sympathetically (Goldberg, 1999).

The potential benefits of staging dark commemorative events could be considerable based on the findings of a small amount of research that has been conducted to date, often in the allied field of dark tourism. We identify six possible benefits. First, it has been suggested that they might help people to confront and come to terms with the idea of their own mortality. Dark tourism may contribute to 'the maintenance and continuity of ontological security and overall well-being' (Stone & Sharpley, 2008, p. 590) by playing a role in 'mediating mortality and linking the living with its resurrected dead' (Stone, 2012, p. 1582). This might be particularly important in a largely secularised society, where death is increasingly avoided as a topic, except in the mass media, where it dominates the news coverage. The often sensationalist treatment of death, viewed at a distance through a television screen or computer, may not adequately prepare people for their own demise (Walter, Littlewood & Pickering, 1995).

Second, dark commemorative events might also provide a sense of resolution, acceptance or *closure* about things that have happened in the past and thus facilitate the grieving process (Coats & Ferguson, 2013; Frost & Laing, 2013). Kang, Scott, Lee and Ballantyne (2012, p. 262), studying visitors to the Jeju April 3rd Peace Park, identified the comfort of meeting an internal obligation to those who have suffered – 'namely a therapeutic effect or sense of psychological healing experienced by visitors'. Similarly, Dunkley, Morgan and Westwood (2011, p. 867) found that some dark tourism and 'the act of commemoration – the personal and collective remembrance – is driven by a moral obligation . . . the opportunity to mark family sacrifice', which might also soothe or provide a cathartic release for pent-up emotions.

Third, some dark commemorative events encourage or facilitate reconciliation between groups of people who have previously been in conflict or aim to give a voice to a previously marginalised group, race or culture. Lowenthal (2003, p. 5) sarcastically labels this 'contrition chic', but others note the positives inherent in this re-reading of history. For example, the centennial re-enactment of the Battle of Little Bighorn allowed Native Americans to challenge the dominant narrative that gave little prominence to their ancestors. Using the centenary as a protest opportunity led to changes in how the National Parks Service managed the battlefield site. These included changing the name from Custer Battlefield National Monument to Little Bighorn Battlefield National Monument and the construction of a monument to those Native Americans who died during the battle (Frost & Laing, 2015; Linenthal, 1991).

Fourth, dark commemorative events may also be a vehicle through which 'a community is reminded of its identity' (Connerton, 1989, p. 70) by facilitating the transfer of social memory. This may help to bond people together, particularly after a difficult or troubled past. According to Stone (2000, p. 55), in relation to the concept of a Holocaust Memorial Day: 'Commemoration is an important event in any society, for it acts as a social 'glue', bringing people together within a shared narrative of heroism, virtue or, in this case, trauma and mourning'. This may also happen on an individual level, with the event contributing to the shaping or construction of personal identity or an existential authentic self, through discovering one's links to a shared national history or national story. Knox (2006, p. 195) refers to the fact that 'many tourists are looking for truths about, and essences of, their home societies', regardless of whether they are difficult or contested.

Fifth, learning or education has been identified as another benefit of a dark tourism experience (Cohen, 2011; Dunkley *et al.*, 2011; Kang *et al.*, 2012; Stone, 2012). This might enhance its meaning and emotional tug on participants. Thus Bird (2016) noted that 'visiting a battlefield provides a unique form of experiential learning that can be emotionally impactful, if not transformative of one's worldview'. Educational motivations were in fact found to be the most important reason given for a visit to the Auschwitz-Birkenau concentration camp (Biran, Poria & Oren, 2011). It may have similar importance in the context of dark commemorative events. For example, Stone (2000), writing about the Imperial War Museum exhibition on the Holocaust, referred to the achievement of educational goals based on visitor comments that mentioned what people felt they had learnt ('an eye opener'; 'the truth').

Sixth, involvement in dark tourism may have a positive effect on family bonding and connections (Kang *et al.*, 2012). A number of studies on battlefield tours have emphasised the role that relationships play in these dark tourism experiences, either in terms of the experience bringing families together or highlighting familial links such as family history (Baldwin & Sharpley, 2009; Clarke & McAuley, in press; Dunkley *et al.*, 2011; Hyde & Harman, 2011).

To better understand these benefits, it might be valuable to utilise Seligman's (2011) theoretical model of well-being known as PERMA (positive emotions, engagement, relationships, meaning and achievement). These benefits are also reminiscent of *eudaimonic* dimensions of well-being such as self-acceptance, positive relations with others, personal growth and purpose in life (see Huta & Waterman, 2014 for an overview of conceptual definitions of eudaimonia). This suggests that there is scope to consider the potential role played by involvement in and attendance at dark commemorative events in promoting well-being.

This chapter aims to explore this phenomenon by focusing on a case study of a contemporary dark commemorative event. Data have been collected about visitor experiences, emotions and reflections in order to explore the potential well-being outcomes. A secondary aim of the chapter is to respond to calls for further research on the positive psychology of events through a study which contributes to our understanding as to how people 'anticipate events, enjoy events, and how they acquire psychological rewards and benefits from event experiences' (Filep, Volic & Lee, 2015, p. 495).

## Method

A qualitative case study approach was adopted in this study. The Centenary of World War One in Australia was selected as a high-profile example of a dark commemorative event, spanning an unusually long period of time – four years (2014–2018) – and thus offering a rich opportunity to study well-being outcomes. This commemoration encompasses a varied program of events, including exhibitions, parades and ceremonies. A description of the background to the case study is included later in this chapter.

While a range of data were collected for this study, this chapter focuses on the analysis of written comments provided by members of the public on the website of Melbourne Museum in relation to two of their exhibitions themed around the Centenary of World War One. The first exhibition was the *WW1 Centenary Exhibition*, which displayed over 350 artefacts from the Imperial War Museum (IWM) in London and ran from April 18 to October 4, 2015. The second exhibition is *WWI: Love & Sorrow* (loveandsorrow.com), which opened on August 30, 2014. It concentrates on the experiences of eight people during World War One and includes over 300 objects and photographs (Figure 5.1). It will run for four years; the entire duration of the Centenary of World War One commemorations.

Comments from 102 individuals were posted online about the *WW1 Centenary Exhibition* between September 11, 2014, and October 23, 2015, while comments

*Figure 5.1  WWI: Love & Sorrow* exhibition
Source: J. Laing

from 48 individuals about *WWI: Love & Sorrow* were posted between August 13, 2014, and December 14, 2015, when the analysis was carried out. The first names provided by the individuals posting the comments were used in reporting the findings, with either the initials *CE* to denote that the comments were about the *WW1 Centenary Exhibition* or *LS* to denote that the comments were about *WWI: Love & Sorrow*. A thematically informed analysis of this data was undertaken, following Miles and Huberman (1994), where data were coded based on themes that emerged.

## Case study background: the centenary of World War One

Even as World War One was in progress, plans were being developed for future commemorations in peacetime. The trends for memorials and events in Britain (Black, 2004; Nicholson, 2009) were influential, though issues with funding and how best to proceed delayed major developments. In contrast, at the local level – particularly in country towns where a high proportion of volunteers had come from – there were rapid developments with annual services, monuments and avenues of honour, with trees representing each fallen serviceman (Inglis, 1998). In some cases, memorials had ongoing local development features. Examples of this include the Great Ocean Road in Victoria and the Lone Pine Koala Sanctuary in Brisbane.

*Figure 5.2* Australian War Memorial, Canberra
Source: J. Laing

In the 1930s, progress finally began to be made on major memorials. The largest of these were the Shrine of Remembrance in Melbourne (1934) and the Australian War Memorial in Canberra (1941) (Figure 5.2). Both functioned as tangible foci for large-scale official commemorative events. This was important as no war dead were repatriated to Australia and the war cemeteries in Western Europe and Turkey were too expensive for most Australians to visit.

Anzac Day – marking the April 25 landings of the Australian and New Zealand Army Corps at Gallipoli – was the most important remembrance day in Australia and became a public holiday in the 1920s (Seal, 2004). The centrepiece of the commemoration is a dawn service, symbolising the time of day when the Australians first came ashore, along with marches in the major capital cities. In the 1960s and 1970s, Anzac Day declined in popularity and seemed likely to disappear. However, a revival of interest began late in the twentieth century. This was primarily due to high levels of government and media interest in the seventy-fifth anniversary in 1990, when a group of veterans were transported to Gallipoli (Seal, 2004).

The lower cost of international travel opened up greater possibilities for Australians to visit Turkey and the April 25 services became highly popular (Frost, Wheeler & Harvey, 2008; Seal, 2004; Slade, 2003). This was particularly the case amongst younger people, with travel to Gallipoli becoming a rite of passage, often within a backpacker experience (Frost *et al.*, 2008; Hyde & Harman, 2011; McKenna & Ward, 2007). In 2005, 20,000 Australians attended the ninetieth anniversary service at Gallipoli (Hall *et al.*, 2011). Indeed, Anzac Day at Gallipoli became so popular that there were concerns about crowding and inappropriate behaviour. For the 2015 centenary, a ballot for ticketed places was introduced, attracting 42,273 applications for just 3,860 double passes.

For the Centenary of World War One, organisational responsibility was given to the Australian Department of Veterans' Affairs. Initially, a National Commission on the Commemoration of the Anzac Centenary was set up to scope out the potential range of activities. Later, a separate Anzac Centenary Advisory Board was formed to oversee the staging of the centenary program. Both bodies were primarily composed of former politicians and military officers.

The National Commission recommended that the main focus be on centenaries of four historical episodes: the first departure of troops in 1914, the Gallipoli Landings in 1915, the Battle of Villers-Bretonneux in 1918 and the Armistice in 1918. In addition, it recommended that anniversaries of other conflicts – including World War Two and the Vietnam War – be included within the official program (National Commission on the Commemoration of the Anzac Centenary, 2011). Local groups were encouraged to develop their own events focusing on a wider range of battles and historical incidents and apply for funding for memorial projects (Anzac Centenary, 2014). The government response to the Report of the Anzac Centenary Advisory Board (Anzac Centenary, 2013) was to broaden the commemoration to

> recognise a century or more of service and sacrifice by Australian servicemen and servicewomen, in all wars, conflicts and peacekeeping operations in which Australia has, and continues to, participate. The Centenary is not simply about what happened a hundred years ago, as if it were past and gone. We fought then on a global scale to defend the values we shared with many other nations and this commitment continues today.

A number of exhibitions have been staged for the Centenary of World War One in Australia, including the two that were specifically the focus of this study. A travelling exhibition, *Spirit of Anzac Centenary Exhibition*, commenced in September 2015, which recognised that as large numbers of people might not be able to travel to the capital, it was appropriate to tour an exhibition through the state capitals and regional cities.

## Well-being outcomes

Six major themes emerged from the analysis that suggested that involvement in the Centenary of World War One enhanced well-being. Five of these themes relate to the five elements of well-being conceptualised by Seligman (2011) in his PERMA model – *positive emotions, engagement, relationships, meaning* and *achievement*. The sixth theme, *identity*, where individuals begin to understand their true selves or discover what they see as their national or collective heritage or story, might be comparable to the dimensions of authenticity, self-identity or social integration within conceptualisations of *eudaimonic* well-being (Huta & Waterman, 2014).

### Positive emotions

Individuals posting about the exhibitions on the web used language that suggested that their emotions had been stirred by what was presented to them. They used words such as 'profoundly moving' (Skye, *LS* and Doreen & Ben, *LS*), 'extraordinarily moving and thought-provoking' (Kate, *LS*) and 'very moving and beautiful' (Evelyn, *CE*). Paul (*LS*) observed that the exhibition he saw highlighted the 'tragic, pitiful and deeply moving cost of war'. This echoes the findings of Winter (2015: 24), where an analysis of visitor books at the Tyne Cot Cemetery in Belgium revealed 'the emotions tourists felt when visiting the cemetery . . . almost half [the comments] were *Very/extremely moving* and many wrote *Touching*, *Very/sad* and *Emotional* and *Overwhelming*'. The comments in the current study suggested that visitors to the exhibition, like those visiting battlefields or other dark tourism sites, experienced 'a strong emotional release' (Coats & Ferguson, 2013, p. 47).

No one posted that they were shocked or angry at what they had seen, nor that they felt that what was presented was one-sided. This was interesting, given that as with all commemorations of conflict, issues of dissonance had emerged that were connected to the Centenary of World War One. These included criticisms of jingoism (excessive national pride), an emphasis on militarism and the glorification of war, commodification, the omission of key events such as the anti-conscription referendum from the official program and concerns that with a four-year program there might eventually be a decline in interest amongst the public (Frost, Laing & Cragg, 2016). In fact, two individuals pointed out the lack of jingoism, which is discussed later under the theme of 'meaning'.

The only negative emotions expressed related to the charging of an entry fee to see the *WW1 Centenary Exhibition*. For some, the mere idea of charging for such an event was anathema, which was reminiscent of concerns that have been raised in the literature that dark tourism sites should be 'free of commercial taint', including fees (e.g. Seaton, 2009): 'One would have thought for such a significant event as the anniversary of WW1 that this would have been a free exhibition. Very disappointing' (Michael, *CE*). One visitor, Ken (*CE*), expressed annoyance that he did not have to pay for a similar exhibition staged at the Imperial War Museum in London. Others did not dispute the need to pay to attend the exhibition, but referred to the 'sneaky' charge to print tickets on top of 'the already some might say inflated entry fee' (Michelle, *CE*) or the small number of exhibits, which were not felt to be worth the entrance fee paid. According to Rhees (*CE*): 'There was too much space in the display, that's why the items were spread out. I finished looking in 30 minutes', while Cliff (*CE*) commented,

> I was shocked at the entry price. A\$32!! That is outrageous. I paid anyway, thinking 'It's the IWM, it must be good'. And when you're in a city

for a short time it's not always possible to be too discriminating. But it left me rather disappointed. Both the quantity and the quality fell short of expectations.

Not all those who saw the original exhibition in London were disappointed in what was brought to Australia. For example, Rob (*CE*) wrote approvingly: 'Having just visited the IWM London, this exhibition is truly stunning in its range and quality. It is wonderful that part of the exhibition is touring'. Others felt that its inherent importance and the high standards of execution warranted what they had paid, such as Scott (*CE*), who referred to it as 'worth every cent'.

### Engagement

There were examples of both positive and negative engagement with the exhibitions, but the former appeared to outweigh the latter. An example of positive engagement can be gleaned from the following comment by Evelyn (*CE*): 'The atmosphere, sound effects, music, objects and letters made me feel like I was there with them'. It made her reflect on what it must have been like to live through the war: 'To see the original objects and the real stories of how this war affected people personally – the soldiers and other personnel (men and women) who were on the field or helping on the homefront – was very sobering'. Mary (*LS*), 'spent quite a long time' at the exhibition, while Cathy (*LS*) wanted 'to go back to take it all in'. The use of eight real-life experiences drew visitors such as Cathy (*LS*) and Skye (*LS*) into the experience, giving them a personal connection with what had happened, with Skye referring to 'some compelling content. I loved the final room containing interviews with living descendants'.

Cliff (*CE*), on the other hand, found the exhibits in the *WWI Centenary Exhibition* 'strangely unengaging'. He elaborated on his disappointment:

In particular I felt that the information/interpretation boards were too simplistic and there was a remarkable lack of depth about the overall progress of the war in the various theatres or of the immense social and political impact . . . Frankly I would have been better off buying a decent book.

Unlike the other contributors to the websites, Cliff was less concerned about the personal stories that were related and more about the bigger picture of what the war represented and its overall meaning. Generally, however, these individual narratives touched those who attended the exhibitions and appeared to be highly absorbing.

The use of technology and interactivity was not mentioned in the postings, which might suggest that they are not necessarily vital to ensure visitor engagement in this context. This latter point needs further research to discern their importance for participants in dark commemorative events and whether they are seen as reducing authenticity or trivialising a serious subject, or simply do not contribute to well-being outcomes.

### Relationships

Findings showed that the exhibitions were seen as activities that families could share or bond over, sometimes, but not necessarily, related to having a family link to World War One. These findings accord with previous work carried out on battlefield tours, discussed earlier in this chapter, which emphasised the importance of familial relations in the experience. A number of people referred to their familial links to World War One, such as Jake (*LS*) who mentioned that 'having family history involved in WW1 this [exhibition] will be awesome' and Shan (*LS*), who queried, 'I'm just wondering whether you uncovered any further info about Herbert Cecil Murray. He is my great great grandfather'. Ann (*CE*) also observed that her 'Great Uncle has 11 items of art work on catalogue in the IWM, of these 11, 7 were done on the battlefield in WW1 . . . and I was wondering to find out if any of these are featured in the exhibition'.

For some, this familial association gave them a sense of a common history, with Scott (*CE*) specifically referring to 'our collective history'. This discourse of nationalism, following Anderson (1991), might have helped 'to construct a form of "imagined community"' (Pretes, 2003, p. 139) for some participants. Rory (*CE*) exemplifies this feeling (words italicised by the authors for emphasis):

> I am looking forward to this exhibition, I can hardly wait. *Like many Australians*, my grandfathers served in WW1, as well as other relatives, including an Aunt who was a nurse. Some of my Uncles didn't make it home. Well done to the museum for getting this exhibition.

Others mentioned seeing the exhibition with their families, with Stephanie (*LS*) noting that 'We saw the exhibition for dad's 80th birthday' and Cathy (*LS*) attending 'with my son, 25, in the Reserves now'. Presumably, the association with her own personal history was partly responsible for her observation: 'We were both very moved by this wonderful exhibition. What a good idea to follow eight people's war experiences!' Scott (*CE*) noted that he had family in New Zealand 'that would love this exhibition'.

In contrast to research by Kang *et al.* (2012), no one commented on feeling fortunate that their family had not been involved in the Great War. Instead, the psychological benefit expressed in the current study was gratitude more generally about the 'peaceful life and stability we have here in Australia' (Evelyn, *LS*).

### Meaning

The current study suggests that viewing an exhibition on a war theme can be highly meaningful for participants. This complements previous research, which has noted the 'meaningful experience' inherent in touring battlefields such as Gallipoli (Slade, 2003; Stone, 2009) or a memorial park (Kang *et al.*, 2012). For some of the exhibition attendees, the meaning was personal or sentimental, with nostalgia expressed for a time in history or family history, possibly before the person posting was born (Clarke & McAuley, 2016). For example, Stephanie (*LS*) wrote,

> Claude Fankhauser's (nicknamed Fank) lawn mower and Braille typewriter are featured in the exhibition. My grandmother was Fank's housekeeper. My dad and uncle used his lawn mower often. After he was blinded in the war he taught them how to fish in Port Phillip Bay.

Others saw meaning in the bigger picture that was presented, which was felt to be balanced and thought-provoking about the nature of war. Kate (*LS*) commended the curators for

> an exhibition that explores the human tragedy of WW1 honestly and with great empathy for those on both sides of the conflict. It places no blame but exposes the ongoing costs of war to families, society and thus ultimately economies.

Scott (*CE*) agreed, noting, 'A great balance between all the major countries involved, and Australia. A dignified retelling of our collective history with strong values of suffering and loss, rather than the contemporary interpretation of heroism and nationalism'. This acknowledgement that the exhibitions were not jingoistic in tone was appreciated, with Paul (*LS*) making his feelings clear that this was in contrast to what was happening elsewhere: 'At a time when we are again involved in a war and flag-wrapped nationalism this exhibition should be compulsory viewing'. None of the individuals posting appeared to feel that they were being asked to forget unpalatable aspects or to avoid memories which they regard as personal or authentic in favour of a *collective* and politically sanctioned memory which is linked to national or cultural identity (Knox, 2006).

## *Achievement*

Seligman (2011) refers to achievement interchangeably with accomplishment and mastery, as an element of well-being that people pursue for its own sake. He notes, however, that it is rarely sought in the absence of at least some of the other dimensions of well-being. Thus 'people who live the achieving life are often absorbed in what they do, they often pursue pleasure avidly' (p. 19). Achievement in the current study relates to improving individual understanding of the historical context of World War One and perhaps learning about stories or groups in society that one did not know about or did not associate with this period in history.

A number of participants referred to the expansion of knowledge that took place or that they thought would occur as a result of seeing one or both exhibitions. There were references to the exhibitions being 'extremely interesting' (Mary, *LS*) and 'thought-provoking' (Kate, *LS*). Some people such as Jill (*LS*) and Ann (*CE*) wrote about the research they had conducted into their forbears, with Ann recording her interest in finding artefacts related to her family in the exhibition.

Other comments were from those involved in formal education. Teachers such as David (*LS*) used the exhibition as part of an online course at Monash University and found that 'responses from students of the course are high in praise for the exhibition'. There were postings from students, such as James (*CE*), who mentioned that he was 'counting down the days' to visit the exhibition with his Year 11 history class and anticipated what he would learn, while Jennifer (*CE*) posted about her learning post-visit:

> I'm currently in year 10 and saw the exhibition last holidays. At school I am studying history and its (sic) basically all about world war 1 and 2. I found this helpful and educational.

The sad and difficult subject matter made some attendees think more deeply about their own lives, as illustrated by this observation by Evelyn (*CE*): 'Really made me feel grateful for the peaceful life and stability we have here in Australia'. This might arguably constitute another form of learning, as well as feelings expressed of gratitude (see the previous theme of positive emotions).

### *Identity*

Some of the data presented earlier could also be conceptualised within the theme of *identity*. The findings of the current study confirm those of previous studies involving dark tourism. Biran *et al.* (2011), for example, found that people with a personal heritage connection to Auschwitz were looking for an emotional experience, which 'points to tourists' desire to maintain their identity by connecting to their own heritage' (p. 836). Similarly, Knox (2006, p. 196) observed that Scottish visitors to the battle sites at Glencoe in Scotland are 'focused on the identity of the home nation and a sense of what it means or is to be a part of that nation'. Slade (2003, p. 780) noted the same phenomenon, where Australians and New Zealanders visiting Gallipoli see it as 'the psychological birthplace of both countries as nations', and integral to how they see themselves. A more recent study suggested that more Australians than New Zealanders associate Gallipoli with their national identity (Hyde & Harman, 2011).

One aspect of identity relevant to the current study involved references to the armed services. People mentioned and thus identified with either having been in the service or having relatives who were currently serving or had served in the past. For example, Rory (*CE*) observed that he had relatives who served in the war 'like many Australians', while others placed emphasis on 'being a service member' (Jake, *LS*) or 'being a military person myself' (Keith, *CE*). Cathy (*LS*) mentioned that she had seen the exhibition with her son '25, in the Reserves now'. This identification with the services or military might constitute a form of *existential authenticity* (Wang, 1999, 2000), where the participants reveal their true selves or who they feel their authentic selves are as a result of their experiences viewing the exhibitions.

Collective terms such as 'our' and 'we' were used when talking about the commemoration. Bev (*CE*) referred to 'a great walk through our military history', while

Scott *(CE)* mentioned 'our collective history'. This might suggest feelings of a common heritage or identity linked to the imagined community (Anderson, 1991; Pretes, 2003) discussed earlier. Brett *(LS)* mentioned that 'being a Queenslander I was still very touched by Victoria's loss'. While this might suggest a division by Australian state boundaries, it also shows that people felt an empathy with the loss of fellow Australians. In this case, the use of ritual language was also observed, with Brett *(LS)* concluding his post with the words 'Lest we forget!' Winter (2015, p. 27) argues that this type of 'linguistic ritual binds [people] together'. It might, therefore, also serve a purpose in shaping identity.

These findings might also evoke eudaimonic well-being outcomes. Huta and Waterman (2014) in their classification of the core elements of eudaimonia identify authenticity, identity, personal expressiveness, autonomy, constitutive goals and integrity as a group of common elements, which would seem to cover the current study context, along with acceptance and self-acceptance. These elements can be both internally directed (e.g. self-identity and insight into the self – see Steger, Shin, Shim & Fitch-Martin, 2013) and socially directed (e.g. social acceptance, social actualization, social contribution, social coherence and social integration – see Keyes, 2002). Further work is needed to explore in depth how they relate to attendance at a dark commemorative event, but the current findings suggest that there are commonalities and thus well-being outcomes for attendees.

Unfortunately, we do not have information about where all the participants in the current study were born, although it is assumed that many were Australians and a number specifically referred to that fact. Four mentioned an international country of origin – Gabriel *(CE)* and Cliff (CE), and possibly Scott *(CE)* – New Zealand – and Keith *(CE)* – USA. Future research might look at whether there are differences in well-being outcomes, particularly with respect to identity, between participants in dark commemorative events from different countries or ethnic origins.

## Conclusion

Studies of visitor's written comments and feedback can elicit useful data about a dark tourism experience (e.g. Winter, 2015). It was therefore felt to be an appropriate method for the current study, which examines the experience of participating in a dark commemorative event. Although exploratory, findings suggest that attending a dark commemorative event, in this case two exhibitions forming part of the Centenary of World War One, had a number of well-being outcomes. Five of these outcomes – positive emotions, engagement, relationships, meaning and achievement – are dimensions of Seligman's (2011) PERMA model. A sixth – identity – is similar to dimensions of eudaimonic well-being (e.g. Keyes, 2002; Steger *et al.*, 2013). Comments suggested that these outcomes affected a broad swathe of individuals, including students, teachers, mothers, service personnel, military history enthusiasts, descendants or relatives of those in active service and family groups. While details of gender were not available, the names used by those posting suggested roughly a 50/50 split between males and females. These findings might be of particular interest to government stakeholders involved in dark commemorative events, in that they support their continued funding because of the societal benefits that they seem to engender to the wider community.

Some limitations are acknowledged with the current study. The ages and cultural backgrounds of people posting on the websites could not be collected, and so no conclusions could be made about their influence. Future research might profit from gathering demographic data on participants in dark commemorative events to examine whether particular groups in the community garner particular well-being outcomes or higher well-being outcomes overall than others. Another limitation is that direct questions could not be put to participants on their postings to elucidate the well-being outcomes in more detail. A future study could collect further data through interviews with participants. Quantitative research could also be conducted using measures of well-being already established in relation to the PERMA model (Diener *et al.*, 2010). The findings of the current study relate only to a particular type of dark commemorative event – dark exhibitions. Studies could extend this research to other types of dark commemorative events to explore whether there are similar findings.

This chapter makes a contribution to the nascent study of *positive events*. It suggests that given the potential outcomes in a number of well-being dimensions experienced by participants in a dark commemorative event, those commissioned with or involved in their staging and management should be looking to enhance these outcomes wherever possible. Further research would be useful (following Coghlan, 2015; Filep *et al.*, 2015) to study the benefits of these events from the organiser perspective or supply side. This research, therefore, continues with a second stage involving interviews with organisers of the Centenary of World War One, including the Australian War Memorial, National Museum of Australia and the Department of Veterans' Affairs in Canberra. It will examine whether there are explicit strategies in place or active attempts made to influence well-being outcomes for event attendees. Findings will help to build a more holistic picture of the ways in which events might play a part in making life worth living.

## References

14–18 NOW. (2014). 14–18 NOW to take poppies art installation around the UK. *14–18 NOW*, 8 November 2014. Retrieved 5 December 2014 from: http://www.1418now.org.uk/14–18-now-take-poppies-around-uk/

Anderson, B. (1991). *Imagined communities: Reflections on the origin and spread of nationalism* (revised ed.). London: Verso.

Anzac Centenary. (2013). *Government Response to the Report of the Anzac Centenary Advisory Board on a Program of Initiatives to Commemorate the Anzac Centenary.* Retrieved 15 January 2015 from: http://www.anzaccentenary.gov.au/sites/default/files/documents/govt_response.doc

Anzac Centenary. (2014). The Program 2014–2018: Significant Commemorative Dates for the Anzac Centenary National Program. Retrieved 15 January 2015 from: www.anzaccentenary.gov.au/program/calendar.htm

Baldwin, F., & Sharpley, R. (2009). Battlefield tourism: Bringing organised violence back to life. In R. Sharpley & P. R. Stone (Eds.), *The darker side of travel: The theory and practice of dark tourism* (pp. 186–206). Bristol: Channel View.

Biran, A., Poria, Y., & Oren, G. (2011). Sought experiences at (dark) heritage sites. *Annals of Tourism Research*, 38(3), 820–841.

Bird, G. (2016). Landscape, soundscape and youth: Memorable moments at the 90th commemoration of the Battle of Vimy Ridge, 2007. In K. Reeves, G. Bird, L. James, B. Stichelbaut & J. Bourgeois (Eds.), *Battlefield events: Landscape, commemoration and heritage* (pp. 109–120). London: Routledge.

Black, J. (2004). Thanks for the memory: War memorials, spectatorship and the trajectories of commemoration 1919–2001. In N. J. Saunders (Ed.), *Matters of conflict: Material culture, memory and the First World War* (pp. 134–148). London and New York: Routledge.

Cesarani, D. (2000). Seizing the day: Why Britain will benefit from Holocaust Memorial Day. *Patterns of Prejudice*, 34(4), 61–66.

Clarke, P., & McAuley, A. (2016). The Fromelles Interment 2010: Dominant narrative and reflexive thanatourism. *Current Issues in Tourism*, 19(11), 1103–1119.

Coats, A., & Ferguson, S. (2013). Rubbernecking or rejuvenation: Post earthquake perceptions and the implications for business practice in a dark tourism context. *Journal of Research for Consumers*, 23, 32–65.

Coghlan, A. (2015). Tourism and health: Using positive psychology principles to maximise participants' wellbeing outcomes: A design concept for charity challenge tourism. *Journal of Sustainable Tourism*, 23(3), 382–400.

Cohen, E. H. (2011). Educational dark tourism at an in populo site: The Holocaust Museum in Jerusalem. *Annals of Tourism Research*, 38(1), 193–209.

Connerton, P. (1989). *How societies remember*. Cambridge: Cambridge University Press.

Cressy, D. (1989). *Bonfires and bells: National memory and the Protestant calendar in Elizabethan and Stuart England* (2004 ed.). Stroud: Sutton.

Cressy, D. (1994). National memory in early modern England. In J. R. Gillis (Ed.), *Commemorations: The politics of national identity* (pp. 61–73). Princeton: Princeton University Press.

Diener, E., Wirtz, D., Tov, W., Kim-Prieto, C., Choi, D. W., Oishi, S., & Biswas-Diener, R. (2010). New well-being measures: Short scales to assess flourishing and positive and negative feelings. *Social Indicators Research*, 97(2), 143–156.

Dunkley, R., Morgan, N., & Westwood, S. (2011). Visiting the trenches: Exploring meanings and motivations in battlefield tourism. *Tourism Management*, 32(4), 860–868.

Filep, S., Volic, I., & Lee, I. S. (2015). On positive psychology of events. *Event Management*, 19, 495–507.

Frost, W., & Laing, J. (2013). *Commemorative events: Memory, identities, conflict*. London: Routledge.

Frost, W., & Laing, J. (2015). *Imagining the American West through film and tourism*. London: Routledge.

Frost, W., Laing, J., & Cragg, D. (2016). Commemorating dissenting voices and stories: The Centenary of the Anti-Conscription Referendum in World War One. In K. Reeves, G. Bird, L. James, B. Stichelbaut & J. Bourgeois (Eds.), *Battlefield events: Landscape, commemoration and heritage* (pp. 109–120). London: Routledge.

Frost, W., Wheeler, F., & Harvey, M. (2008). Commemorative events: Sacrifice, identity and dissonance. In J. Ali-Knight, M. Roberston, A. Fyall & A. Larkins (Eds.), *International perspectives on festivals and events: Paradigms of analysis* (pp. 161–172). London: Academic.

Goldberg, S. (1999). The Enola Gay affair: What evidence counts when we commemorate historical events? *Osiris*, 14, 176–186.

Hall, J., Basarin, V. J., & Lockstone-Binney, L. (2011). Pre and post-trip factors influencing the visitor experience at a battlefield commemorative event. *Tourism Analysis*, 16(4), 419–429.

Huta, V., & Waterman, A. S. (2014). Eudaimonia and its distinction from hedonia: Developing a classification and terminology for understanding conceptual and operational definitions. *Journal of Happiness Studies*, 15, 1425–1456.

Hyde, K. F., & Harman, S. (2011). Motives for a secular pilgrimage to the Gallipoli battlefields. *Tourism Management*, 32(6), 1343–1351.

Inglis, K. S. (1998). *Sacred places: War memorials in the Australian landscape*. Melbourne: Miegunyah.

Kang, E. J., Scott, N., Lee, T. J., & Ballantyne, R. (2012). Benefits of visiting a 'dark tourism' site: The case of the Jeju April 3rd Peace Park, Korea. *Tourism Management*, 33(2), 257–265.

Keyes, C. L. (2002). The mental health continuum: From languishing to flourishing in life. *Journal of Health and Social Behavior*, 43, 207–222.

Knox, D. (2006). The sacralised landscapes of Glencoe: From massacre to mass tourism, and back again. *International Journal of Tourism Research*, 8, 185–197.

Linenthal, E. T. (1991). *Sacred ground: Americans and their battlefields*. Urbana and Chicago: University of Illinois Press.

Lowenthal, D. (2003). Tragic traces on the Rhodian shore. *Historic Environment*, 17(1), 3–7.

McKenna, M., & Ward, S. (2007). 'It was really moving, mate': The Gallipoli pilgrimage and sentimental nationalism in Australia. *Australian Historical Studies*, 38(129), 141–151.

Miles, M. B., & Huberman, A. M. (1994). *Qualitative data analysis: An expanded sourcebook*. Thousand Oaks: Sage.

National Commission on the Commemoration of the Anzac Centenary. (2011). *How Australia may commemorate the Anzac centenary*. Canberra: Government of Australia.

Nicholson, J. (2009). *The great silence 1918–1920: Living in the shadow of the Great War*. London: John Murray.

Pretes, M. (2003). Tourism and nationalism. *Annals of Tourism Research*, 30(1), 125–142.

Seal, G. (2004). *Inventing ANZAC: The digger and national mythology*. Brisbane: University of Queensland Press.

Seaton, A. V. (1999). War and thanatourism: Waterloo 1815–1914. *Annals of Tourism Research*, 26(1), 130–158.

Seaton, T. (2009). Purposeful otherness: Approaches to the management of thanatourism. In R. Sharpley & P. R. Stone (Eds.), *The darker side of travel: The theory and practice of dark tourism* (pp. 75–108). Bristol: Channel View.

Seligman, M. E. P. (2011). *Flourish*. Sydney: Random House.

Sharpe, J. A. (2005). *Remember, remember: A cultural history of Guy Fawkes Day*. Cambridge, MA: Harvard University Press.

Slade, P. (2003). Gallipoli thanatourism: The meaning of ANZAC. *Annals of Tourism Research*, 30(4), 779–794.

Steger, M. F., Shin, J. Y., Shim, Y., & Fitch-Martin, A. (2013). Is meaning in life a flagship indicator of well-being? In A. Waterman (Ed.), *Eudaimonia* (pp. 159–182). Washington, DC: APA Press.

Stone, D. (2000). Day of remembrance or day of forgetting? Or, why Britain does not need a Holocaust Memorial Day. *Patterns of Prejudice*, 34(4), 53–59.

Stone, P. R. (2006). A dark tourism spectrum: Towards a typology of death and macabre related tourist sites, attractions and exhibitions. *Tourism*, 54(2), 145–160.

Stone, P. R. (2009). Making absent death present: Consuming dark tourism in contemporary society. In R. Sharpley & P. R. Stone (Eds.), *The darker side of travel: The theory and practice of dark tourism* (pp. 23–38). Bristol: Channel View.

Stone, P. R. (2011). Dark tourism: Towards a new post-disciplinary research agenda. *International Journal of Tourism Anthropology*, 1(3–4), 318–332.

Stone, P. R. (2012). Dark tourism and significant other death: Towards a model of mortality mediation. *Annals of Tourism Research*, 39(3), 1565–1587.

Stone, P. R., & Sharpley, R. (2008). Consuming dark tourism: A thanatological perspective. *Annals of Tourism Research*, 35(2), 574–595.

Strange, C., & Kempa, M. (2003). Shades of dark tourism: Alcatraz and Robben Island. *Annals of Tourism Research*, 30(2), 386–405.

Walter, T., Littlewood, J., & Pickering, M. (1995). Death in the news: The public invigilation of private emotion. *Sociology*, 29(4), 579–596.

Wang, N. (1999). Rethinking authenticity in tourism experience. *Annals of Tourism Research*, 26, 349–370.

Wang, N. (2000). *Tourism and modernity: A sociological approach*. Oxford: Pergamon.

Winter, C. (2015). Ritual, remembrance and war: Social memory at Tyne Cot. *Annals of Tourism Research*, 54, 16–29.

# 6  The role of humour in contributing to tourism experiences

*Anja Pabel*

## Introduction

Going on a holiday or visiting a tourism attraction with family and friends is considered by most people a pleasant activity. There are many tourism businesses that are already using humour and fun as part of their experience offerings for reasons of entertainment and enjoyment. The theme parks of Disney World are a good example of a global tourism business that uses fun and entertainment for its many audiences (Ritzer, 1999). Csikszentmihalyi (in Filep & Pearce, 2014) stated that it is difficult to understand why tourism research does not have a stronger presence in positive psychology since it is an intervention that can add so much to people's quality of life.

Considering that holidays are normally associated with relaxation and fun, the role of humour in tourism experiences needs to be explored as a way of enhancing people's subjective well-being. The role of positive emotions created through humour and attendant sociability in tourism operations has been supported empirically by Mitas, Yarnal and Chick (2012). Their study identified four themes that generated positive emotions at two tourism settings: amusement from humour, warmth of friendship, interest in activities and sublime reactions to loss (Mitas *et al.*, 2012). The theme most applicable to the present study is amusement from humour in the creation of positive emotions. These positive emotions add value to the tourism experiences by helping to build a community among the regular attendants of the tourism activities in Mitas, Yarnal and Chick's study (2012).

Three distinctions can be made in tourism humour. There is humour about tourists, humour provided for tourists and humour created and perceived by tourists themselves. Humour *about* tourists was examined by Cohen (2010), who explored the relationship between jokes about tourists and the stereotypical image of the modern tourist. Another study by Cohen (2011) included an analysis of 100 cartoons which were entered into the 2009 *First International Tourism Cartoon Competition* and explored how the humour in these cartoons was produced. He found that the ordinary tourists in these cartoons were depicted as facing various extraordinary, exaggerated and incongruous situations.

Humour *for* tourists can be found on official tourism websites where humour is used for general appeal and to build favourable relationships with various audiences of multicultural backgrounds (Kang & Mastin, 2008). A study by Carden (2005) revealed that humour and entertainment appeals exceed factual appeals in travel and tourism public relations efforts. Sometimes tourists themselves become the butt of critical satire because they are perceived as stereotypically funny by the general public either because of the way they dress or behave or both (Cohen, 2010, 2011).

The biggest research gaps exist in the area of humour *by* tourists. The book *Tourism and Humour* by Pearce and Pabel (2015) casts some light on tourists' perspectives on humour in tourism settings. They state that the relevance of humour in tourism presentations as well as the naturalness of its delivery were top considerations.

In terms of theory development on the tourism-humour relationship, a conceptualisation by Pearce (2009) named the 'tourism and humour patterns and pathways' framework shows the many components and interactions which are possible in the tourism-humour relationship. This multifaceted model also illustrates the various pathways which can be studied in the tourist-humour relationship, including humour source, humour target, tourist context, nature of content, technique, medium, humour type, appropriateness filter and outcomes.

Exploring the area of humour in tourism settings is a broad new space that has not been well researched. There are many questions that remain unanswered about how exactly humour contributes to tourism experiences, and it is the purpose of this study to begin to fill this void. If used deliberately and appropriately, humour should contribute to the quality of the tourism experience. Consequently, it is important to find out what perspectives tourists hold about humour. For this reason, the aim of this study was to identify in what ways humour affected tourism experiences. A focus group study with tourists was conducted at four tourism settings in Far North Queensland, Australia, to address this aim.

## *Introduction to humour from a positive psychology perspective*

Humour was given only peripheral importance in psychology for most of the twentieth century. A small beginning was made in the 1970s with a focus on the cognitive aspects of humour studied experimentally (Ruch, 2008). The emergence of positive psychology at the start of the twenty-first century highlighted the need for a complete science of psychology which should include an understanding of not only suffering, disorders and stressors but also how happiness is achieved (Park, Peterson & Seligman, 2005; Seligman, Steen, Park & Peterson, 2005). In this manner, positive psychology tries to investigate the full spectrum of the human experience, and, naturally, this also includes finding ways of making life fun and worth living (Seligman & Csikszentmihalyi, 2000).

Peterson and Seligman's (2004) Values in Action (VIA) Classification of Strengths and Virtues highlights the character strengths and virtues that are needed for human thriving and therefore contribute to a good life. According to the VIA, there are six overarching virtues which are desired by every culture across the world: wisdom, courage, humanity, justice, temperance and transcendence. A total of 24 character strengths were assigned to these 6 virtues. In this framework, humour as character strength is listed under the virtue of transcendence, which is associated with a hopeful and optimistic perspective on life. In fact, previous research has found humour to be amongst one of the highest recognised strengths to produce correlations with subjective well-being and life satisfaction (Park, Peterson & Seligman, 2005). Research by Beermann and Ruch (2009) revealed that humour was also strongly compatible with the virtues of humanity, wisdom and transcendence because it appears to integrate goodwill.

Certain aspects of humour can lead to positive effects on life satisfaction and can indeed be viewed as virtuous, particularly when the humour has included spreading good cheer and an ability to be amused by one's own embarrassing episodes (Beermann & Ruch, 2009). The ability to 'laugh at oneself' is often considered a core component of the sense of humour. Peterson and Seligman (2004) argue that it is also up to individuals to create their own environments. In this view, people are active seekers of environments, situations and cognitive states of cheerfulness and playfulness. This personal creativity links to the work of Martin, Puhlik-Doris, Larsen, Gray and Weir (2003) in terms of self-enhancing humour and self-defeating humour. Self-enhancing humour is about having a humorous outlook on life in general and embracing humour as a coping strategy to deal with all sorts of situations. Self-defeating kinds of humour are about using humour at one's own expense and being able to laugh at oneself.

### *The benefits of humour and laughter*

Physiologically, humour and laughter have positive effects on human functioning such as making us feel relaxed by reducing the heart rate, blood pressure, muscle tension and stress-linked chemicals and at the same time increasing oxygen in the blood and emitting endorphins (Costa & Kallick, 2000; Morreall, 2010). Laughter is also helpful in reducing anxieties and boosting activities of the immune system, which are key reasons for introducing humour rooms and clowns into hospitals and retirement homes (Baumann & Staedeli, 2005; Franzini, 2012; Morreall, 2010; Ruch & Mueller, 2009). These humour therapies encourage a more cheerful atmosphere for patients (Ruch & Mueller, 2009) because visits by clowns, for example, can create a positive distraction for patients, make them laugh and improve the quality of their stay. People in today's society are even encouraged to learn how to improve their sense of humour, and a huge industry exists to encourage more amusement in our lives such as self-help books, laughing yoga and laughing clubs which appear to be increasing in popularity (Baumann & Staedeli, 2005).

Being able to cultivate positive emotions is also important for psychological growth and well-being (Fredrickson, 2001). Frequent positive emotional states build an individual's personal resources (Crawford & Caltabiano, 2011). Fredrickson (1998, 2001) explains in her 'broaden-and-build theory' the importance of positive emotions such as mirth and exhilaration to increase people's social and psychological resources. Although Gorovoy (2009) acknowledges that the relationship between cheerfulness and life satisfaction is indirect and complex, she states that having this character strength may result in a subjective evaluation where the individual can be more satisfied with life. This might be due to cheerful people having a larger social network, better developed social skills and relationships, as well as the resulting higher self-esteem these people experience.

### The conceptual model

The theoretical perspective guiding this work is Pearce's (2009) model of the comfort-concentration-connection outcomes of humour. Pearce (2009) used three humorous tourism settings (namely the Jungle Cruise in California's Disneyland, the Polynesian Cultural Center in Hawaii and the Canyon Swing in New Zealand) as a base for his research on humour. He examined material available on the Internet and his own observations after visiting these three tourism settings to develop a comfort-concentration-connection construct for the tourism-humour relationship. He found that humour in tourism settings can play three roles: 'it establishes visitor comfort levels, it assists visitor concentration and it establishes connections to tourism presenters' (Pearce, 2009, p. 639). It was this comfort-concentration-connection model that was chosen to guide this research by using perceptions from tourists who have been exposed to humorous tourism experiences in Far North Queensland, Australia.

Each of these three components can be explained through a theoretical underpinning. The comfort outcome can be linked to Goffman's (1974) frame analysis because it helps people in novel tourism activities interpret what is going on. For Goffman, a frame is an act of interpretation which allows individuals to understand and appraise the context of a situation. The frame of using humour in a tourism activity is mostly based on the idea that it lightens the atmosphere and lets people know that they are in for a good time. The concentration outcome can be linked to Langer's (1989) mindfulness theory. Through the telling of humorous stories, it is possible to establish if people are actually mindful and are paying attention, which is necessary for them to understand a punchline. There are various examples of adventure tourism activities, such as skydiving and bungee jumping, where humour is used to ascertain if tourists understand the humour, which informs the tour guide about tourists' level of English and likelihood of following safety instructions. The connection outcome relates to Fredrickson's (1998, 2001) 'broaden-and-build theory' since this theory outlines how feeling positive emotions makes people more willing to interact with others. A quote by Victor Borge describes laughter 'as the shortest distance between two people', which indicates quite well that it can function as a means to connect people, and this is a desirable characteristic for most tourism experiences.

## Method

### Appropriateness of focus groups as a research method

Focus groups were the chosen method for this research for two key reasons. First, focus groups are a useful method, especially for exploratory research where only little is known about a topic (Stewart, Shamdasani & Rook, 2007). Second, focus groups are based on the free flow of information which enables participants to listen to others and reflect on their own experiences and build on responses of one another's comments (Kirsch, 2001; Smith, 2010). This dynamic makes it possible to collect information on the different opinions and attitudes that research participants have when discussing the multifaceted construct of humour. Rich data were collected and expressed in the participants' own words (Smith, 2010).

## Selection of tourism operators

The design of this study ensured that the tourism businesses considered were different in nature and did in fact include humour in their communications and interactions with tourists. Pearce (2011) pointed out that considerable attention is usually given to selecting individual participants, but sampling actual examples of the tourism phenomenon of interest can be just as important. As an external justification, TripAdvisor was used to identify tourism businesses that were already using humour successfully. As a review website, TripAdvisor enables consumers to leave comments about a range of tourism-related services and experiences such as accommodations, restaurants, attractions and tour operators. The researcher thoroughly reviewed TripAdvisor comments on various tourism businesses to identify tours and attractions where the use of humour was a persistent theme. In order to enhance the range and scope of humour applications being studied, the following types of tourism experiences were chosen: a wildlife tourism operator, a nature-based tourism operator, an adventure tourism operator and a Great Barrier Reef (GBR) tourism operator.

## Descriptions of the tourism operations

The wildlife attraction, situated approximately 40 minutes north of Cairns, offers educational and entertaining presentations about crocodiles, snakes, cassowaries, koalas and other wildlife at several times throughout the day. The nature-based tourism operator offers one-day guided tours to the many natural attractions of the Atherton Tablelands, a picturesque rural area inland from Cairns. The adventure tourism operation is based on white-water rafting, which takes place daily on the Tully River. The GBR tourism operation includes guided snorkelling tours, glass bottom boat tours, scuba diving and scenic helicopter flights.

## On-site procedure

Focus groups were conducted at the various tourism settings from June to November 2012. At each tourism setting, focus groups were conducted towards the end of the tourism experience. This approach ensured that participants had spent a reasonable amount of time on-site and therefore had sufficient opportunity to experience the humour on offer. Focus groups lasted from 10–30 minutes. Overall, 29 focus groups with 103 participants were conducted. Each focus group was limited to smaller groups of up to six participants to ensure that everyone had the opportunity to express their views (Krueger & Casey, 2001). All focus group discussions were audio-recorded for later transcription.

## Analysis of focus groups

Focus groups transcripts were analysed using the NVivo software which was based on the identification of relevant themes or categories based on frequency of comments and agreement with the topic (Krueger & Casey, 2001). Since Pearce's (2009) comfort-concentration-connection model was used to guide the questioning during the focus groups, the transcripts were scrutinised for information to contribute to this model. When participants' responses addressed more than one category, then these responses were coded under each category that they addressed. Findings in this study are supported by quotations from the research participants (Kirsch, 2001). In using appropriate quotes as evidence, the research reflects the voice of the participants and builds trust in the findings (Creswell, 2007).

## Profile of respondents

As shown in Table 6.1, focus group participants were quite diverse in terms of gender mix, age groups and nationalities.

*Table 6.1* Demographic details of focus group participants (n = 103)

| Wildlife attraction | n = 31 | Nature-based tour | n = 23 | Adventure tourism operator | n = 28 | GBR tourism operator | n = 21 |
|---|---|---|---|---|---|---|---|
| **Gender** | | | | | | | |
| Male | 14 | Male | 7 | Male | 15 | Male | 10 |
| Female | 17 | Female | 16 | Female | 13 | Female | 11 |
| **Age group** | | | | | | | |
| < 20 | 5 | < 20 | 2 | < 20 | 0 | < 20 | 1 |
| 21–30 | 14 | 21–30 | 19 | 21–30 | 22 | 21–30 | 7 |
| 31–40 | 0 | 31–40 | 1 | 31–40 | 4 | 31–40 | 8 |
| 41–50 | 0 | 41–50 | 1 | 41–50 | 1 | 41–50 | 3 |
| 51–60 | 3 | 51–60 | 0 | 51–60 | 1 | 51–60 | 1 |
| > 60 | 9 | > 60 | 0 | > 60 | 0 | > 60 | 1 |
| **Nationality** | | | | | | | |
| NZ | 4 | USA | 6 | Ireland | 6 | Belgium | 2 |
| UK | 4 | Germany | 3 | Australia | 1 | Sweden | 1 |
| Germany | 5 | UK | 4 | UK | 8 | Canada | 1 |
| Australia | 14 | Canada | 6 | Germany | 3 | Italy | 1 |
| Canada | 2 | Netherlands | 1 | Netherlands | 3 | UK | 8 |
| Austria | 2 | Belgium | 1 | Canada | 1 | Brazil | 3 |
| | | Ireland | 2 | China | 4 | Switzerland | 2 |
| | | | | India | 2 | Australia | 3 |

*Table 6.2* Findings based on Pearce's (2009) comfort-concentration-connection model

| COMFORT | |
| --- | --- |
| **The role of humour:**<br>– Good start to the day<br>– Creation of a relaxing and positive atmosphere<br>– Contribution to the overall experience | **This was achieved because:**<br>– Filling downtime<br>– Reducing apprehension |

| CONCENTRATION | |
| --- | --- |
| **The role of humour:**<br>*During on-site experience*<br>– Captures and maintains interest<br>– Reinforces the message<br>*Post experience*<br>– Creation of positive memories to take home | **This was achieved because:**<br>– Humour breaks messages into smaller pieces<br>– Humour-filled interpretation makes learning a more positive and engaging experience |

| CONNECTION | |
| --- | --- |
| The role of humour:<br>*Connections with other tourists on-site*<br>– Humour makes the experience more engaging<br>*Connections with tour guide*<br>– A more personable and approachable tourism presenter<br>– Getting to know the tourism presenter | **This was achieved because:**<br>– Laughing together<br>– Reducing the unease when approaching others |

## Findings

The aim of the study was to identify in what ways humour affected tourism experiences. Pearce's (2009) comfort-concentration-connection model was used to highlight how each of the three categories materialised from the perspective of the focus group participants. Table 6.2 outlines the findings based on content analysis of focus group transcripts.

The following paragraphs discuss each of the three components in more detail and include focus group participants' quotes to exemplify their views.

## Comfort

### *The role of humour in creating comfort*

*Humour helps to get the day/tour off to a good start*

Most tour guides used humour right at the start of the tour experience. Therefore humour plays its role in signalling what is to come, as this respondent stated: 'He sets you at ease. It kind of really gives you that feeling where, "OK, I think it's going to be a good day"'. Another respondent thought: 'It was very good. It makes the experience more enjoyable. It puts you in a good mood for the rest of the trip basically. A good start'. Moreover, applying humour during safety briefings at the start of the tour acted as an ice breaker: 'It kind of breaks the tension and they use it as an ice breaker because we are all from different parts of the world'.

*Humour creates a relaxing atmosphere on-site*

Many respondents commented on how the humour affected the ambiance overall. Agreement was achieved by participants describing humour as having the following effect: 'easy-going, relaxing, entertaining, it made things more dynamic, enjoyable, it lightens the atmosphere'. Humour is something that most people could associate with, and it was therefore helpful in creating a positive atmosphere that was easily picked up by everyone: 'Actually humour bridges language because even when they don't understand, when people laugh that is a common bond'. Some respondents indicated that it can sometimes be difficult to understand all of the humour; however, the sight and sound of laughter can also influence people's moods. The following comment illustrates this point: 'Well, I think with the many nationalities even those that couldn't speak English, which I noticed there was a few, they tend to laugh or seemed to join in and feel relaxed'.

*Humour contributes to the experience*

The tour guides' humour appeared to add to the enjoyment of the day at all four tourism settings. One participant said, 'He was funny and he made the bus trip enjoyable because of that'. It also seemed that the humorous style set their tour experience apart from what other tours were offering: 'I guess the other thing is that it is just so different from what you can expect from a tour, it makes it more enjoyable'. Being able to laugh and have fun also had an impact on how the overall tourism experience was perceived. One respondent acknowledged that laughing so much made her trip a better one: 'It just kind of makes your day a bit more fun if you are laughing'.

## How was this achieved?

While the previous section stated in what ways humour enhanced respondents' comfort levels, the next paragraphs outline how this was achieved – that is, by filling downtime and by reducing awkwardness and apprehension.

*Filling downtime through humour*

One way in which humour was used to enhance the comfort of the tourists was by filling downtimes using humour. Each tourism setting had its times when tourists were merely sitting around and watching, and it was up to the tour guides to keep the audience interested and entertained. A respondent at the wildlife attraction noticed,

> For quite a long period the crocodile is sitting under the water not doing anything. So you are there to watch the crocodile but the guide is talking for

15 minutes and joking with the audience, so you are definitely keeping more attention.

The river guides of the adventure tourism operator also played an important part in making the downtime as comfortable and fun for the tourists in the rafts as possible as this participants mentioned: 'There were no real awkward moments for anything because he filled the gaps when we were rowing and the downtime'. The humour-induced safety briefing performed on the reef boat was also noticed: 'It distracts from the journey' which shows yet again that humour fills gaps when it is necessary.

### *Humour reduces apprehension*

Respondents considered humour as a great way to defuse some of their nervousness about being exposed to unfamiliar settings or taking part in novel activities such as scuba diving and white-water rafting. One respondent referred to this unfamiliarity as being 'out of your element and if somebody is going to make you laugh then you are going to open up'. Another respondent stated after his first white-water rafting experience, 'A few of our ladies felt nervous and scared. He included humour to make them feel easy and be calm'. Humour can also be helpful in reducing people's fear about crocodiles: 'I can imagine if you are serious about the whole issue it makes the audience more anxious'.

## Concentration

The attention-grabbing properties of humour appeared to be highly relevant while the tourism experience was taking place. The concentration component of humour was created in two ways: during the actual tourism experience as well as after the experience through the creation of positive memories.

### *During the on-site tourism experience*

### *Humour captures the participants' interest*

Humour was helpful during the tourism presentations because it helped to draw tourists' attention to what was said, which was appreciated by many respondents. For example, the humour assisted in making the presentations appear less rigid, as this participant noted: 'It keeps people interested in a way that isn't too structured. I think people are more interested when it's something funny, more so than if it is just information being told to you'. Participants also mentioned that it felt like they were subconsciously drawn to what was being said: 'I didn't feel like I had to listen but it increased my interest. I wanted to hear what was going on next'. Another respondent noticed that safety announcements and other instructional information delivered throughout the day was filled with humour: 'I thought it was good with serious information, you know information that people have to know but it was funny'.

*Reinforcing the message*

The attention-grabbing properties of humour were mentioned by several participants who said that humour was successfully used to reinforce messages that needed
to be delivered. A respondent noticed, 'They were educating travellers about physiological things and safety around snakes and crocodiles and they used the humour
as part of that education'. Explanations including humour were well-received, as
this participant explained: 'We enjoyed the experience more I think rather than the
dry "This is a crocodile, it is 500 million years old bla". It just lightened it up and
made it more interesting'. Furthermore, non-English-speaking respondents noted
that including humour in the presentations allowed them to understand some topics better. This response was received from a Swiss participant: 'Sometimes I only
understand very little of what is being said but when they use humour I understand
a lot more because it's an easy language. That works very well for me'.

## Post experience

*Creation of positive memories to take home*

The analysis of focus group transcripts revealed that humour was not just important
during the on-site experience but also the post experience in terms of positive memories that tourists would be able to take home with them. Explaining that laughter
would help him remember the pleasant time he had, this participant said, 'I think
most people when they say they enjoyed something, it's because they enjoyed the
laughing and having a good time and so you are more likely to remember it'. Some
respondents compared previous tourism experiences with their humour-filled experience. An example comment was, 'It helps make the tour more memorable. You
remember it for these reasons. We've been on many tours and you know and the
ones that we remember most are the ones with funny guides'. Hence the feeling
of happiness that was generated throughout the day because of the humorous tour
guides is helpful in creating a remembered happiness, which tourists are likely to
share with family and friends once they are back at their place of origin.

## How was this achieved?

The following section outlines in what ways post experience concentration outcomes were achieved – that is, by using humour to break down information into
smaller pieces and by making presentations more entertaining through humour-
induced interpretation.

*Breaking information into smaller pieces*

Several respondents recognised that the inclusion of humorous stories was helpful
in breaking the educational messages into smaller, digestible pieces. A respondent
recalled, 'I thought that it really added to the experience. I think that's part of what

makes them interesting, the humour thrown in with the info. I think it broke it up a bit rather than it just to be like a lecture'. While it is indeed possible for tourists to disconnect with the material being delivered, a little bit of humour might be helpful in bringing them back to the information, as this participant explained: 'I think a joke from time to time is really good for the attention of the customer because then you can relax a bit and then after the joke or after the laughter you can focus again'.

### The importance of humour-induced interpretation

Good interpretation needs to be attention arresting and this is achieved, amongst others, through using humour. The entertainment factor of humour ensured that tourists kept paying attention to what was said, as this respondent explained: 'If you keep the audience entertained they don't go and quiet off'. Another respondent compared her humour-induced tour experience with previous tours she had been on where humour apparently did not play a noteworthy role: 'He wasn't just all jokes, he would put a lot of facts into what he was saying. And so when he got on his microphone, I noticed I paid attention to that a lot more than what I have on previous tours'. It also mattered that there was the right mix of information and jokes: 'There was also a lot of serious value, a lot of serious information about the environment but he did that in a funny way'.

## Connections

Building connections with others was present in two ways: connections with other tourists on-site and connections with the tour guide.

### Connections with other tourists on tour/on-site

#### Humour makes the experience more engaging

Many respondents at the various tourism settings expressed that they thought humour made the experience more engaging and gave them the opportunity to participate. A participant on the reef vessel expressed, 'It makes you feel part of something as opposed to just being a spectator. So when we were on the boat, I felt part of a big group and we were having a laugh and it was a giggle'. A participant in the white-water activity commented, 'If you tell a joke and everybody is laughing, you do something together. So this makes you feel like a team'. The humour used at the nature-based tourism operation appeared to create a conversation booster: 'It gives you kind of a pathway to actually talk if you know what I mean. It creates conversation for you'. For all these various reasons, it appeared that tourists forming connections did not happen in isolation; they first had to feel comfortable to do so, and humour seemed to play a crucial role in breaking down initial boundaries.

## Connections with the tour guide

*A more personable and approachable tourism presenter*

Participants at all four settings mentioned that humour made their tour guides more approachable. A respondent at the adventure tourism setting commented, 'It made him seem a bit more down to earth and easier to talk to'. Tour guides at the wildlife attraction also appeared more accessible: 'I felt comfortable enough to walk to him afterwards and ask him questions. They seemed like approachable nice people and not stiff, not scary, not boring'. This response was given by a focus group participant on the nature-based tour: 'There are things in the forest that I wanted to know about. I love rainforests and I felt comfortable saying "I need to know about this"'. A similar response was given by a respondent on the reef vessel: 'You could have approached any one of those guides and ask a question (. . .) they were very approachable, which makes you feel relaxed, you can approach them, and it's not a silly question'.

*Getting to know the tourism presenter*

Due to the tour guides' humour, many respondents felt they became fairly familiar with their guides. One respondent said, 'It feels like you got to know them a bit better'. The humour also made the tour guides seem very likeable: 'He is not like a tour guide; he is more like a friend showing you around'. Something that was noticed across almost all settings by respondents was the perception of a lack of a divide between the tour group and the tour guide: 'It separates the divide in between the person who is giving the presentation and the audience. It kind of makes you feel like you are more included and that barrier is broken'.

## How was this achieved?

The previous paragraphs outlined how connections with other tourists on-site and with the tour guides were fostered. The following paragraphs identify in what ways these connections were achieved, notably by laughing together and through using humour to reduce any uneasiness in approaching others.

*Laughing together*

Having a laugh together was noted as a great bonding agent by this respondent who said, 'Humour is a good way to build a bridge'. It may be exactly this 'bridge-building' character of humour that provides people with a little bit of self-assurance when approaching others. For humour to work in tourism settings, it has to be reasonably easy to understand and universal in nature so that the majority of the tourism audience can appreciate it. One participant on the reef vessel referred to the sick bag joke as an example of simple but effective humour. She described how a crew member pointed out that if people were unsure about how to use a sick bag, they could look inside and find instructions written in 14 different languages at the bottom of the bag. She added, 'I think that works for wherever you are from because they have sick bags on the airplanes all the time and every single person can relate to that'.

*Humour reduces uneasiness in approaching others*

For the younger market joining the nature-based tour, there seemed to be some apprehension regarding whom they were going to meet on the tour. A person explained, 'Because we all didn't know each other, you are kind of sitting there waiting, who is going to say something and how are we going to talk to each other. The guide gave us something to talk to each other'. The river guides have a similar approach of using humour to get people in the boats to connect to one another. A respondent recalled, 'He wasn't making fun of people; he was more making jokes at himself and that gave people the opportunity to perhaps become familiar with others and they came out of their shell later on'.

## Discussion

As this research illustrated, humour presented by tour guides was not only helpful in creating a positive atmosphere but also made it easier for tourists to start a conversation with others and therefore acted as a successful ice breaker or initiator-boosting conversation. The following section discusses each of the three outcomes in relation to previously published literature.

### Comfort

For the majority of participants, the humour provided a great deal of enjoyment irrespective of the various settings. The findings across the four settings indicate that humour was influential in making tourism experiences more enjoyable by providing positive emotions and fun. Humour was applied to reduce downtime, which is helpful in creating comfort because it reduces feelings of awkwardness. It also distracts the tourists' attention from uninteresting periods such as when it was required to wait for the next rapids when white-water rafting or when waiting for a crocodile to display the death roll.

Another important finding of this study was that humour provided a good start during the various tourism experiences by creating a relaxing atmosphere that was easy to be absorbed by everyone. The ability to foster a welcoming atmosphere relates back to Goffman's (1974) work on frame analysis, in that humour provided a key to let tourists know that they are about to have an enjoyable and entertaining time. The generated laughter made research participants feel happy to be part of their tourism experiences. Moreover, the contagious nature of humour and laughter also made it possible for people whose English might not be as good to pick up on the positive atmosphere. Christrup (2008) found that emotions are contagious in that they can be read physically, consciously or unconsciously. Therefore, even tourists whose level of English is not proficient enough to understand all of the humour can still see and hear the laughter of other people and recognise the fun and share in the atmosphere. This laughter contagion effect works for friends as well as for strangers (Provine, 2000).

Research by Mitas *et al.* (2012) found that positive emotions such as amusement, warmth, interest and awe play a crucial part in tourists' experiences. At the four selected tourism settings in this study, humour was indeed part of the experience offering. The tour guides used humour to expertly manipulate the atmosphere to one where people felt comfortable to be in novel situations such as white-water rafting or scuba diving. The role that emotions play can be highly relevant for stagers and designers of tourism experiences. Experiences that entertain and provide fun are the kinds of experiences that leave customers with positive impressions. Such positive perceptions could lead to positive recommendations made to others by word of mouth or on social media, as well as provide a competitive advantage over others in the marketplace by generating repeat business. This is in line with the work by Pine and Gilmore (1999) who state that enjoyable and memorable experiences can provide opportunities for differentiation from others in the marketplace.

### *Concentration*

The findings of this study showed that humour was used to enliven interpretation material and safety instructions to gain tourists' attention, which is obviously useful not just for classroom settings (Meeus & Mahieu, 2009). Nowadays, tourists prefer to be actively engaged while having sensory and emotional reactions to their experiences instead of simply passively absorbing information (Smith, MacLeod & Robertson, 2010). Humour was successfully used to break up educational messages into smaller digestible pieces, to provide entertainment value and to reinforce relevant parts of the message. This finding concurs with the study by Mitas *et al.* (2012) where humorous fillers were also welcomed as a break in between all the facts, names and numbers.

Overall, many participants stated that they felt more engaged and actually part of their tourism experiences as a result of humour, which is likely to have a positive effect on their attention and learning. This is in line with Langer's (1989) mindfulness theory, in that respondents were actively paying attention and therefore felt more involved with their experience. Previous research has also found that people who are in a positive mood seem to pay more attention and are open to receive new information (Powell & Andresen, 1985; Schmidt, 1991).

It has been recognised that emotions and cognition are not occurring separately but are linked to one another and that affective states can clearly influence what we learn, what we remember and also the kinds of evaluations and judgments we make (Forgas, 2001; Medina, 2008). The mood-biased evaluation of tourism services in the memories of tourists is something that tourism operators can use to their advantage. When people are made to feel welcome and positive due to humour at a tourism setting, they are likely to form positive impressions, not only of the tour guides who deliver the humour but also of the tourism attraction which later may be a part of the tourists' recollection of their holiday experiences. Using humour in such a way that tourists leave a tourism setting in a positive frame of mind can have an impact on satisfaction ratings of experiences (Sirakaya, Petrick & Choi, 2004).

One fairly surprising finding for the researcher was that participants thought that humour would contribute not just to their on-site tourism experience but also have an effect after their actual tourism experiences through the creation of memories. As shown in the numerous comments by participants, they felt that their experiences would stay with them longer because they created positive memories of them. The emotional distinctiveness of some experiences, where strong emotional responses are created, makes them more easily remembered (Schmidt, 1991). Therefore, having pleasant memories of one's fun holiday experiences is likely to play a role after the holiday has already ended.

Remembering such funny travel experiences and reliving the happiness associated with those experiences may lead to mental benefits such as increased well-being and social benefits because memories of this kind can reinstate positive frames of mind (Neal, Sirgy & Uysal, 1999). This line of argument also links to Fredrickson's (2001) work that stated the importance of positive emotions as a durable personal resource. Positive emotions go beyond their acquisition and can act as a reserve that can be drawn on when we are in different emotional states (Fredrickson, 2001). Savouring one's pleasant holiday memories can prolong the positive emotions linked to the humorous experience, and this can also act as a reserve to be drawn on during a sombre day.

### *Connections*

The findings illustrated that humour played a role in making tourism experiences more interactive and transactional because respondents perceived it was easier to initiate a conversation with others and because humour created a positive social setting that acted as a successful ice breaker in a bus or boat full of strangers. Tour guides, as the social facilitators of tourism activities, play an important part in encouraging interactions between group members (Pastorelli, 2003). To participants, the use of humour indicated that their tour guides were very knowledgeable about delivering safety and education messages, which is essential before any humorous appeals could be applied to tourism presentations.

Numerous illustrative examples were provided by focus group participants who felt that they connected with their tour guides on a more personal level because of their humorous presentations. Indeed, joke telling was actually found to be quite powerful in conveying something personal about the tour guides. Norrick (2003, p. 1344) recognised that humour can make 'a person's presence more strongly felt in a multi-party conversation'. Effective tour guiding is dependent on the guide's ability to build good connections with the people her or she is guiding. This seems to be in accord with the literature where, apart from roles such as leader and communicator, a tour guide also needs to be an entertainer aiming to produce positive feelings and a warm atmosphere (Heung, 2008), as well as ensuring that tourists feel comfortable irrespective of the tour setting (Black & Weiler, 2005).

While humour in this research was mainly delivered by the tourism presenters, it can also be initiated or co-created by the tourists on-site to keep the laughter of a tour group going. Mitas *et al.* (2012) urge providers of tourism experiences to take note of the processes that link positive emotions to the social contexts of tourism activities. Positive emotions created during tourism experiences add value to these experiences because they can be relationship enhancing and make an audience feel uplifted and joyful (Franzini, 2012). The research findings showed that humour played an important role in creating an atmosphere where tourists felt comfortable starting a conversation and forming connections with others. Fredrickson (1998, 2001) explained in her 'broaden-and-build theory' the importance of positive emotions to broaden one's momentary thought-action repertoire. Positive emotions not only broaden a person's attention, but they also build his or her social resources.

Sharing humour can be helpful in creating powerful social bonds and closer emotional relationships between the humour presenter and the audience, especially since laughing together is a sign of belonging and signals similarity, and this similarity breeds closeness (Kuipers, 2009). These relationship-enhancing properties appear to be especially visible with humour. Mitas *et al.* (2012) stated that when participants laughed because of a joke and funny story that was delivered by a tour guide, they appeared to be moving physically and emotionally closer to one another. However, for humour to build rapport between people, it has to be thoughtful and sensitive (Franzini, 2012). Pearce and Pabel (2015) have considered some of the negative effects of humour on tourism experiences such as using too much humour or it being misinterpreted.

## Conclusion

This study looked at the role of humour in contributing to tourism experiences as perceived by tourists at four different tourism settings. Pearce's (2009) comfort-concentration-connection model was used to organise the empirical material into categories which emerged from focus group discussions. The findings of this study illustrate that the concentration outcome of humour does not only occur during on-site tourism experiences but also that humour appears to contribute to the formation of positive memories for tourists to take home. Moreover, humour was not only helpful in establishing connections to tourism presenters, but it also played an important role in fostering connections with other tourists who might be present at a tourism setting. Lastly, the interrelatedness of the three categories of comfort, concentration and connection should be pointed out. The findings show that none of the three categories were likely to happen in isolation, because being comfortable in a tourism setting allowed tourists to socially connect with the tour guide as well as other people in their tour group. Similarly, when humour was used to capture the tourists' interest and attention, it was done in a humorous way.

## References

Baumann, S., & Staedeli, I. (2005). *Laecheln, Lachen und experimentell induzierter Schmerz: Eine FACS Studie*. Zurich: Universitaet Zuerich.
Beermann, U., & Ruch, W. (2009). How virtuous is humor? Evidence from everyday behavior. *Humor: International Journal of Humor Research*, 22(4), 395–417.
Black, R., & Weiler, B. (2005). Quality assurance and regulatory mechanisms in the tour guiding industry: A systematic review. *The Journal of Tourism Studies*, 16(1), 24–37.
Carden, A. R. (2005). The use of persuasive appeals and public relations in the travel and tourism industry post-9/11. *Journal of Hospitality Marketing & Management*, 12(1), 79–95.
Christrup, H. (2008). On sense and sensibility in performative processes. In J. Sundbo & P. Darmer (Eds.), *Creating experiences in the experience economy* (p. 203). Cheltenham, UK: Edward Elgar.
Cohen, E. (2010). Confirmation versus contestation of tourism theories in tourist jokes. *Tourism Analysis*, 15, 3–16.
Cohen, E. (2011). The people of tourism cartoons. *Anatolia: An International Journal of Tourism and Hospitality Research*, 22(3), 326–349.
Costa, A. L., & Kallick, B. (2000). *Describing 16 Habits of Mind*. Retrieved 17 May 2012 from: http://www.ccsnh.edu/sites/default/files/content/documents/CCSNH%20MLC%20HABITS%20OF%20MIND%20COSTA-KALLICK%20DESCRIPTION%201-8-10.pdf
Crawford, S. A., & Caltabiano, N. J. (2011). Promoting emotional well-being through the use of humour. *Journal of Positive Psychology*, 6(3), 237–252.
Creswell, J. W. (2007). *Qualitative inquiry & research design: Choosing among five approaches* (2nd ed.). Thousand Oaks, CA: Sage Publications.
Filep, S., & Pearce, P. L. (2014). *Tourist experience and fulfillment: Insights from positive psychology*. London: Routledge.
Forgas, J. P. (2001). Affective intelligence: The role of affect in social thinking and behaviour. In J. Ciarrochi, J. P. Forgas & J. D. Mayer (Eds.), *Emotional intelligence in everyday life: A scientific inquiry* (pp. 45–79). New York: Psychology Press.
Franzini, L. R. (2012). *Just kidding: Using humour effectively*. Plymouth: Rowman and Littlefield.
Fredrickson, B. L. (1998). What good are positive emotions? *Review of General Psychology*, 2(3), 300–319.
Fredrickson, B. L. (2001). The role of positive emotions in positive psychology: The broaden-and-build theory of positive emotions. *American Psychologist*, 56(3), 218–226.
Goffman, E. (1974). *Frame analysis*. Cambridge, MA: Harvard University Press.
Gorovoy, I. (2009). *Best predictors of quality of life (QOL) based on character strengths of gratitude, curiosity and cheerfulness*. Melbourne: (Honours), Victoria University.
Heung, V. C. S. (2008). Effects of tour leader's service quality on agency's reputation and customers' word-of-mouth. *Journal of Vacation Marketing*, 14(4), 305–315.
Kang, D. S., & Mastin, T. (2008). How cultural difference affects international tourism public relations websites: A comparative analysis using Hofstede's cultural dimensions. *Public Relations Review*, 34, 54–56.
Kirsch, S. (2001). Ethnographic methods: Concepts and field techniques. In R. A. Krueger, M. A. Casey, J. Donner, S. Kirsch & J. N. Maack (Eds.), *Social analysis: Selected tools and techniques* (p. 50). Washington, DC: Social Development Family of the World Bank.

Krueger, R. A., & Casey, M. A. (2001). Designing and conducting focus group interviews. In R. A. Krueger, M. A. Casey, J. Donner, S. Kirsch & J. N. Maack (Eds.), *Social analysis: Selected tools and techniques* (pp. 4–23). Washington, DC: Social Development Family of the World Bank.

Kuipers, G. (2009). Humor styles and symbolic boundaries. *Journal of Literary Theory*, 3(2), 219–239.

Langer, E. J. (1989). *Mindfulness*. Reading, MA: Addison-Wesley.

Martin, R. A., Puhlik-Doris, P., Larsen, G., Gray, J., & Weir, K. (2003). Individual differences in uses of humor and their relation to psychological well-being: Development of the humor styles questionnaire. *Journal of Research in Personality*, 37, 48–75.

Medina, J. (2008). *Brain rules*. Brunswick: Scribe Publications Pty Ltd.

Meeus, W., & Mahieu, P. (2009). You can see the funny side, can't you? Pupil humour with the teacher as target. *Educational Studies*, 35(5), 553–560.

Mitas, O., Yarnal, C., & Chick, G. (2012). Jokes build community: Mature tourists' positive emotions. *Annals of Tourism Research*, 39, 1884–1905.

Morreall, J. (2010). Comic vices and comic virtues. *Humor: International Journal of Humor Research*, 23(1), 1–26.

Neal, J. D., Sirgy, M. J., & Uysal, M. (1999). The role of satisfaction with leisure travel/ tourism services and experience in satisfaction with leisure life and overall life. *Journal of Business Research*, 44, 153–163.

Norrick, N. R. (2003). Issues in conversational joking. *Journal of Pragmatics*, 35, 1333–1359.

Park, N., Peterson, C., & Seligman, M. E. P. (2005). *Character strengths in forty nations and fifty states*. Unpublished manuscript, Kingston, RI: University of Rhode Island.

Pastorelli, J. (2003). *An interpretive approach to tour guiding: Enriching the experience*. French Forest, NSW: Pearson Education Australia.

Pearce, P. L. (2009). Now that is funny: Humour in tourism settings. *Annals of Tourism Research*, 36(4), 627–644.

Pearce, P. L. (2011). *Tourist behaviour and the contemporary world*. Bristol: Channel View.

Pearce, P. L., & Pabel, A. (2015). *Tourism and humour*. Bristol: Channel View.

Peterson, C., & Seligman, M. E. P. (2004). *Character strengths and virtues: A handbook and classification*. Washington, DC: American Psychological Association.

Pine, B. J., & Gilmore, J. H. (1999). *The experience economy: Work is theatre and every business a stage*. Boston, MA: Harvard Business Review Press.

Powell, J. P., & Andresen, L. W. (1985). Humour and teaching in higher education. *Studies in Higher Education*, 10(1), 79–90.

Provine, R. (2000). *Laughter: A scientific investigation*. New York: Viking.

Ritzer, G. (1999). *Enchanting a disenchanted world: Revolutionising the means of consumption*. Thousand Oaks, CA: Pine Forge Press.

Ruch, W. (2008). Psychology of humor. In V. Raskn (Ed.), *A primer of humor* (pp. 17–100). Berlin: Mouton de Gruyter.

Ruch, W., & Mueller, L. (2009). Wenn Heiterkeit Therapie wird. *Geriatrie*, 3, 22–24.

Schmidt, S. R. (1991). Can we have a distinctive theory of memory? *Memory & Cognition*, 19(6), 523–542.

Seligman, M. E. P., & Csikszentmihalyi, M. (2000). Positive psychology: An introduction *American Psychologist*, 55(1), 5–14.

Seligman, M. E. P., Steen, T. A., Park, N., & Peterson, C. (2005). Positive psychology progress: Empirical validation of interventions. *American Psychologist*, 60(5), 410–421.

Sirakaya, E., Petrick, J., & Choi, H. (2004). The role of mood on tourism product evaluation. *Annals of Tourism Research*, 31(3), 517–539.

Smith, M., MacLeod, N., & Robertson, M. H. (2010). *Key concepts in tourist studies.* London: Sage Publications.

Smith, S. L. J. (2010). *Practical tourism research.* Wallingford: CABI.

Stewart, D. W., Shamdasani, P. N., & Rook, D. W. (2007). *Focus groups theory and practice* (2nd ed.). Thousand Oaks, CA: Sage Publications.

# 7 Employing hedonia and eudaimonia to explore differences between three groups of wellness tourists on the experiential, the motivational and the global level

*Cornelia Voigt*

## Introduction

Since the meteoric rise of the field of positive psychology in 2000, an increase of interest in the concept of well-being can also be noticed in tourism research. Despite tourism being an epitome of freedom, self-fulfilment and choice, there is still limited knowledge on how well-being relates to tourism. This lack of research seems to be particularly puzzling in the context of wellness tourism, since here the tourists are motivated by maintaining or increasing their well-being per definition.

Wellness tourism has been defined as

> the sum of all phenomena resulting from a journey by individuals whose motive in whole or in part is to maintain or promote their health and well-being, and who stay at least one night at a facility that is specifically designed to holistically enable and enhance people's physical, psychological, spiritual and/or social well-being, and that ideally also takes into account environmental and community wellness in a sustainable manner.
>
> (Voigt, 2014, p. 33)

Although wellness tourism is often equated with spa visitation, many authors agree that it subsumes different experiences and that wellness tourists cannot be considered as one homogenous group (e.g. Smith & Puczkó, 2009). In this research, three different groups of wellness tourists have been defined for comparison: (1) beauty spa visitors, (2) lifestyle resort visitors and (3) spiritual retreat visitors. The major focus of beauty spas is on non-invasive beauty and body treatments, which often incorporate water-based and sweat-bathing facilities. Tourists generally tend to be passive recipients of the treatments provided to them. Lifestyle resort visitors are typically enrolled in a comprehensive program covering a range of health-promoting domains, such as nutrition, stress management and exercise, with the aim of helping tourists to achieve a healthier lifestyle. Spiritual retreats emphasise spiritual development and enlightenment. They can be religious or non-religious, but always include meditation in various forms (Voigt, 2014).

The research reported in this chapter does *not* assess the effects of a wellness tourism vacation on the well-being of tourists, but whether different groups of tourists report different patterns of well-being. How the concept of well-being is understood varies according to different disciplines such as philosophy, theology, sociology and economics. The theoretical framework of this research is based in the field of positive psychology, specifically the two principal approaches of hedonic and eudaimonic well-being. In this research, hedonia and eudaimonia have been explored on three different levels: the experiential, the motivational and the global level. In terms of tourist experiences, it has been analysed whether and how hedonia and eudaimonia play a role in reflective accounts of the three different wellness tourism experiences (i.e. in form of subjective states while being engaged in the activity, as well as a result of the activity). On the motivational level, the aim of this study was to determine the benefits sought by wellness tourists and to explore whether the content of these benefits can be described as distinctly hedonic or eudaimonic. Furthermore, in this research, the global well-being (i.e. the general subjective assessment of well-being, independent of tourism experiences) of wellness tourists has been assessed. To summarise, the aims of this study were twofold: to explore and compare the well-being of three groups of wellness tourists on the experiential, the motivational and the global level and to examine the usefulness of employing hedonia and eudaimonia to establish particular patterns of well-being per wellness tourist group.

## The concept of well-being in positive psychology

Although the term 'positive psychology' was coined by Maslow in the last chapter of his book *Motivation and Personality* (1954), and although positive psychology draws substantially on works by him and other humanistic psychologists, it has only been established as a field fairly recently. For most of its history, researchers of psychology have been concerned with examining factors that ail the human mind rather than with the factors that foster and promote individual and group well-being. The positive psychology movement has made major advances toward improving this imbalance. In 2000, Seligman and Csikszentmihalyi edited a special issue of the *American Psychologist* and wrote a seminal introductory article on positive psychology. Ever since that special issue, there has been an explosive growth of positive psychology all over the world (e.g. Gable & Haidt, 2005; Rusk & Waters, 2013). Even within the field of positive psychology, numerous approaches to conceptualise and measure well-being exist. Next, the two principal approaches, hedonic and eudaimonic well-being will be described.

### *Hedonic and eudaimonic well-being*

Much of the current research on positive psychological well-being is based on one of two broad philosophical traditions concerned with the meaning of a 'good life' (Keyes, 2002; Ryan & Deci, 2001). One is the pursuit of 'happiness', which is the hedonic view, while the eudaimonic tradition focuses on personal growth and a meaningful life. The birth of hedonism can be attributed to the Greek philosopher Aristippus of Cyrene (435–366 BCE), who held that feelings of 'hedone' (Greek for pleasure) were the supreme good in life. They argued that all living creatures pursue pleasure and avoid pain by nature. 'Eudaimonia' is a concept introduced by Aristotle (384–322 BCE) and is also often translated as 'happiness'. However, for Aristotle, present pleasures did not constitute the highest good; for him, it was realising one's 'daimon' or 'true self' (Waterman, 1993) in the long-term. In other words, the effort to live in accordance to one's 'daimon', the congruence between one's potential and one's life activities, leads to the experience of eudaimonia.

Positive psychologists have drawn on these ancient philosophies to develop scientific measurement tools in relation to these different perspectives on well-being. Among those psychologists who have focused on a hedonic conceptualisation of well-being, there seems to be a general consensus that it is measured by one's general satisfaction with life or subjective happiness assessments, as well as frequent positive affect and infrequent negative affect (e.g. Diener 1984; Lyubomirsky & Lepper, 1999). One reason for this agreement may be that hedonic well-being has been researched since the 1970s and thus a larger body of research had been built even before the positive psychology movement commenced. Also, it is arguably not as complex as eudaimonic well-being. In the literature, hedonic well-being is often referred to as 'subjective well-being' (SWB), which is somewhat misleading because hedonic and eudaimonic well-being are both essentially subjective. The establishment of eudaimonic well-being indicators has been less straightforward and is much more heterogenic (Henderson & Knight, 2012). Arguably, one of the best-known sets of indicators to assess eudaimonic well-being is Ryff's conceptualisation of 'psychological well-being' , which includes six dimensions: purpose in life, personal growth, self-acceptance, environmental mastery, autonomy and positive relations with others (Ryff & Keyes, 1995; Ryff & Singer, 1998). In a recent review of different eudaimonic approaches, Huta and Waterman (2014) discussed four central eudaimonic dimensions that are found in most conceptualisations: growth (i.e. self-actualisation, realisation of personal goals), meaning (i.e. identification of purpose in life, understanding a bigger picture and contributing to it), excellence (i.e. striving for higher standards of one's behaviours) and authenticity (i.e. identifying and staying connected with one's true self).

Although initially there was a vigorous debate on the merits of each approach to understanding well-being (e.g. Kashdan, 2004 ; Waterman, 2008), there now seems to be a consensus that both approaches should be integrated to comprehensively understand psychological well-being (Henderson & Knight, 2012). Nevertheless, the bulk of existing research seems to be subscribed to either the hedonic or the eudaimonic approach, and there still seems to be limited knowledge as to how hedonic and eudaimonic well-being relate to each other. Perhaps most inclusively, Keyes, Smothkin and Ryff (2002, p. 1018) have argued that, depending on the theory used, one can 'see both forms of well-being usefully construed as antecedent, consequent, or even mediating variable'.

Consequently, another issue that leads to the complexity of hedonia and eudaimonia is that they cannot only be assessed at the global level but also on the experiential/activity and motivational levels. Waterman and colleagues (Waterman, 2008; Waterman *et al.*, 2003, 2008) produced a body of research where hedonia and eudaimonia were assessed on the experiential level. They were interested in how hedonia and eudaimonia are connected to the concept of intrinsic motivation and thus suggested a new set of indicators for intrinsic motivation that takes eudaimonia into account. They included a set of predictor variables of intrinsic motivation – namely (a) self-determination, (b) balance of challenge and skills, (c) effort and (d) self-realisation values (i.e. whether one promotes one's best potentials) and a set of outcome variables– namely, the hedonic outcomes of (a) enjoyment and (b) interest, as well as the eudaimonic outcomes of (c) flow and (d) feelings of personal expressiveness (i.e. embodiment of one's personal identity). In a series of studies, it was found that hedonia and eudaimonia are highly related but distinct states because they correlated with distinct patterns of variables. Hedonic enjoyment correlated more strongly with self-determination, while eudaimonic outcomes had stronger correlations with the balance of challenges and skills, self-realisation values and effort (Waterman, 2008; Waterman *et al.*, 2003, 2008).

On the motivational level, psychologists have been interested in how motivational constructs such as goal contents and motives contribute to people's psychological well-being. Recently, a series of studies investigated the effect of hedonic motives on multiple measures of psychological well-being – namely, positive affect, negative life satisfaction, carefreeness, vitality, meaning and elevating experience (Huta & Ryan, 2010). The authors developed the HEMA scale, which includes four items to assess hedonic motives and four items to evaluate eudaimonic ones. Thus this scale appraises general motivational tendencies that are not tied to a specific activity or experience. The results showed that hedonic motives were related to greater positive and lower negative affect, as well as carefreeness, whilst eudaimonic motives were related more strongly with meaning and elevating experiences. The authors furthermore examined the effects of hedonia and eudaimonia over time and found that hedonically motivated activities were associated with greater immediate well-being, while eudaimonically motivated activities were related to greater long-term well-being. Finally, Huta and Ryan (2010) found that those individuals with high levels of both hedonic and eudaimonic well-being had the highest degree of well-being in all dimensions, particularly when compared with those who were low in both motives or predominantly motivated by either hedonia or eudaimonia. Consequently, they concluded that hedonically and eudaimonically motivated pursuits are related and that they are both necessary for optimal psychological well-being.

## Hedonic and eudaimonic well-being in tourism

In no other context in life are individuals as free to choose the nature of their experiences as in leisure and tourism – in tourism perhaps even more intensively because tourism experiences tend to be separated from everyday life chores and commitments. Thus tourism has the potential to lead to well-being. Surprisingly, up until the 2000s, empirical research into well-being of tourists largely does not exist. However, since the positive psychology movement facilitated the scientific assessment of previously somewhat elusive constructs, there have been calls for drawing upon positive psychology to study the linkages between tourism and well-being (Filep, 2012; Pearce, 2009). Since then the relationship between tourism and well-being has slowly become one of the main topics in current tourism publications and research collections have begun to be issued (Filep & Pearce, 2014; Pearce, Filep & Ross, 2011). In a recent review of existing works, however, Filep (2012) notes that nearly all existing empirical studies in tourism solely focus on hedonic well-being (in other words, SWB). He specifically promotes a more inclusive conceptualisation of well-being that incorporates eudaimonia. It also appears that in tourism well-being is mostly assessed at the global outcome level, rather than the experiential or motivational level.

## Stebbins's theory of casual versus serious leisure: a focus on experiences

Indirectly, Stebbins's theory of casual versus serious leisure can be employed in the tourism context to differentiate hedonic and eudaimonic experiences. Stebbins (1997a) describes casual leisure as immediately rewarding, enjoyable experiences for which positive outcomes are relatively short-lived. Importantly, Stebbins argues that the central characteristic of casual leisure experiences is that they can all be described as *hedonic*. Stebbins lists six types of casual leisure types: relaxation, passive entertainment, active entertainment, sensory stimulation, social conversation and play (Stebbins, 1997a, 2001). Significantly, Stebbins specifies that all casual leisure experiences can be pursued in combination; for instance, all experiences can be perceived as relaxing, or play can accompany sensory stimulation (Stebbins, 2008). Consequently, the fact that these experiences are characterised as relaxing, fun, stimulating and pleasurable and the fact that these rewards are short-lived could be considered indicators of hedonic tourism and leisure experiences.

Serious leisure is defined as the committed pursuit of activities or hobbies, which typically encompasses acquiring and expressing special skills and knowledge (Stebbins, 1997b). There are several characteristics that distinguish serious from casual leisure experiences. People engaging in serious leisure experiences make a significant *effort* that results in the attainment of special *knowledge, training or skills*. Furthermore, serious leisure participants tend to follow a *career path*, characterised by increasing involvement and achievement. When engaged in an activity for a time, people become entrenched in a *special social world* – a community with shared values, attitudes and beliefs. A further characteristic of serious leisure is that it provides a source of *identity*. Serious leisure experiences are thought to produce a number of *durable* benefits that are supposed to be long-lived in contrast to the short-term benefits of casual leisure (Stebbins, 2008). While Stebbins apparently has not referred to the concept of eudaimonia in his writings, the durable benefits he describes reflect eudaimonia as described in positive psychology. He specifically notes that serious leisure can be enjoyed and perceived as pleasurable, but that these outcomes are not as pronounced and can be considered a side effect (Stebbins, 1997b). Stebbins specifically notes that serious leisure does not exclude negative emotions and that another serious leisure quality is that participants are going to *persevere* despite experiencing adversity (Stebbins, 2008).

## *The motivational level*

Tourist motivation is one central topic in tourism research, and the concept of benefits sought is widely used. On the psychological level, a benefit can be defined as a positive outcome received from a tourism experience. Benefits sought are future oriented; however, after their experience, tourists are naturally able to reflect on why they travelled to a certain destination and undertook certain activities in the first place. It is beyond the scope of this chapter to review the literature on tourist motivation, but despite different underlying theories, it is obvious that certain motives consistently recur, even in dissimilar tourism contexts. With regard to the benefits sought by wellness tourists, Smith and Puczkó (2009, p. 133) concluded that there has been little research investigating the motives or benefits sought by wellness tourists. Existing studies tend to focus only on spa visitation (Mak, Wong & Chang, 2009; Naylor and Kleiser 2002), which is why it was necessary to establish the benefits sought by wellness tourists in this study.

## *Hedonia, eudaimonia and wellness tourism*

While to the knowledge of the author there is no prior empirical research in regard to hedonic and eudaimonic well-being in the wellness tourism context, the notion of hedonia has been theoretically linked to wellness tourism. For instance, Henderson (2004, p. 113) designates wellness tourism as consisting of 'hedonistic indulgences of spas and alternative therapies'. Often the concept of hedonia carries negative connotations. For instance, Dann and Nordstrand (2009, p. 127) propose that spa visitation appeals to 'hedonistic sybarites' and Steiner and Reisinger (2006, p. 12) postulate that much of wellness tourism focuses on the 'superficial quest for merely feeling well'. Steiner and Reisinger continue to argue that only those tourists who focus on transcendence and spirituality (i.e. more eudaimonic outcomes) should be regarded as wellness tourists. This distinction between tourists who 'only' look for somewhat superficial pleasures and those with allegedly 'higher' aims of meaningful self-development and transcendence is mirrored in the general tourism literature by authors who have linked mass tourists with the former and individual tourists with the latter (e.g. Boorstin, 1992; Cohen, 2004). In other words, some works engender the impression that eudaimonic pursuits of meaning, self-actualisation and spirituality of individual tourists are seen as more worthy than the hedonic quest of pleasure, enjoyment, fun and relaxation connected to mass tourists or, in this case, spa tourists.

In order to explore and compare patterns of hedonic and eudaimonic well-being in three groups of wellness tourists across three different levels, a mixed methods approach was employed which will be outlined in the following section.

# Methods

## *Qualitative study*

In 2008, data were collected using semi-structured, in-depth interviews with 27 Australian wellness tourists and analysed using thematic analysis (Boyatzis, 1998). Snowball sampling was used to obtain the purposive sample. Four of the interviewees engaged in two of the three different wellness tourism experiences, which they recounted separately. This raised the final sample to 15 tourists describing their spa experiences, 6 individuals with lifestyle resort experiences and 10 tourists portraying their spiritual retreat experiences. The opening prompt of the interview guide was, 'Please tell me of your experiences as a wellness tourist'. In order to specifically address the benefits wellness tourists seek, the following questions were asked: 'What are the benefits you seek from your wellness tourism experience?' and 'Why do you have wellness tourism holidays?' The digitally recorded interviews were transcribed verbatim, and the qualitative analysis software NVivo7 was used to facilitate data analysis and code recognition.

The themes identified in regard to the hedonic or eudaimonic nature of the three different types of wellness tourism experiences are based on a priori established theory based on the previously discussed works of Stebbins and Waterman. Accordingly, the distinction between hedonia and eudaimonia encompasses emotions, cognitive appraisals and temporal differences. Specifically, casual/hedonic characteristics are characterised by (a) pleasure, (b) relaxation and (c) sensory stimulation, all of which are (d) short-lived. In contrast, serious/eudaimonic characteristics include (a) belongingness to a special social world, (b) career development, (c) effort and perseverance and (d) knowledge, training and skills, which are (e) fulfilling and identity-building and which (f) have a long-lasting effect. The themes in regard to the benefits wellness tourists seek were derived from the data.

## *Quantitative study*

As no overall sampling frame of Australian wellness tourists exists, participants were recruited using quota sampling in the second stage of the research. In quota sampling, the target population is divided into sub-groups; in this case, the three categories of wellness tourists. The sample was drawn from databases provided by three wellness tourism associations or operators (the Australasian Spa Association membership list, an Australian health resort chain and a South Australian spiritual retreat operator). A self-administered survey was mailed to the wellness tourists who had been targeted. The final sample included 509 cases comprising 91 beauty spa visitors, 316 lifestyle resort visitors and 102 spiritual retreat visitors.

The following measures relevant for this chapter were included in the survey:

- *The newly developed Benefits of Wellness Tourism Scale (BWTS)* to measure benefits sought (Voigt, Brown & Howat, 2011). Based on the in-depth interviews conducted in the qualitative stage of the research scale, items were drawn from a pool of 210 benefit statements expressed in the interviews. After a culling process with four other tourism academics and representatives from each of the participating organisations, 46 benefit items remained. These were randomly mixed and respondents were asked to 'rate the importance of each of the following benefits you hope to attain' on a seven-point, Likert-response format, ranging from 1 (not at all important) to 7 (extremely important).

- *Subjective Happiness Scale (SHS)* to measure hedonic well-being (Lyubomirsky & Lepper, 1999), consisting of four items. The first two items ask respondents to describe themselves in relation to others, and the last two items provide descriptions of happy and unhappy individuals and ask participants to what extent the descriptions apply to them. The SHS has been nominated as one of the most appropriate instruments to measure happiness in the hedonic sense (Kashdan, 2004). Internal consistency in this study was high ($\alpha = 0.88$).

- *Eighteen-item version of the Psychological Well-Being Scale (PWBS)* to measure eudaimonic well-being (Ryff, 1989; Ryff & Keyes, 1995; Ryff & Singer, 1998). The short version of the PWBS uses three items to measure each of the six dimensions of psychological well-being: self-acceptance, positive relations, environmental mastery, personal growth, autonomy and purpose in life. Respondents are asked to indicate their level of agreement with each item on a seven-point Likert scale, with higher scores indicating higher appraisals. As with previous studies, in this research, Exploratory Factor Analysis (EFA) did not support the six-dimensional structure as proposed by Ryff and colleagues. Therefore, a composite index of eudaimonic well-being was created ($\alpha = 0.84$).

## Results

### Qualitative study

Table 7.1 shows the relative percentage of participants expressing casual/hedonic and serious/eudaimonic experience characteristics expressed by interviewees of the three different wellness tourist groups, revealing distinct differences. Beauty spa experiences were solely associated with casual/hedonic characteristics, whereas spiritual retreat experience accounts almost exclusively incorporated serious/eudaimonic characteristics. Lifestyle resort experiences were described with mixed characteristics, although serious/eudaimonic themes outweighed the casual/hedonic ones. It is outside the scope of this chapter to present sample data for each theme; for more detail refer to Voigt (2010) and Voigt, Howat and Brown (2010). One example quote that was coded with the casual/hedonic experience characteristic of *Pleasure* and *Relaxation* reads:

> With the spa in England, that was mainly for me, just a treat for myself. I didn't really go with any other purpose in mind, other than just to relax and

enjoy it. And I did, it was very nice . . . . And I did that mainly for relaxation, just for my own pleasure. There was no particular aim involved other than must have a good time.

Beauty spa visitation was predominantly associated with experiencing complete relaxation, but also pleasure. The *sensory stimulation* consisting of the touch of the spa therapists, warm room temperatures that made individuals feel 'cocooned', soothing, meditative music and the pleasant smells of aromatic oils contributed to their enjoyment. However, these positive outcomes tended to be *short-lived* – ranging from one day up to a week. Like *sensory stimulation*, this casual/hedonic experience characteristic was solely coded in beauty spa experience accounts. Nevertheless, in the short time that relaxation and pleasure were experienced, these positive experiences seemed to be very strong and profound. Participants frequently discussed that their spa experiences stand in stark contrast to their everyday lives, where they tend to be the ones that always give (their time and their emotions), while during the spa experience, they could put themselves first for a change and feel nurtured, pampered and cared for.

In comparison, relaxation and, to even to a lesser extent, pleasure featured a lot less often in lifestyle resorts and spiritual retreat experience accounts. Even then it became clear that *relaxation* was understood in an active manner, something one must actively work towards, not something that is passively attained. This does not mean that lifestyle resort and spiritual retreat experiences are not enjoyable, just that hedonic outcomes did not come readily to mind when participants recalled their experiences. The serious/eudaimonic characteristic *knowledge,*

*Table 7.1* Relative percentage of three groups of wellness tourists expressing casual/ hedonic and serious/eudaimonic experience characteristics

|  | *Beauty spa visitors* | *Lifestyle resort visitors* | *Spiritual retreat visitors* |
|---|---|---|---|
| **Casual/hedonic experience characteristics** | | | |
| Pleasure | 40% | 33% | – |
| Relaxation | 93% | 17% | 10% |
| Sensory stimulation | 35% | – | – |
| Short-lived | 73% | – | – |
| **Serious/eudaimonic experience characteristics** | | | |
| Belongingness to a special social world | – | – | 10% |
| Career development | – | – | 50% |
| Effort & perseverance | – | 50% | 40% |
| Knowledge, training & skills | – | 67% | 80% |
| Fulfilling & identity-building | – | 67% | 70% |
| Long-lived | – | 67% | 70% |

*training & skills* was the most frequently mentioned theme overall. Lifestyle resort and spiritual retreat visitors can gain knowledge in very different areas. On one hand, they learn specific techniques, therapies and health-promoting behaviours (e.g. yoga, meditation styles and how to identify personal goals and to eat in a more healthful manner). In particular, lifestyle resort participants sometimes explained that while they did not always learn things that were new to them, they still learned tools and techniques that helped them to implement lasting behaviour changes in their everyday lives. On the other hand, they learned a lot about themselves, about who they are and what is truly important to them. It appears that lifestyle resort visitation, and particularly spiritual retreat visitation, supports people's construction of identity. It seems that lifestyle resort and spiritual retreat experiences can cause major shifts in perspective and encourage tourists to see the world and the self with new eyes. Thus the things tourists learn during their experiences either blend into their daily lifestyles in the form of behavioural changes (e.g. participants start to meditate regularly or eat more consciously) or in the form of trait changes that really alter the person in terms of who he/she is. Sometimes the experiences also worked as a catalyst for major life decisions. For instance, after visiting a spiritual retreat, one participant gave up his stressful job and decided to be a stay-at-home dad for a while. Importantly, it became clear that these changes of skills and traits are long lasting, as they become part of visitors' daily lives and of who they are.

All these major, often existential, changes require effort, which often does not exclude negative emotions – an important characteristic of eudaimonia. Accordingly, some lifestyle resort and spiritual retreat visitors described parts of their experiences as 'hard', 'tough', 'demanding', 'slightly uncomfortable', 'frustrating' and something one has 'to put a lot of effort into'. However, many participants then described their experiences as deeply satisfying, fulfilling and meaningful once they had overcome the hurdles and persevered through the struggle.

Finally, the theme *career development* came up only in experience accounts of spiritual retreat visitors. Half of these interviewees described their spiritual development in a manner that can be compared to a career development. All of them started this development by first being involved in a formal religion and then questioning that religion and becoming anti-religious for a while. They then realised that they still craved spiritual meaning in their lives, which heightened their interest in yoga, meditation and spiritual retreats. The term 'journey' was actually used frequently to describe this kind of progress.

### Quantitative study

#### Benefits sought: factors and group differences

To explore the benefits sought by wellness tourists, the 46 items of the BWTS scale were subjected to principal axis factoring (PAF) with direct oblimin oblique rotation as the rotation method. Prior to performing PAF, the Kaiser-Meyer-Olkin (KMO) test and Bartlett's test of sphericity were used to assess the suitability of the data for factor analysis. In this research, the KMO value was 0.918, and the Bartlett's test of sphericity demonstrated significance at the level of $p < 0.001$, therefore signifying appropriateness of factor analysis. A series of PAF solutions were examined, ranging from a three-factor to a six-factor solution. The three- and five-factor solutions were difficult to interpret. Compared to the four-factor solution, the six-factor solution had fewer cross-loadings, much higher communalities and was most interpretable. Jolliffe (cited in Field, 2009) argues that an eigenvalue threshold of 1.0 can be too strict when the number of variables is more than 30, and the resulting communalities are not all greater than 0.7. For these reasons, the six-factor solution was selected, although the sixth factor did not have an eigenvalue above 1.0. As suggested by Tabachnick and Fidell (2007), freeloading items and items with high cross-loadings were candidates for elimination. Thus the final solution retained 42 across the following 6 factors:

- Factor *transcendence* (10 items; eigenvalue = 11.64; α = 0.93): contains items describing the benefits of meditation, contemplation, experiencing peace and calmness and finding one's true self.
- Factor *physical health and appearance* (10 items; eigenvalue = 6.24; α = 0.92): includes benefits of physical fitness and exercise, general health improvement and also improvement of appearance.
- Factor *escape and relax* (7 items; eigenvalue = 2.7; α = 0.87): covers benefits of getting away from demands of everyday life to letting go of problems and stressors and becoming deeply relaxed and refreshed.
- Factor *important others and novelty* (7 items; eigenvalue = 2.43; α = 0.79): encompasses benefits either reflecting social benefits of being with others or impressing others, as well as benefits of experiencing something new.
- Factor *re-establish self-esteem* (4 items; eigenvalue = 1.22; α = 0.77): includes benefit items related to overcoming negative life events and regaining confidence and self-esteem.
- Factor *indulgence* (4 items; eigenvalue = 0.81; α = 0.72): comprises benefits of indulging and pampering the self.

Some of these benefit factors can be easily described as more hedonic or eudaimonic in content. While the factor *transcendence* can be clearly seen as eudaimonic, *indulgence* and *escape and relax* are more hedonic. The importance of positive relationships with others is seen by some as signifying eudaimonia (Ryff, 1989; Ryff & Keyes, 1995), but not through impressing others.

A MANOVA was utilised to investigate differences in benefits sought according to the wellness tourist category. The dependent variables consisted of the six benefit factors identified in the EFA and the independent variable was the wellness tourist category (i.e. beauty spa, lifestyle resort or spiritual retreat visitor). Using Pillai's trace, there was a statistically significant difference between beauty spa, lifestyle resort and spiritual retreat visitors across the dependent variables, $V = 0.962$, $F (12, 1004) = 77.60$, $p < 0.001$. Follow-up ANOVAs were subsequently undertaken to investigate the source of the significant differences. These statistical tests revealed significant differences in four out of six benefit factors. Importantly, another series of MANOVAs was performed to ensure that effects of the wellness tourist category on benefits sought could not be explained by underlying demographic differences. No interaction effects were found.

The benefit factor of *transcendence* was significantly more important to spiritual visitors *(M* = 5.85) than to beauty spa *(M* = 4.11) and lifestyle resort visitors *(M* = 4.34). The benefit factor of *physical health and appearance* was significantly more important for lifestyle resort visitors *(M* = 5.19) than for beauty spa *(M* =3.66) and spiritual retreat visitors *(M* = 2.86), and spiritual retreat visitors found it to be significantly less important than both of the other wellness tourist groups. There were no significant group differences in relation to the benefit factor of *escape and relaxation,* but it was rated high by all groups (beauty spa visitors *M* = 5.61; lifestyle resort visitors *M* = 5.46 and spiritual retreat visitors *M* = 5.23). Beauty spa visitors *(M* = 3.06) rated the factor of *important others and novelty* as significantly more important than lifestyle resort *(M* = 2.72) and spiritual retreat visitors *(M* = 2.13), but overall this benefit factor did not receive high ratings, which makes sense, as most wellness tourists travel by themselves (Voigt *et al.*, 2010). There were no significant group differences in relation to *re-establish self-esteem,* and it was generally ranked relatively low (beauty spa visitors *M* = 3.33, lifestyle resort visitors *M* = 3.44 and spiritual retreat visitors *M* = 3.34). Beauty spa visitors *(M* = 5.04) rated the factor of *indulgence* significantly higher than lifestyle resort *(M* = 4.50) or spiritual retreat visitors *(M* = 2.92), and spiritual retreat visitors found it significantly less important than the other two groups.

*Hedonic and eudaimonic well-being: correlation and group differences*

Pearson product-moment correlation coefficient was used to investigate whether there was a positive correlation between hedonic and eudaimonic well-being. The results indicated a strong positive relationship between the two variables, $r =$ 0.696, $N$ = 509, $p$ (one-tailed) < 0.01.

A one-way MANOVA was utilised to assess differences in hedonic and eudaimonic well-being according to the wellness tourist group. The MANOVA demonstrated significant differences in positive psychological well-being between wellness tourist groups, $V$ = 0.024, $F$ (4, 1012) = 3.01, $p$ < 0.001). The source of significant variance was then located by ANOVAs and Bonferrroni post-hoc tests. Bonferroni post-hoc tests revealed that beauty spa visitors rated hedonic well-being significantly higher *(M* = 5.62) than lifestyle resort *(M* = 5.31) and spiritual retreat visitors *(M* = 5.15). There were no statistically significant group differences in regard to eudaimonic well-being (beauty spa visitors *M* = 5.57, lifestyle resort visitors *M* = 5.38 and spiritual retreat visitors *M* = 5.43). Again, a series of MANOVAs ascertained that the group differences could not be explained by demographic differences.

## Discussion

The study described in this chapter represents an interdisciplinary mixed-method approach to examine the concepts of hedonic and eudaimonic well-being on three different levels in the context of wellness tourism: the experiential, the motivational and the global levels.

With regard to all three levels of well-being, there were distinct differences between the three groups of wellness tourists. Differentiating hedonia and eudaimonia was especially useful in relation to the experiential level. Linking positive psychology research by Waterman, Huta and colleagues with Stebbins's theory of casual versus serious leisure, a pool of specific hedonic and eudaimonic indicators could be generated. When applying these to the experience accounts of the three wellness tourist groups, distinct patterns of well-being were revealed. One can think of a continuum with pure hedonic experiences on the left and pure eudaimonic experiences on the right. Beauty spa visitation is clearly located on the far left side, whereas spiritual retreat visitation can be placed on the right side of this continuum. Lifestyle resort visitation sits more in the middle of the continuum but leans toward the right side. On one hand, this result supports literature that portrays beauty spa visitation as a hedonic tourism activity. It does not, however, concur with the negativity that sometimes accompanies such a portrayal. Beauty spa visitation is about taking time for oneself to feel nourished and cared for, to lose oneself completely in the present moment, to forget worries and to enjoy the experiences with all senses. The immediate well-being outcomes for spa tourists are intense, blissful pleasure as well as profound relaxation and replenishment that, however, lasts for only a short period of time. While these experiences may be about emptying or clearing the mind, one cannot conclude that spa visitors are mindless tourists; their experiences are not unhealthy or deviant, but a legitimate and genuine avenue to achieve higher levels of (hedonic) well-being. On the other hand, spiritual retreat visitation and to a little lesser degree lifestyle resort visitation can be linked to eudaimonic rather than hedonic well-being. These kinds of experiences are perceived to be deeply meaningful and self-actualising. It appears that these kinds of tourism experiences help people to construct their identities, to better understand themselves and their place in the larger scheme of things. What individuals learn in these kinds of retreats stays with them for a long time; in fact, for some, retreat visitation acted as a catalyst for profound life changes. Importantly, spiritual retreat and lifestyle resort visitation does not exclude negative emotions. To achieve self-awareness, one often must overcome one's comfort zones, as well as negative feelings such as anxiety or fear of losing self-control. Often, it is an effort and a struggle to reach self-awareness and a state of existential authenticity.

On the motivational level, distinguishing hedonia and eudaimonia has not been as straightforward because, based on the existing theories, not all contents of the benefit factors can be easily ascribed to either hedonia or eudaimonia. Nevertheless, the benefit factor of *indulgence* can be clearly described as hedonic and the benefit factor of *transcendence* as eudaimonic. In regard to group differences, the aforementioned pattern was thus repeated on the motivational level. Beauty spa visitors rated the hedonic benefit factor of *indulgence* significantly higher and spiritual retreat visitors significantly lower than the other three groups of wellness tourists. In contrast, spiritual retreat visitors found the eudaimonic benefit factor of *transcendence* significantly more important than the other two groups. On the surface, the content of the benefit factor *escape and relaxation* seems to be hedonic. Here, however, the three groups did not differ significantly and the factor was generally rated with high levels of importance across the three groups. From the qualitative experience accounts it is known, however, that escape and relaxation can be understood differently. Whereas beauty spa visitors want to forget their everyday life problems and achieve relaxation passively, mainly through the restorative techniques of therapists, spiritual retreat and lifestyle resort visitors are actively involved in their relaxation, either in the form of exercise and mind/body activities such as yoga and meditation and/ or through an inner journey of mindful contemplation and self-realisation. This benefit factor shows that not all indicators can be easily divided into the dichotomy of hedonia versus eudaimonia.

Differences between the groups were also explored on the global level. It was not necessarily expected that the same patterns of global well-being would emerge as on the experiential and motivational levels, because a single wellness holiday is of course only one factor of many that contribute to people's psychological well-being. Interestingly, however, beauty spa visitors whose experience accounts can be clearly described as hedonic and whose highly ranked motives are also hedonic in content also had significantly higher levels of hedonic well-being on the global level. However, while lifestyle resort and spiritual retreat visitors ranked global eudaimonic well-being with higher importance than global hedonic well-being, there were no significant group differences.

Future research is needed to further explore if and how hedonia and eudaimonia at the experiential and motivational levels are linked to global hedonic and eudaimonic well-being. Is it possible that those people who value hedonic outcomes and life goals more than eudaimonic ones tend to choose tourism experiences that more easily yield these outcomes and vice versa? In this research, beauty spa visitors, who had a significantly higher level of hedonic well-being on the global level also placed significantly more importance on hedonic motives and their tourism experience can be described as hedonic. However, although eudaimonia dominated in regard to spiritual retreat and lifestyle resort visitors on the experiential and motivational levels, this pattern was not replicated on the global level. It might also be that people are consciously or subconsciously aware that they have a deficit in one of the well-being dimensions and try to compensate this through their leisure and tourism experiences.

## Conclusion

Outside, but especially inside the field of tourism, it is rare that hedonia and eudaimonia are assessed in parallel terms, but such kinds of studies are necessary to better understand the interrelationships and the undoubted complexity of different dimensions and signifiers of psychological well-being.

All together this research demonstrates that hedonia and eudaimonia are useful concepts to compare and differentiate between groups of tourists and to distinguish certain kinds of tourism experiences. In this context of wellness tourism, different patterns of hedonia and eudaimonia were discernible on the experiential, the motivational and the global levels of psychological well-being. In positive psychology, research on hedonic and eudaimonic well-being is far from complete. There is still much debate on appropriate conceptualisations, and measures are constantly refined or newly developed. There also needs to be a discussion on how to investigate these constructs in the context of tourism. Without a doubt, well-being plays a major role in tourists' motivation and in having satisfying tourism experiences. Hedonia and eudaimonia seem to be crucial, complementary pathways to achieve well-being and to explain differences between groups of tourists. More research is needed to understand hedonic and eudaimonic well-being patterns within and across tourism activities, experiences and motivations, in particular how these patterns relate to tourists' global subjective well-being.

## References

Boorstin, D. J. (1992). *The image: A guide to pseudo-events in America*. New York: Vintage Books.

Boyatzis, R. E. (1998). *Transforming qualitative information: Thematic analysis and code development*. Thousand Oaks, CA: Sage Publications.

Cohen, E. (2004). *Contemporary tourism: Diversity and change*. Amsterdam: Elsevier.

Dann, G. M. S., & Nordstrand, K. B. (2009). Promoting well-being via multisensory tourism. In R. Bushell & P. J. Sheldon (Eds.), *Wellness and tourism: Mind, body, spirit, place* (pp. 125–137). New York: Cognizant Communication Corporation.

Diener, E. (1984). Subjective well-being. *Psychological Bulletin*, 95, 542–575.

Field, A. P. (2009). *Discovering statistics using SPSS* (3rd ed.). London: Sage.

Filep, S. (2012). Moving beyond subjective well-being: A tourism critique. *Journal of Hospitality and Tourism Research*, 38, 266–274.

Filep, S., & Pearce, P. L. (2014). *Tourist experience and fulfilment: Insights from positive psychology*. New York: Routledge.

Gable, S. L., & Haidt, J. (2005). What (and why) is positive psychology? *Review of General Psychology*, 9, 103–110.

Henderson, J. C. (2004). Healthcare tourism in Southeast Asia. *Tourism Review International*, 7, 111–121.

Henderson, L. W., & Knight, T. (2012). Integrating the hedonic and eudaimonic perspectives to more comprehensively understand well-being and pathways to well-being. *International Journal of Well-Being*, 2, 196–221.

Huta, V., & Ryan, R. M. (2010). Pursuing pleasure or virtue: The differential and overlapping well-being benefits of hedonic and eudaimonic motives. *Journal of Happiness Studies*, 11, 735–762.

Huta, V., & Waterman, A. S. (2014). Eudaimonia and its distinction from hedonia: Developing a classification and terminology for understanding conceptual and operational definitions. *Journal of Happiness Studies*, 15, 1425–1456.

Kashdan, T. B. (2004). The assessment of subjective well-being (issues raised by the Oxford Happiness Questionnaire). *Personality and Individual Differences*, 36, 1225–1232.

Keyes, C. L. M. (2002). The mental health continuum: From languishing to flourishing in life. *Journal of Health and Social Behavior*, 43, 207–222.

Keyes, C. L. M., Smothkin, D., & Ryff, C. D. (2002). Optimizing well-being: The empirical encounter of two traditions. *Journal of Personality and Social Psychology*, 82, 1007–1022.

Lyubomirsky, S., & Lepper, H. S. (1999). A measure of subjective happiness: Preliminary reliability and construct validation. *Social Indicators Research*, 46, 137–155.

Mak, A. H. N., Wong, K. K. F., & Chang, R. C. Y. (2009). Health or self-indulgence? The motivations and characteristics of spa-goers. *International Journal of Tourism Research*, 11, 185–199.

Maslow, A. (1954). *Motivation and personality*. New York: Harper.

Naylor, G., & Kleiser, S. B. (2002). Exploring the differences in perceptions of satisfaction across lifestyle segments. *Journal of Vacation Marketing*, 8, 343–351.

Pearce, P. L. (2009). The relationship between positive psychology and tourist behavior studies. *Tourism Analysis*, 14, 37–48.

Pearce, P. L., Filep S., & Ross, G. F. (2011). *Tourists, tourism and the good life*. New York: Routledge.

Rusk, R. D., & Waters, L. E. (2013). Tracing the size, reach, impact, and breadth of positive psychology. *Journal of Positive Psychology*, 8, 207–221.

Ryan, R. M., & Deci, E. L. (2001). On happiness and human potentials: A review of research on hedonic and eudaimonic well-being. *Annual Review of Psychology*, 52, 141–166.

Ryff, C. D. (1989). Happiness is everything, or is it? Explorations on the meaning of psychological well-being. *Journal of Personality and Social Psychology*, 57, 1069–1081.

Ryff, C. D., & Keyes, C. L. M. (1995). The structure of psychological well-being revisited. *Journal of Personality and Social Psychology*, 69, 719–727.

Ryff, C. D., & Singer, B. (1998). The contours of positive human health. *Psychological Inquiry*, 9, 1–28.

Seligman, M. E. P., & Csikszentmihalyi, M. (2000). Positive psychology: An introduction. *American Psychologist*, 55, 5–14.

Smith, M., & Puczkó, L. (2009). *Health and wellness tourism*. Oxford: Butterworth-Heinemann.

Stebbins, R. A. (1997a). Casual leisure: A conceptual statement. *Leisure Studies*, 16, 17–25.

Stebbins, R. A. (1997b). Serious leisure and well-being. In J. T. Haworth & S. E. Iso-Ahola (Eds.), *Work, leisure and well-being* (pp. 67–79). New York: Routledge.

Stebbins, R. A. (2001). The costs and benefits of hedonism: Some consequences of taking casual leisure seriously. *Leisure Studies*, 20, 305–309.

Stebbins, R. A. (2008). *Serious leisure: A perspective for our time*. New Brunswick: Transaction Publishers.

Steiner, C. J., & Reisinger, Y. (2006). Ringing the fourfold: A philosophical framework for thinking about wellness tourism. *Tourism Recreation Research*, 31, 5–14.

Tabachnick, B. G., & Fidell, L. S. (2007). *Using multivariate statistics* (5th ed.). Boston: Pearson/Allyn & Bacon.

Voigt, C. (2010). *Understanding wellness tourism: An analysis of benefits sought, health-promoting behaviours and positive psychological well-being*. Unpublished doctoral dissertation, Adelaide: University of South Australia.

Voigt, C. (2014). Towards a conceptualisation of wellness tourism. In C. Voigt & C. Pforr (Eds.), *Wellness tourism: A destination perspective* (pp. 19–44). London: Routledge.

Voigt, C., Brown, G., & Howat, G. (2011). Wellness tourists: In search for transformation. *Tourism Review*, 66, 16–30.

Voigt, C., Howat, G., & Brown, G. (2010). Hedonic and eudaimonic experiences among wellness tourists: An exploratory inquiry. *Annals of Leisure Research*, 13, 541–562.

Waterman, A. S. (1993). Two conceptions of happiness: Contrasts of personal expressiveness (eudaimonia) and hedonic enjoyment. *Journal of Personality and Social Psychology*, 64, 678–691.

Waterman, A. S. (2008). Reconsidering happiness: A eudaimonist's perspective. *Journal of Positive Psychology*, 3, 234–352.

Waterman, A. S., Schwartz, S. J., & Conti, R. (2008). The implications of two conceptions of happiness (hedonic enjoyment and eudaimonia) for the understanding of intrinsic motivation. *Journal of Happiness Studies*, 9, 41–79.

Waterman, A. S., Schwartz, S. J., Goldbacher, E., Green, H., Miller, C., & Philip, S. (2003). Predicting the subjective experience of intrinsic motivation: The roles of self-determination, the balance of challenges and skills, and self-realization value. *Personality and Social Psychology Bulletin*, 29, 1447–1458.

# 8   Why do we travel?

## A positive psychological model for travel motivation

*Mihaly Csikszentmihalyi and John Coffey*

For as far as we know, humanity has been a mobile species. In order to survive, our ancestors had to learn to move as the seasons changed to follow their source of food or to avoid clashing with neighbouring tribes. As more severe changes occurred – ice ages, severe draughts, foreign invasions – they had to find new places to settle by covering great distances. At the beginning of human history, travel must have been a dreaded necessity, dangerous and unpleasant – a last resort in life-threatening circumstances.

Of course, as human beings differ in their genetic makeup and their life experiences, there probably were always some individuals who differed from the rest in their curiosity and tolerance for risk and undertook travelling by choice to find out what the world looked like beyond the familiar spaces of their customary lives. Thus, even in earlier times, motivations for travel almost certainly varied and were not always limited to a single motivational factor.

As human groups learned how to grow grains and vegetables for their subsistence, they developed permanent settlements next to land that could be cultivated and irrigated. This new adaptation provided a much more stable and comfortable lifestyle. On the other hand, this new lifestyle could become boring and constraining. Thus the option of travelling to new places became attractive to some of the more active and curious members of the population. But it was still a very slow process of change. Even as late as 25 centuries ago, few people left their village or town voluntarily. The few exceptions went abroad for a variety of complex reasons. A good example of an early traveller was Herodotus, a Greek who has been called the first western historian, the father of geography, an early anthropologist and who might even be considered the first western tourist on record.

Herodotus gave a variety of reasons for why he crisscrossed the western world. Some of these could be seen as gathering military intelligence: as a native of the eastern colonies of Greece, threatened by the invasion of the Median armies from further east, he wanted to learn more about Persian customs, Persian life – in short, get to know the strengths and weaknesses of the enemy. But while that might have been his initial reason, he was soon distracted by other reasons for travelling. As soon as he reached Egypt, for instance, he became fascinated by the question of where the Nile originated. It was known that the Nile River was the main source of energy for the ancient and powerful Egyptian civilisation. Every year it provided the water for the rich crops of wheat that made the pharaohs the wealthiest rulers of the known world. The stately river provided an ideal highway for the transport of troops and merchandise up and down the country. On its banks, idyllic groves of palm trees could shelter towns and cities built from the stone that barges carried down the river from mountain quarries. As crucial as the Nile was to the existence of Egypt, its sources remained a mystery. Where did it actually come from?

This question sparked Herodotus's interest and got him to walk endless trails in North Africa searching for the mystery of the origins of the Nile. He never got to answer that question, but fortunately he became fascinated by many of the tales and customs he encountered along the way and recorded in detail. Many of the incredible stories he reported about his travels turned out with time not to be as far-fetched as they had seemed; for instance, the story of the giant ants that the inhabitants of the Caucasus Mountains used to mine for gold. This story was widely considered one of the 'lies' made up by Herodotus – which lately has been explained: in those regions, there are marmots living in the mountains that in the process of building their tunnels underground bring to the surface gold dust and even small nuggets that the local villagers melt into jewellery. How the marmots got morphed into ants remains a mystery, but the substance of the story has a definite resemblance to reality. There are other accounts that still stretch credulity, such as the flying snakes Herodotus reports from Egypt, but given the difficulty in translating terms, and in transcribing texts many generation after the author's death, one could say that the histories of Herodotus were subjective and imaginative, but rooted in reality.

This extended example illustrates in an embryonic form the many reasons why people took up travelling as a voluntary activity and the way motivation might shift during travel. In the intervening centuries after Herodotus, people decided to travel for a variety of reasons. In the Middle Ages, most travellers were merchants or craftsmen for whom travel was part of their way of making a living. During religious festivals, Christian pilgrims made their way to sacred places such as Jerusalem, Rome or Santiago de Campostela, and Moslem pilgrims travelled great distances to visit the tomb of the Prophet in Mecca. Then the great voyages of exploration started from the maritime kingdoms of the Mediterranean, and for a short period, from the fleets of the Chinese emperors.

As with Herodotus, the motives of these explorations were a mixture of military preparations and economic incentives, with a smattering of curiosity and the thrill of discovering something new, regardless of utility. Much later in Europe, travelling became a status symbol; young men of wealthy families were expected to round out their education by participating in some version of the Grand Tour that took them from their native England or Germany to visit the classic historical sites around the Mediterranean, and if the family was really wealthy, all the way to India and China. During the relatively peaceful period in Europe in the eighteenth and nineteenth centuries, the practice of 'tourism' could be seen to evolve in the form it has now: travel motivated by the sheer experience of visiting new places, with no intent of military, economic or scientific purpose. Travel just for the sake of travelling. As such, understanding motivations for travel or tourism remains an important topic to this field that has resulted in multiple tourism and leisure models (e.g. Crompton, 1979; Pearce & Lee, 2005).

This development seems at first sight to simplify matters considerably: tourism is a form of travel motivated by the experience of travelling. But this apparently simple explanation turns out to be really no explanation at all. Why is the experience of travelling so rewarding – under some circumstances – that people look forward to it, spend large sums of money on it and often remember it as a high point of their lives?

## A model of reasons to travel for the sake of travelling

When we try to answer the aforementioned question about the reasons and rewards of travel, so many reasons come to mind that any single answer seems incomplete. Indeed, many other researchers have taken on this task (e.g. Chen, Mak & McKercher, 2011; Coghlan & Pearce, 2010; Harril & Potts, 2002; Iso-Ahola, 1982; Moscardo, 2011; Pearce, 2005; Pearce & Lee, 2005). A recent study identified escape, relaxation, relationship enhancement and self-development as the core components of travellers' motivation (Pearce & Lee, 2005). Even more recently, Pearce and Packer (2013) suggested that tourism researchers can benefit from integrating themes from contemporary psychology. We feel that contemporary positive psychology offers a new way to conceptualize motivation for tourism that recognizes how there might be co-existing or shifting motivation during a vacation. This conceptualization will also allow for examination of how benefits (and consequences) vary with tourists' shifting motivations.

Therefore, we wish to consider a model that, while quite simple, is capable of generating systematically a great number of relevant answers as to why people decide to temporarily leave their homes and go on a tour. Furthermore, the model is designed to be used online (i.e. in real time), such that motivations can be tracked at different points throughout the day (independent of memory biases) as to allow for a better understanding of how multiple or changing motives might be associated with well-being (e.g. Coghlan & Pearce, 2010). Finally, as research has highlighted how motivations can vary across cultures (e.g. Kozak, 2002; You, O'Leary, Morrison & Hong, 2000), we expect this model will work for cross-cultural understanding of motivations and well-being.

The travel motivation model (see Figure 8.1) consists of two orthogonal dimensions. The first one is the degree to which the traveller is engaging in the voyage because of extrinsic or because of intrinsic reasons (this would be the y-axis of the model). A person who is forced to travel, or is expected to travel by those in power, or is forced to go shopping with their partner, or is travelling because his job requires it, or is travelling for religious reasons, would be low on this axis – towards the extrinsic end of the y-axis. A person would be said to be high on this axis if he chose to travel for the sake of the journey itself: to relax, see new sights, voluntarily go shopping, taste new food, meet different people and learn about different places or cultures. It could very well happen that an extrinsically motivated trip becomes intrinsically rewarding; for instance, a parent agreeing to chaperone

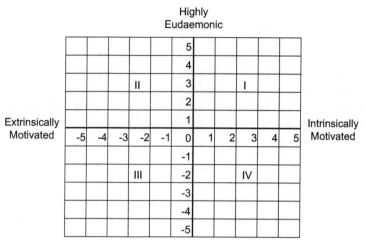

*Figure 8.1* Travel motivation matrix

a class trip to Japan falls in love with the sights and the culture. The opposite can also happen: a businessman flies to Hawaii to relax and enjoy the beaches, makes the acquaintance of a supplier vacationing at the same resort and spends the rest of the vacation planning a joint venture. In other words, it is perfectly possible for extrinsic and intrinsic motives to be involved in the same tourist excursion, either sequentially or at the same time; however, at any given time point, one of these motives is usually the predominant factor.

This model can be used to understand motivations to travel and associated benefits or consequences of travel experiences within each quadrant.

The x-axis of the model that describes a travel experience could be hedonic (i.e. pleasurable) or eudaimonic (i.e. involve personal growth and development). A person low on this count would be one whose main goal is to have a good time, to enjoy the new locale, the food and the people he encounters. At the other end, the one representing eudaimonia, would be a person who is more interested in travel as a growth experience – a chance to learn about the history or culture of the places, the variety of the cuisine and the beliefs and values of the people. Again, it is perfectly possible for a person to start a trip with a purely hedonic purpose and after a while start wondering about the local architecture, about the way people work, about the reasons for their differing beliefs – who knows, perhaps even to the point of learning a bit about the history and the language of the place. And it is equally possible for a person to enjoy a travel experience for its hedonic rewards while also growing emotionally or intellectually in the process. Later we highlight how this model can help deal with the fluid or evolving motives of travel. However, for the sake of simplicity, we will assume that one or the other of these two kinds of goals, but not both, are definitely more salient.

Placing any real-life tourist on the grid defined by these two axes would be relatively easy. A 'typical' tourist would be high on the y-axis of the model and probably low on the x-axis. In other words, he or she would be intrinsically motivated by hedonic goals. But as we have said, many combinations are possible, with different combinations and intensities of the two defining motives that might provide a broad understanding of which of these motives is associated with better psychological and physiological well-being.

For instance, many religious pilgrims from Northern Europe fell in love with the natural beauty, the lifestyle and the artistic splendour of the southern nations they visited originally for extrinsic reasons and returned again to savour the intrinsic elements of the cultures they visited. A few went farther in order to enlarge their understanding of the world and of their own selves by learning from the experience and thereby becoming more complex individuals. Or to use another example, many GIs who had no choice but to go and fight on the trenches of Europe during WWI and WWII returned voluntarily after the war to bask in the lifestyle of Paris or of Rome. Now the Vietnam War veterans are beginning to take their families on tours of Saigon and the inland of that country rich in history and natural beauty.

If we wanted to single out one position on the matrix that represents the ideal tourist vacation, it would probably be one that was high on both axes: a voluntary trip that afforded opportunities for expanding the self intellectually and emotionally – in other words, experientially. It would be a trip after which one could truthfully say, 'I am so glad I decided to go. I learned so much from this trip about this area and the culture of the people here. I really feel like a different person. I am looking forward to going again. Even if I won't have a chance to go again, I think my life is going to be richer from now on'.

By contrast, travel that would definitely not be thought of as tourism would fall in the lower left corner of the matrix as being both extrinsically motivated and focused on hedonic, rather than eudaimonic outcomes. Such a person would be someone who took a trip he really did not want to take, but felt he had to because of professional or family obligations, and once abroad could hardly wait to get back home. Besides these extreme types, several other combinations are possible: the intrinsically motivated traveller who is only interested in the pleasures of tourism, or the extrinsically motivated one who becomes aware of the potential for growth opportunities in exploring strange places. And of course, any one traveller might move all over the map of the matrix as the experiences he encounters increase or decrease his intrinsic motivation, or the kind of rewards he gains from the experience.

To see more concretely the various possibilities of the model, it might make sense to use the matrix in Figure 8.1 as a conceptual tool. We suggest that as an example you try to remember one tourist experience you had in the past that stands out as having been closest to an absolute disaster. Now look at Figure 8.1, and after you have understood its parameters, try tracing the itinerary of the trip from beginning to end. What were the conditions at the start of the trip? Did you feel you wanted to do it, or that you had to do it? Did you expect to enjoy the pleasures of the trip, or to learn something from it? Having identified the starting point of

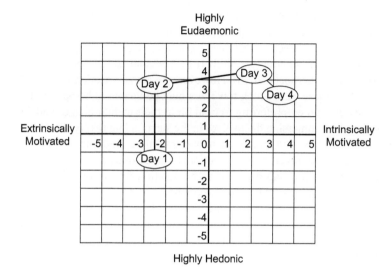

*Figure 8.2* Travel motivation matrix: example of a four-day trip

your journey, you can then trace your motivations from day to day until the end of your trip. We created a hypothetical example in Figure 8.2.

Within the motivation matrix, individual activities and overall daily motivations can be plotted. Plots like these can be used to examine overall well-being of the individual.

And now you may want to think of a tourist experience you had that stands out as being as close to your ideal as possible. Repeat the imaginary journey tracing your motivations day by day (it might be clearer if you photocopied the two itineraries and drew a line on each to represent your experience) or even activity by activity. How do the two lines differ from each other? Does this exercise help you make sense of why one trip was a disaster and the other a delight?

Of course, no tourist experience is delightful, or disastrous, from beginning to end. In a matter of a few minutes, we might switch from one frame of mind into its opposite. But, by and large, you probably can remember trips that you could hardly wait to end and other that you wished would never end (Coffey & Csikszentmihalyi, in press).

Using the model in this way should help one understand the complexities of the tourist experience in a new way. And by understanding the experiences better, it is possible to prepare for a journey more efficiently so that one will have a chance to get the most benefits from the experience. Preparing oneself by reading about the history and the culture of the places one plans to visit can help a great deal in transforming the trip from a purely hedonic to a eudaimonic experience. The same holds for looking at pictures of the sights, for studying typical menus of local foods and for learning a few sentences in the local language.

Like everything else, preparation can be overdone. One sometimes hears from returning tourists the rueful admission that the best part of their trip was the preparation for it, when they eagerly fantasized about what they would see and do during the journey. Indeed, researchers have found that anticipation of a vacation offers a number of benefits (e.g. Gilbert & Abdullah, 2002; Nawijn, Marchand, Veenhoven & Vingerhoets, 2010). However, the actual vacation might not go as anticipated. In these cases, such travellers may be unable to be open to the alien reality they encounter, preferring to hold on to their mental images and expectations rather than immersing themselves in the surrounding reality. That seems like a huge waste of time and money. Armchair travelling might be pleasant, but it is unlikely to help the traveller grow emotionally or cognitively as much as immersing oneself into a location can. But as preparation for the real thing, it can be enormously enhancing of the actual experience.

A particular strength of this model is that this broad approach is individualized and less prescriptive. The motives (and related benefits and consequences) remain the central focus of the model rather than fixating on specific types of vacations (e.g. relaxing beach get away, visit to see a college friend) or even the activities on the vacation (e.g. snorkelling on the ocean, ice fishing). Indeed, two people could engage in the same activity for completely different motives, thus resulting in completely different benefits or consequences to psychological and physiological well-being.

Thus this model might also help to highlight a number of elements related to tourists' well-being (and satisfaction). For example, one could examine the range of motivations (e.g. shifts or variations) in relation to concurrent and post-vacation well-being, or one could compare the broad motivations to specific activities to determine when one might be a better indicator of well-being (Coffey & Csikszentmihalyi, in press). This would allow for a greater understanding of person-activity fit.

## A simplified and individualized way of tracking well-being

As highlighted earlier, the tourism industry often advertises that their destination or experience will promote some form of improved well-being. Sometimes they promise happiness or pleasure, others promise relaxation or adventure, some are designed to connect you to others, some promote learning and engagement and others argue for improved fitness or spiritual enlightenment. Some might even go so far as to argue that they will change your life. Claims such as these are made because they seek to attract individuals with these desires. Indeed, modern society has adopted the idea that tourism is good for our psychological and physiological health (Coffey & Csikszentmihalyi, in press; Hobson & Dietrich, 1995).

Research has supported at least some of these claims. For example, a recent review of 98 papers, 29 of which tested travel benefits, found that tourism is associated with some psychological and physiological benefits across a range of different samples (Chen & Petrick, 2013). Yet many of the benefits of vacations are only shown to last as little as a few days (e.g. Nawijn *et al.*, 2010) to two to three weeks (e.g. de Bloom *et al.*, 2011; de Bloom *et al.*, 2010; Westman & Eden,

1997). Thus some researchers identified how certain types of tourism motivations (e.g. adventure/novelty, escape/relaxation, self-development, relationship building) are associated with well-being (e.g. Moscardo, 2011; Pearce, 1993; Pearce & Lee, 2005; Pearce & Packer, 2013). Although these are useful and worthwhile endeavours, our model presents individuals' motivations as the focal point rather than the actual activities. Simply put, well-being is multidimensional and pursued in many different ways (e.g. Coffey, Wray-Lake, Mashek & Branand, 2016; Ryan & Deci, 2000; Ryff, 1989; Seligman, 2011, even on vacation. Thus our model allows for new forms of analyses which could help to answer a range of questions centred on the travellers (i.e. tourism industry consumers).

How are these motivational influences associated with well-being? Are these motivations more important than the actual activities used to reach them? For example, one person might be intrinsically motivated to find more meaning in life by visiting a new culture, while another might be intrinsically motivated to find more meaning in life while visiting family. In our model, these two people would be treated the same despite doing very different activities. Even more to this point, trying to get individuals to take a vacation that is of little interest to them is likely to result in significantly worse outcomes than for the person who organically chose the same type of vacation. Thus our model allows researchers to determine how motivations are associated with well-being. In doing so, individuals can begin to identify types of vacations and activities, while planning their next holiday, that are particularly healthy for them.

Finally, this model will allow researchers to explore how and when travellers in one domain versus the others are more likely to experience psychological and physiological benefits or consequences. As other positive psychology research has suggested intrinsic and eudaimonic motivations are generally more beneficial then extrinsic and hedonic motivations (e.g. Fredrickson *et al.*, 2013; Huta & Ryan, 2010; Nelson, Fuller, Choi & Lyubomirsky, 2014; Ryan & Deci, 2001), we expect this will be the quadrant associated with the greatest benefits to psychological and physiological well-being. That said, nuances are likely to emerge, as there are benefits to extrinsically motivated experiences and hedonically motivated experiences (e.g. Huta & Ryan, 2010; Kopperud & Vitters, 2008; Nelson, Kushlev, Dunn & Lyubomirsky, 2014; Ryan & Deci, 2001). Other positive psychology research highlighted cross-cultural differences in such motivations (e.g. Delle Fave, Brdar, Freire, Vella-Brodrick & Wissing, 2011; Delle Fave, Massimini & Bassi, 2011). In measuring these differences, travellers will be better prepared to pick vacations that really will better their lives.

## Modern measurement

Just as individuals' motivations might change before and during a vacation, their perceived happiness is also susceptible to fluctuation (e.g. Coghlan & Pearce, 2010; de Bloom *et al.*, 2009; Nawijn, 2011). Thus we propose that an optimal way to conduct research using this model might utilise the experience sampling method (ESM; see Hektner, Schmidt & Csikszentmihalyi, 2006) along with examining overall pre-post-vacation well-being. ESM allows individuals to report in on their motivations and individual well-being throughout a vacation. Modern ESM utilises smartphone applications to randomly buzz or alert participants in real time such that they can quickly report on their motivations and well-being (e.g. Song, Foo & Uy, 2008; Wirtz, Chiu, Diener & Oishi, 2009).

By utilising ESM, an online reading can be made rather than a retrospective assessment of one's vacation motivations. Using ESM is particularly useful because a comparison with post-vacation memories has shown that after the vacation, people rely primarily on positive experiences from their past vacations, even when they reported negative experiences and emotions at the time of the vacation (Wirtz *et al.*, 2009; Wirtz, Kruger, Scollon & Diener, 2003). Furthermore, collecting data using ESM would allow for a broad range of factors to be examined. For example, one could examine different points or activities during the vacation, amount of variation in motivations, amount of time spent within each quadrant or by classifying the vacation more broadly.

Although a common concern about ESM is that it might be distracting, this has rarely been reported as a problem in past studies (see Hektner, Schmidt & Csikszentmihalyi, 2006). The questions are generally quick and focused on the present activity, so they do not tend to distract the individuals in an overly disruptive manner. Daily diaries are an alternative option that have been used in travel contexts (for more information, see Coghlan & Pearce, 2010).

## Summary

In this chapter, we have proposed a simple two-dimensional model for tracking motivation as it relates to physiological and psychological well-being during self-initiated travel. The first dimension examines intrinsic versus extrinsic motivation, while the second dimension evaluates expected benefits as hedonic or eudaimonic. This model is focused on the consumer side of the tourism industry such that the central goal is to determine how differences in these motivations are related to benefits or consequences for those seeking enhanced well-being. Although specific activities and destinations are important considerations better explored by our colleagues (e.g. Moscardo, 2011; Pearce & Lee, 2005; Pearce & Packer, 2013), this model allows for a broader understanding across these experiences and contexts that is focused specifically on the travellers' broad motivations. Furthermore, this model should work with motivations and well-being that might vary by culture. In doing so, we hope that this model will help travellers to better understand themselves and select vacations that will offer them the optimal chances for improving their own well-being.

## References

Chen, C. C., & Petrick, J. F. (2013). Health and wellness benefits of travel experiences a literature review. *Journal of Travel Research*, 52(6), 709–719. doi: 10.1177/0047287513496477

Chen, Y., Mak, B., & McKercher, B. (2011). What drives people to travel: Integrating the tourist motivation paradigms. *Journal of China Tourism Research*, 7, 120–136. doi: 10.1080/19388160.2011.576927

Coffey, J. K., & Csikszentmihalyi, M. (in press). Finding flow as a tourist. In L. Puczkó & M. Smith (Eds.), *Handbook of health tourism*. London: Routledge.

Coffey, J. K., Wray-Lake, L., Mashek, D., & Branand, B. (2016). A longitudinal examination of a multidimensional well-being model in college and community samples. *Journal of Happiness Studies*, 57, 187–211. doi: 10.1007/s10902-014-9590-8

Coghlan, A., & Pearce, P. L. (2010). Tracking affective components of satisfaction. *Journal of Tourism and Hospitality Research*, 10(1), 1–17.

Crompton, J. L. (1979). Motivations for pleasure vacation. *Annals of Tourism Research*, 6(4), 408–424. doi: 10.1177/004728758001900185

de Bloom, J., Geurts, S. A. E., Sonnentag, S., Taris, T., de Weerth, C., & Kompier, M. A. J. (2011). How does a vacation from work affect employee health and well-being? *Psychology & Health*, 26(12), 1606–1622. doi: 10.1080/08870446.2010.546860

de Bloom, J., Geurts, S. A. E., Toon, W. T., Sonnentag, S., de Weerth, C., & Kompier, M. A. J. (2010). Effects of vacation from work on health and well-being: Lots of fun, quickly gone. *Work & Stress*, 24(2), 196–216. doi: 10.1080/02678373.2010.493385

de Bloom, J., Kompier, M., Geurts, S., de Weerth, C., Taris, T., & Sonnentag, S. (2009). Do we recover from vacation? Meta-analysis of vacation effects on health and well-being. *Journal of Occupational Health*, 51(1), 13–25.

Delle Fave, A., Brdar, I., Freire, T., Vella-Brodrick, D., & Wissing, M. P. (2011). The eudaimonic and hedonic components of happiness: Qualitative and quantitative findings. *Social Indicators Research*, 100(2), 185–207. doi: 10.1007/s11205-010-9632-5

Delle Fave, A., Massimini, F., & Bassi, M. (2011). Hedonism and eudaimonism in positive psychology. In A. Delle Fave, F. Massimini, and M. Bassi (Eds.), *Psychological selection and optimal experience across cultures* (pp. 3–18). Dordrecht: Springer.

Fredrickson, B. L., Grewen, K. M., Coffey, K. A., Algoe, S. B., Firestine, A. M., Arevalo, J. M., . . . & Cole, S. W. (2013). A functional genomic perspective on human well-being. *Proceedings of the National Academy of Sciences*, 110(33), 13684–13689. doi: 10.1073/pnas.1305419110

Gilbert, D., & Abdullah, J. (2002). A study of the impact of the expectation of a holiday on an individual's sense of wellbeing. *Journal of Vacation Marketing*, 8, 353–361. doi: 10.1177/135676670200800406

Harril, R., & Potts, T. D. (2002). Social psychological theories of tourist motivation: Exploration, debate, and transition. *Tourism Analysis*, 7, 105–114.

Hektner, J., Schmidt, J., & Csikszentmihalyi, M. (2006). *Experience sampling: Measuring the quality of everyday life*. Thousand Oaks, CA: Sage Publications.

Hobson, J. P., & Dietrich, U. C. (1995). Tourism, health and quality of life: Challenging the responsibility of using the traditional tenets of sun, sea, sand, and sex in tourism marketing. *Journal of Travel & Tourism Marketing*, 3(4), 21–38. doi: 10.1300/J073v03n04_02

Huta, V., & Ryan, R. M. (2010). Pursuing pleasure or virtue: The differential and overlapping well-being benefits of hedonic and eudaimonic motives. *Journal of Happiness Studies*, 11(6), 735–762. doi: 10.1007/s10902-009-9171-4

Iso-Ahola, S. E. (1982). Towards a social psychological theory of tourism motivation: A rejoinder. *Annals of Tourism Research*, 9(2), 256–262. doi: 10.1016/0160-7383(82)90049-4

Kopperud, K. H., & Vitters, J. (2008). Distinctions between hedonic and eudaimonic well-being: Results from a day reconstruction study among Norwegian jobholders. *Journal of Positive Psychology*, 3(3), 174–181. doi: 10.1080/17439760801999420

Kozak, M. (2002). Comparative analysis of tourist motivations by nationality and destinations. *Tourism Management*, 23(3), 221–232.

Moscardo, G. (2011). Searching for well-being: Exploring change in tourist motivation. *Tourism Recreation Research*, 36(1), 15–26. doi: 10.1080/02508281.2011.11081656

Nawijn, J. (2011). Determinants of daily happiness on vacation. *Journal of Travel Research*, 50(5), 559–566. doi: 10.1177/0047287510379164

Nawijn, J., Marchand, M. A., Veenhoven, R., & Vingerhoets, A. J. (2010). Vacationers happier, but most not happier after a holiday. *Applied Research in Quality of Life*, 5(1), 35–47. doi: 10.1007/s11482-009-9091-9

Nelson, S. K., Fuller, J. A. K., Choi, I., & Lyubomirsky, S. (2014). Beyond self-protection: Self-affirmation benefits hedonic and eudaimonic well-being. *Personality and Social Psychology Bulletin*, 40, 998–1011. doi: 10.1177/0146167214533389

Nelson, S. K., Kushlev, K., Dunn, E. W., & Lyubomirsky, S. (2014). Parents are slightly happier than nonparents, but causality still cannot be inferred: A reply to Bhargava, Kassam, and Loewenstein. *Psychological Science*, 25, 303–304. doi: 10.1177/0956797613508561

Pearce, P. L. (1993). Fundamentals of tourist motivation. In D. Pearce & R. Butler (Eds.), *Tourism research: Critiques and challenges* (pp. 85–105). London: Routledge.

Pearce, P. L. (2005). *Tourist behaviour: Themes and conceptual schemes*. Clevedon: Channel View.

Pearce, P. L., & Lee, U. (2005). Developing the travel career approach to tourist motivation. *Journal of Travel Research*, 43(3), 226–237. doi: 10.1177/0047287504272020

Pearce, P. L., & Packer, J. (2013). Minds on the move: New links from psychology to tourism. *Annals of Tourism Research*, 40, 386–411. doi: 10.1016/j.annals 2012.10.002. doi: 10.1016/j.annals.2012.10.002

Ryan, R., & Deci, E. (2000). Self-determination theory and the facilitation of intrinsic motivation, social development, and well-being. *American Psychologist*, 55(1), 68–78. doi: 10.1037/0003-066X.55.1.68

Ryan, R., & Deci, E. (2001). On happiness and human potentials: A review of research on hedonic and eudaimonic well-being. *Annual Review of Psychology*, 52, 141–166. doi: 10.1146/annurev.psych.52.1.141

Ryff, C. (1989). Happiness is everything, or is it? Explorations on the meaning of psychological well-being. *Journal of Personality and Social Psychology*, 57(6), 1069–1081. doi: 10.1037/0022-3514.57.6.1069

Seligman, M. (2011). *Flourish: A visionary new understanding of happiness and well-being*. New York: Free Press.

Song, Z., Foo, M. D., & Uy, M. A. (2008). Mood spillover and crossover among dual-earner couples: A cell phone event sampling study. *Journal of Applied Psychology*, 93(2), 443–452. doi: 10.1037/0021-9010.93.2.443

Westman, M., & Eden, D. (1997). Effects of a respite from work on burnout: Vacation relief and fade out. *Journal of Applied Psychology*, 82(4), 516–527.

Wirtz, D., Chiu, C., Diener, E., & Oishi, S. (2009). What constitutes a good life? Cultural differences in the role of positive and negative affect in subjective well-being. *Journal of Personality*, 77(4), 1167–1196. doi: 10.1111/j.1467-6494.2009.00578.x

Wirtz, D., Kruger, J., Scollon, C. N., & Diener, E. (2003). What to do on spring break? The role of predicted, on-line, and remembered experience in future choice. *Psychological Science*, 14(5), 520–524. doi: 10.1111/1467-9280.03455

You, X., O'Leary, J., Morrison, A., & Hong, G. S. (2000). A cross-cultural comparison of travel push and pull factors: United Kingdom vs. Japan. *International Journal of Hospitality & Tourism Administration*, 1(2), 1–26. doi: 10.1300/J149v01n02_01

# Part III
# Positive host communities

# 9 Examining kindness of strangers in tourism

## Trail magic on the Appalachian Trail

*Troy D. Glover and Sebastian Filep*

Taking a civic approach to understanding host communities, this chapter examines tourist and host interactions on the Appalachian Trail (AT) – a large hiking track in the eastern United States. The AT is well known for 'trail magic' – that is, acts of kindness, gifts and other tangible and intangible forms of encouragement given to thru-hikers, sometimes anonymously and often unexpectedly, either from strangers who live along a section of the trail or from former thru-hikers who return to the trail to reciprocate the kindness they once received. This chapter seeks to understand (1) the motives of 'trail angels', the people who gift acts of kindness to thru-hikers and (2) the responses of thru-hikers to the receipt of trail magic. What drives donors of kindness to give in tourism contexts? And how do recipients of such kindness respond? In exploring these questions, the chapter answers Glover and Filep's (2015) call for a more concerted social science research agenda on the kindness of strangers and gratitude in tourism contexts. The chapter also aims to add to the contemporary positive psychology works on kindness (Otake, Shimai, Tanaka-Matsumi & Fredrickson, 2006) and gratitude (Emmons & Crumpler, 2000) by introducing the new tourism context and advances some key discussions in the tourism literature. Specifically, it extends works on tourists' attitudes toward the people they visit (Bowen & Clarke, 2009; Murphy & Murphy, 2004; Pearce, 2011) by focusing on gratitude and the generosity of strangers. It also aims to enhance understandings of contemporary tourist motivations (Pearce, 2011; Pearce & Lee, 2005) by further explaining the role and the value of the need for social interactions (Larsen, Urry & Axhausen, 2007).

We begin this chapter with a review of literature pertaining to the kindness of strangers before describing the methods involved and then report findings from a thematic analysis of 50 travel blogs by thru-hikers and the trail magic providers. The chapter continues with a discussion of the findings and concludes with recommendations for future research.

## Literature review

Why would strangers act with kindness towards other strangers in tourism contexts? The answer is somewhat perplexing, given Derrida's (2000) notion that hospitality – which embodies the nature of interactions within tourism contexts – presents the risky possibility that guests could become adversaries or freeloaders of their host's generosity. This sentiment complements Bauman's (1995) belief that individuals in contemporary society fear encounters with strangers because such interactions could entangle both parties in mutual obligation. Additionally, there is a debate in the literature (Wijesinghe, 2013) suggesting that virtue and genuine acts of kindness have been eroded in tourism and hospitality contexts because of profit-maximizing commercialism imperatives.

Given these complex conditions, strangers will sometimes go to great lengths to avoid each other in public and deliberately keep 'the stranger at arm's length' (Bauman, 1995, p. 45). In the tourism literature, we see this sort of behaviour when we consider the 'tourist bubble' in which visitors often restrict themselves (see Cohen, 1972). Though perhaps unfortunate, such behaviour stems naturally from a preference amongst people – including tourists – to confine themselves to engaging with others similar to themselves (McPherson, Smith-Lovin & Cook, 2001). Tourists often face uncomfortable scenarios in which they must negotiate egoism and sociality (Simpson & Willer, 2015).

Of course, norms in tourism contexts do press hosts and guests to act in generous ways. In particular, acts of kindness may be anticipated when helping is part of the donor's social role (Buchanan & Bardi, 2010). We would expect tourism professionals and hospitality workers, for example, to assist tourists in circumstances that warrant helping behaviour. Even so, strangers who interact in tourism contexts are not always formal service providers – they may be locals disconnected formally from the tourism product or other disinterested tourists. Under these circumstances, tourists may still expect to receive acts of kindness from others based on principles of reciprocity, social exchange or equity. These so-called descriptive norms 'are simply regularities of behaviour, what most people do in a given situation' (Simpson & Willer, 2015, p. 46).

Interestingly, research on kindness shows that individuals tend to respond to acts of kindness by subsequently behaving more generously with third parties – what many refer to as 'paying it forward' (Tsvetkova & Macy 2014). We see this behaviour when locals not associated with the tourism product come to the assistance of tourists in need. This form of generalized reciprocity in which those who benefit from the kindness of strangers become more generous towards others in the future is driven by injunctive norms. An injunctive norm refers to 'a normative obligation to express one's gratitude at being helped not by repaying the helper but by acting as the helper acted' (Tsvetkova & Macy, 2014, p. 2). The kindness a tourist receives, therefore, may stem from kindness the donor received from someone else.

These understandings of kindness remain surprisingly neglected areas of empirical study in the social sciences (Baskerville *et al.*, 2000; Nowak & Roch, 2007, including in tourism (Glover & Filep, 2015). Tourism, which by its very nature has the potential to draw relative strangers together, even if only on a temporary basis, represents a particularly unique context in which to study kindness. Indeed, many tourists can and do share stories of benefiting from the kindness of strangers during their travels. Tourists regularly welcome the generosity of and assistance of others, but rarely retain ties to those from whose generosity they benefit. Far from a negative scenario, Torche and Valenzuela (2011) argued trust in such situations facilitates interactions between strangers even when weak third-party guarantees of compliance exist and without the burdensome need to convert the stranger into a personal connection. That is, Torche and Valenzuela reasoned that trust differs from other situations in which a rational cost-benefit analysis prevails because it is embedded within a universalistic ethic of personal responsibility, which rests on the basic assumption that all interaction partners keep commitments made to others. In short, host behaviours often reflect a general ethic of care towards guests.

This study aims to better understand this phenomenon by examining acts of 'trail magic' on the Appalachian Trail. The AT is characterized by its unique social environment, which encourages an active culture of kindness and therefore represents a suitable site for the study of kindness of strangers in tourism. While there is a history of associating long-distance walking as a tourist and leisure activity that leads to contemplation, self-development, achievement and self-transformation (Edensor, 2000; Saunders, Laing & Weiler, 2014), we found no previous academic works on kindness of strangers in this context. We begin our next section by describing our study context in greater detail.

## Appalachian Trail (AT)

This chapter explores bloggers' observations of their encounters with trail magic on the AT. The AT, as mentioned, is an approximately 3,500 km marked trail consisting mostly of forest and wild lands with some portions of it traversing towns, roads and farms. Over its entire length, it passes over 138 mountain tops, across several rivers and streams and negotiates the scenic, wooded, pastoral, wild and culturally resonant lands of the Appalachian Mountains. Typically, hikers travel south to north from Springer Mountain, Georgia, to Mount Katahdin, Maine. Together, the trail spans 14 eastern American states. Accordingly, it is commonly referred to as the 'people's path' because nearly two-thirds of all Americans reside within a day's drive from the trail.

Most thru-hikers take between five and seven months to complete the full thru-hike. There is no formal thru-hiking registration system, but the Appalachian Trail Conservancy (ATC) encourages hikers to register voluntarily to help guide start dates and to alleviate crowding. The ATC estimates that two to three million visitors hike a portion of the AT each year (ATC, 2015). Most enjoy day hikes and short backpacking trips, but each year a small percentage complete the entire trail. Since 1936, the ATC reports more than 15,000 hike completions have been recorded, including thru-hikes and multi-year section hikes. Thru-hikers who complete the entire trail are referred to as '2,000-milers'.

The AT is relevant to this study because of its enduring culture of kindness on the trail. As the AT is known for its 'trail magic', thru-hikers are typically exposed to random acts of kindness from so-called 'trail angels' who provide assistance in a variety of ways. As Clara Hughes, a Canadian Olympic athlete who blogged about her experience as a thru-hiker on the AT, wrote:

> Trail magic comes in many forms. It can be something serendipitous where you just happen to meet someone, they know you're hiking, they offer food. It can be intentional where a person goes to a high volume section at the right time and place and set up an impromptu hot dog/hamburger stand. It can be catching a ride into town before your thumb goes up. It can be a fellow hiker offering a sip of bourbon he got from another weekend hiker the night before. It is any form of random act of kindness intentional or not.

These acts of kindness are reciprocated amongst thru-hikers, thereby establishing a unique environment of generosity among strangers.

## Method

To learn more about trail magic and trail angels, we drew on blog entries as our data. As Banyai and Glover (2012, p. 269) noted, 'Blogs offer the opportunity to reveal tourists' interpretations of tourism products and experience, and to express tourists' impressions, perceptions, thoughts, and feelings, all that may otherwise not be revealed in a more constrained research environment such as personal interviews'. The rich information supplied by the bloggers in this study enabled us to draw upon the insight, articulate descriptions and meaning-making bloggers engage in by sharing their perspectives on their AT experience.

Our data collection began by googling the keywords 'travel blog', 'Appalachian Trail', and 'trail magic', which resulted in 362 results. In order of appearance, we viewed each site linked to the online search and read through the material of each result to determine if it provided relevant information to our research. Our criteria for inclusion in the study were (1) the site had to be an actual blog – that is, it profiled 'online diaries and stories meant to provide information and engage the reader in the travel experience' (Banyai & Glover, 2012, p. 269) – no bulletin boards, virtual communities (e.g. Facebook), or consumer review sites (e.g. TripAdvisor) were included; (2) trail magic had to be the main focus of the blog entry, not simply an incidental reference; and (3) the entry had to include sufficient text from which to glean content; in other words, all sites included in this study provided useable content for analysis. Photo blogs (with little text) were excluded. Once we identified 50 blogs that fit our inclusion criteria, we ended our search and began our analysis. Though the total was arbitrary, it was believed, based on the inclusion criteria, to provide sufficient content for a thorough analysis.

Approximately three-quarters of the blogs (n = 36) were maintained by thru-hikers or individuals who had either already attempted or were attempting to hike the AT in a single season. Doing so successfully can take up to seven months, though only 15 per cent of hikers achieve this outcome. The remainder of the blog entries were maintained by hiking enthusiasts who had hiked only portions of the

trail. They are referred to as section hikers. Most blogs were maintained independently of any formal organization (i.e. using blogging sites such as wordpress.
com or blogspot.com), though a few were blog entries profiled by a commercial
organization (e.g. L.L.Bean, Runner's World, Thunder Island Brewing). There
was a relatively equal gender split among the bloggers included in the study with
28 male and 22 female bloggers. The blogs analysed varied in length from 3 paragraphs of text to 36.

Data were analysed using open coding within and between blog texts to identify
recurrent conceptual themes. Each blog text was first analysed using open categories to develop initial descriptive categories (e.g. 'restoring faith in humanity').
Focused or selective coding was then used to compare categories both within and
between interviews and to look for emerging conceptual themes (e.g. 'the implications of gratitude'). Subsequently, patterns of relationships among themes were
also examined (such as the relationship between 'gratitude' and 'kindness'). These
patterns of relationships were developed into the major themes for this chapter
(e.g. 'paying it forward'). Although the blog transcripts were analysed through
the development of themes, the group of blog transcripts were also analysed as
a whole to compare and contrast developing patterns of relationships among the
participants' comments and experiences. In this regard, the themes were inclusive
of data across blog entries.

## Findings

The following section provides the results of our data analysis. For ease of presentation, the content falls under two sub-headings: (1) trail angels and (2) recipients
of trail magic. These sub-sections focus on those who gift trail magic to others
and the thru-hiker beneficiaries of these acts of kindness, respectively. Consistent
with the purpose of our study, the findings explore the impact and intentions of
trail magic on the AT.

### *Trail angels: paying it forward*

Overwhelmingly, bloggers emphasized the notion that trail angels 'asked for nothing in return' for their gestures of kindness. Trail angels were often described
by recipients of trail magic as 'complete strangers who want[ed] nothing more
than to see the smile on your face' (Damien Tougas). Upon closer examination,
trail magic appeared to benefit trail angels too. As Paul 'Big Tex' Bunker wrote,
'people want to do Trail Magic because it makes you feel good and fills a void
that exists'. This void appears, in many cases, to be connected to trail angels'
past experiences thru-hiking the AT. While some were never thru-hikers and just
wanted to be close to the AT and its community of hikers, many trail angels were
former thru-hikers who felt a strong emotional pull to return to the trail and 'give
back' to it in repayment for the trail magic they received during their hiking experiences. Indeed, in reflecting upon his experience as a trail angel, one blogger
confessed, 'It felt good, like I was giving back to the trail I love so much' (Dusty

Camel). In this sense, trail angels seemingly sought to renew their ties to the trail through their acts of kindness.

References to the 'trail' transcended the physical landscape. 'It's not just the [physical] trail I miss', wrote Bunker. 'It's the community, the people, the strangers, that made you part of their community without question and judgement'. This culture of acceptance led Katherine Imp to describe the AT community as 'this alternative universe'. She added, 'It's a place where everyone is welcomed and respected, regardless of where you came from or what brought you here. It's a place where people do kind things for one another and don't expect anything in return'. Consequently, 'Trail angels and trail magic are just a couple of the phenomena woven into AT culture' (Damien Tougas). For many bloggers, trail magic is what sets the AT apart from most other wilderness experiences.

Ultimately, the kindness encountered on the trail was regarded by most trail angels as something truly unique and characterized the AT as 'not the real world' (Katherine Imp). This sentiment pervaded amongst trail angels. To sensitize those unfamiliar with AT culture, Damien Tougas wrote, 'After being habituated to our "normal" lives where nothing comes for free, receiving intentional and generous kindness from complete strangers who want nothing more than to see the smile on your face is really a unique experience'. Accordingly, 'Post-trail depression can set in as hikers leave the freedom of the wilderness to return to their structured roles in society' (Hayley Benton). Evidently, the antidote for this depression was to return to the AT as a trail angel.

Because many trail angels were recipients of trail magic themselves, they often regarded their acts of kindness as a way to 'pay it forward'. In SectionHiker's words,

> I go out of my way to contribute to the pool of trail magic whenever I can by doing what I can for other hikers who need a hand or by giving people who I know are regular trail angels a little extra cash to pass along to someone who needs it more than I do. It evens out in the end and you never know when you'll need a little trail magic, yourself.

This norm of reciprocity was affirmed by other trail angels. Earlylite, who commented on SectionHiker's post, wrote, 'I've gotten a lot of trail magic over the years, and want to give back'. This sort of behaviour has become expected on the AT. In writing about an encounter with a trail angel, Crystal Hoffman recalled the advice she received from her donor:

> All I ask is that when you get out there, you tell your story with as much excitement to every single person you meet. Tell it as if you were telling it for the first time. One day it will be your turn to make a little trail magic happen for someone. You'll receive a lot of miracles out there. And you'll earn all of it.

As a result, trail angels viewed the act of sharing on the AT as a 'privilege' that enabled them to return to the environment that profoundly influenced their lives and make a difference in the experiences of a new generation of thru-hikers.

### Recipients of trail magic: gratitude and acculturation

By and large, bloggers praised trail magic for enriching the thru-hiking experience on the AT. Most credited trail magic with contributing to their completion of the full hike: 'I sometimes wonder if I would have made three successful back to back thru hikes without the help and kindness that was shown to me by complete strangers'. Indeed, they regarded trail magic as deeply kind gestures that significantly enhanced their thru-hiking experience: 'Would I of [sic] finished the trail without magic? There is a very good chance I would. Would I of [sic] had such an enjoyable and rewarding experience without it? NO. That's for sure!' (Paul 'Big Tex' Bunker). Whatever their perspective, bloggers acknowledged that trail magic consisted of 'moments an AT Hiker can't ever forget' (ggray).

The unforgettable nature of trail magic corresponded with what bloggers described as uplifting experiences of incredible acts of kindness on the trail. As Chris Spencer explained, 'Trail Magic can be one of the most extreme highs of any trail experience'. In fleshing this idea out further, Bunker noted, 'when we did encounter [trail magic], it was often at the time I needed it most: Tired. Fed up. Injured and in need of assistance. Wet, cold and miserable. Or just ready to quit'. Ray Anderson offered a similar explanation:

> Imagine yourself tired, cranky, and beat up from the trail. Most of all you are thirsty. You're low on water and what water you have is warm. All of a sudden, you see a piece of cardboard fastened to a tree. **ICE COLD DRINKS STRAIGHT AHEAD ON RIGHT!** it says. Really? Can this be true? Sure enough, there's a cooler stashed beneath a pine just off the trail. You swing up the lid and packed in ice are Mountain Dews, Cokes, Gatorades – bottled ice water!
>
> (Original emphasis)

In other words, '[Trail Magic was] a big spirit lifter out there' (Stephanie) because it provided 'a quick shot of life energy' (Zack Davis) at a time when it was truly needed.

Not surprisingly, appreciation for these acts of kindness came easily on the trail because of the gruelling experience the thru-hikers shared. Time and time again, bloggers underscored the incredible physical and emotional demands of thru-hiking the AT. 'People outside of the trail community often do not realize how kind gestures could have such a big impact on a long distance hiker's mental attitude', wrote Niki. The mostly unexpected nature of trail magic, '[was] part of the thrill. You just never know when it's going to happen' (Robert Sutherland). As a result, these unexpected encounters gave thru-hikers a greater sense of perspective.

Katherine Imp admitted,

> Sometimes the weather is awful. And the uphill inclines never seem to end. And let's face it, the privies (outdoor toilets) are disgusting. But when you

look at the big picture, these negatives seem to fade away in the distance and the beauty of trail magic shines through.

(Katherine Imp, para 6–7)

In Zack Davis's words, 'Just when you're reaching your peak misery level, something will happen to remind you of life's simple beauties'.

Under these circumstances, most bloggers naturally felt 'overwhelmed with gratitude' upon encountering trail magic. 'Never before had I ever been grateful to have a level place to sleep, or a dry place to sleep, or hot food. So I was grateful just for simple things. When I came off the trail, I was absolutely overwhelmed with gratitude', said Jordan, who was quoted in Rebecca Williams' post. When trail angels were present at the time thru-hikers encountered trail magic, the thru-hikers would greet them with 'huge smiles and glowing faces' (Paul 'Big Tex' Bunker). It was not uncommon for thru-hikers to 'literally tear up and launch into smelly sweaty hugs at the sight of magic' (Scott Shipley). Where no trail angels could be found, bloggers often took to social media to express their sincere appreciation.

In many cases, the experience of receiving trail magic encouraged bloggers to become trail angels themselves during their hikes. 'If you give someone a meal, someone else giving you a meal becomes more likely in your frame of reality. Your neural pathways are honed for it', explained Crystal Hoffman. In Crystal's case, she ended up '[giving] away two-thirds of the things that [she] started with on [her] walk and nearly everything that was gifted to [her] found a perfect home with someone further down the road'. These and other similar acts of generosity reflected a larger culture of kindness on the AT that made the trail unique from other environments. Reflecting upon his own experience, Damien Tougas wrote,

> The trail and the AT culture has given to [thru-hikers] more than they could have ever asked for, and what they gain from the experience often compels them to give back and get involved . . . When you hike the Appalachian Trail you become a part of this loop, experiencing the AT's culture first-hand and hopefully, adding your own contribution to the people and places, the community, that make the trail what it is.

For these reasons, Brian Kenney described the AT as 'good for the soul'. Indeed, a strong theme among bloggers who were thru-hikers was the notion that '[trail magic] had restored [their] hope in humanity and that good people did exist in the world'. Described another way, thru-hikers came to appreciate 'There's just really good people out there, and it just seems like the A.T. – the whole length – is just a magnet for goodness' (Gary Sizer quoted in Hayley Benton's blog). This attitude led Chris Spencer to 'enthusiastically encourage anyone to attempt a thru hike. You will learn a great deal about yourself and humanity even if you do not have the good fortune of finishing'.

# Discussion

Most trail angels discussed in this chapter appeared to give back to the AT in the form of trail magic because of their past positive experiences as thru-hikers. As they reflected on their own experiences, both in their blogs and in their everyday lives, they expressed a deep sense of gratitude. Gratitude, derived from the Latin *gratia* meaning graciousness, grace, gratefulness, has been defined by moral philosophers as a virtue and considered in classical Hebrew, Christian and Graeco-Roman writings as a highly valued human disposition (Emmons & Shelton, 2002; Zagzebski, 1996). In positive psychology, however, it is understood as an emotional response to life: 'a felt sense of wonder, thankfulness, and appreciation for life' (Emmons & Shelton, 2002, p. 460). In this psychological sense, the participants were grateful for their receipt of trail magic on the AT. They recognized the intention of the hosts and rewarded it with gratitude. The sense of gratitude for the receipt of trail magic links well with the formal theory of reciprocity, which explains that individuals reward kind actions and punish unkind ones. The theory suggests that people assess the kindness of an action by the intention underlying this action as well as by its consequences (Falk & Fischbacher, 1999), just like the bloggers have done.

The often unexpected nature of being on the receiving end of acts of kindness aimed at strangers seemed to make trail magic even more powerful in terms of its impact on recipients' feelings of gratitude. As Buchanan and Bardi's (2010, p. 54) research on kindness revealed, non-normative kindness – that which is out of the norm – 'grabs people's attention' and can be met with 'amazement'. Indeed, all of the bloggers described the extraordinary experience of receiving timely acts of kindness from complete strangers, an experience they rarely encountered in their everyday lives away from the trail, during a particularly challenging physical and emotional activity. As reported, bloggers described being 'overwhelmed with gratitude' when happening upon trail magic. Accordingly, for most of the bloggers profiled in this chapter, trail magic restored their hope in humanity. Their gratitude functioned as a moral barometer insofar as it sensitized them to a change in their social relationships with their fellow thru-hikers; they became aware of the provision of a benefit by someone else that enhanced their own well-being (McCullough, Kilpatrick, Emmons & Larson, 2001).

In addition to contributing to life satisfaction (Emmons & McCullough, 2003; McCullough *et al.*, 2001), the gratitude trail angels experienced led to action in the form of trail magic, either by returning to the trail to dispense acts of generosity or by extending kindness to their fellow thru-hikers while continuing on their hikes. As Emmons and Shelton (2002, p. 464) noted, gratitude 'serves to remind [people] of their need to reciprocate'. Indeed, McCullough *et al.* (2001) posited that gratitude functions as a moral motive, prompting grateful people to behave pro-socially themselves. Trail magic appeared to have this effect on the bloggers in this study.

That most trail angels in this study were thru-hikers themselves is a relevant factor to consider, for they were recipients of trail magic themselves. In other words, 'Functionally, gratitude motivates the person to reward the other's pro-social behavior' (Emmons & Shelton, 2002, p. 462). For the bloggers profiled in this chapter, generosity towards strangers proved to be socially contagious (Tsvetkova & Macy, 2014, p. 1). The bloggers' gratitude for their receipt of trail magic led them to contribute to an already established norm of upstream reciprocity (see Nowak & Roch, 2007) – better known as paying it forward – on the trail, thereby (re)producing a persistent culture of giving and generosity. This finding is consistent with research that shows how kindness flows through social networks, influencing the behaviours of people degrees removed from the original contributor (Fowler & Christakis, 2010).

Consistent with paying it *forward*, acts of kindness on the AT did not extend to the original benefactor (i.e. the person who provided the trail magic); rather, it entailed giving back to strangers – namely, unknown thru-hikers on the trail. This response supports the outgroup salience hypothesis, which suggests that recalling an experience of kindness from a stranger increases charitable donations because it primes the idea of giving between strangers (Buchanan & Bardi, 2010). That bloggers in this study paid kindness forward, responding to acts of trail magic by subsequently behaving more generously with third parties (i.e. other thru-hikers), is supported by both field and laboratory experiments in the psychological literature (Tsvetkova & Macy, 2014; Willer *et al.*, 2014 as cited in Simpson & Willer, 2015).

Importantly, the acts of trail magic reported by the bloggers in this study were also *random* acts of kindness insofar as they represented 'something one does for an unknown other that they hope will benefit that individual' (Baskerville *et al.*, 2000, p. 294). For this reason, recipients of trail magic largely viewed the kindness they received as acts of altruism. Understandably, recipients interpreted trail angels' giving 'as freely offered' and recognized it as something that 'proved costly to or incurred hardship for the benefactor' (Emmons & Shelton, 2002, p. 461). Indeed, in several cases, trail angels travelled to the AT from faraway distances to give back to the trail community.

In terms of fostering the AT's culture of kindness, encouragement to gift trail magic to others by the very trail angels who assisted the recipient appeared to make a difference. Such face-to-face interactions likely contributed to the impact of the receipt of the kindness. As Capraro and Marcelletti (2014) argued, face-to-face contact is profoundly different from anonymous interactions and may be more effective at driving the spread of prosocial actions. In their view, face-to-face, positive interactions associated with kindness not only provide recipients with needed resources but also improve the recipients' mood. Importantly, though, 'in dealing with someone [directly] you learn something not only about him [or her], but also about others in his [or her] society' (Dasgupta, 1988, pp. 64–65, as cited in Glanville, Andersson & Paxton, 2013). Indeed, Tsvetkova and Macy (2015, p. 140) explained, 'hearing about or seeing other people who benefit from the kindness of strangers increases contributions [of kindness to others]. As a result, a relatively small number of persistent altruists can trigger the spread of helping behaviour'. This spread, as it were, is referred to as third-party influence:

cases in which those who observe kindness between strangers become more generous towards a stranger (Tsvetkova & Macy, 2014, p. 2). Not surprisingly, then, norms and expectations on the AT have emerged over time through observation and communication amongst thru-hikers and trail angels (Ostrom, 2000), thereby establishing an environment in which norms of kindness prevail.

## Conclusion

This chapter explores kindness among strangers on the AT, a site that supports a vibrant culture of kindness. In so doing, it provides insight into the motives and responses to acts of kindness in tourism. While the hiking leisure experiences we described could broadly fall under the umbrella of nature-based tourism (Saunders *et al.*, 2014), the AT is a unique context in which to study kindness, as it differs significantly from everyday or even other tourist environments. Social relations on the trail were characterized by emotional commitment, feelings of moral obligation, interest in the welfare of others and reduced uncertainty about the other's likely behaviour, all of which promoted pro-sociality amongst present-day and former thru-hikers (Simpson & Willer, 2015). Future research on kindness amongst tourists in environments in which kindness is not such an established part of the culture would further enable an understanding of the relationships at play. Even so, there is much to gain from understanding the relationship between kindness and gratitude on the AT. Clearly, kindness and gratitude are linked, not only conceptually, but practically. Acts of kindness result in gratitude, which can in turn lead to separate acts of kindness towards strangers. Getting tourists to a point where they anticipate kindness, yet still retain some uncertainty and curiosity associated with it, will ultimately likely make their experiences more rewarding and meaningful (Otake *et al.*, 2006; Wilson, Centerbar, Kermer & Gilbert, 2005).

## References

Appalachian Trail Conservancy. (2015). *2000 milers*. Retrieved from: http://www.appala chiantrail.org/2000-milers

Banyai, M., & Glover, T. D. (2012). Evaluating research methods on travel blogs. *Journal of Travel Research*, 51(3), 267–277.

Baskerville, K., Johnson, K., Monk-Turner, E., Slone, Q., Standley, H., Stansbury, S., & Young, J. (2000). Reactions to random acts of kindness. *The Social Science Journal*, 37(2), 293–298.

Bauman, Z. (1995). *Life in fragments*. Cambridge: Blackwell.

Bowen, D., & Clarke, J. (2009). *Contemporary tourist behaviour*. Wallingford, UK: CABI.

Buchanan, K. E., & Bardi, A. (2010). Acts of kindness and acts of novelty affect life satisfaction. *Journal of Social Psychology*, 150(3), 235–237.

Capraro, V., & Marcelletti, A. (2014). Do good actions inspire good actions in others? *Scientific Reports*, 4, 7470.

Cohen, E. (1972). Towards a sociology of international tourism. *Social Research*, 39, 164–189.

Dasgupta, P. (1988). Trust as a commodity. In D. Gambetta (Ed.), *Trust: Making and breaking cooperative relations* (pp. 49–72). Oxford: Blackwell.

Derrida, J. (2000). *Of hospitality: Anne Dufourmantelle invites Jacques Derrida to respond* (trans. R. Bowlby). Stanford, CA: Stanford University Press.

Edensor, T. (2000). Walking in the British countryside: Reflexivity, embodied practices and ways to escape. *Body and Society*, 6(3–4), 81–106.

Emmons, R. A., & Crumpler, C. A. (2000). Gratitude as human strength: Appraising the evidence. *Journal of Social and Clinical Psychology*, 19, 56–69.

Emmons, R. A., & McCullough, M. E. (2003). Counting blessings versus burdens: An experimental investigation of gratitude and subjective well-being in daily life. *Journal of Personality and Social Psychology*, 84(2), 377–389.

Emmons, R. A., & Shelton, C. M. (2002). Gratitude and the science of positive psychology. *Handbook of Positive Psychology*, 18, 459–471.

Falk, A., & Fischbacher, U. (1999). *A theory of reciprocity*. Zürich: University of Zürich, Institute for Empirical Research in Economics.

Fowler, J. H., & Christakis, N. A. (2010). Cooperative behavior cascades in human social networks. *Proceedings of the National Academy of Sciences*, 107(12), 5334–5338.

Glanville, J. L., Andersson, M. A., & Paxton, P. (2013). Do social connections create trust? An examination using new longitudinal data. *Social Forces*, 92, 545–562.

Glover, T. D., & Filep, S. (2015). On kindness of strangers in tourism. *Annals of Tourism Research*, 50, 159–162.

Larsen, J., Urry, J., & Axhausen, K. W. (2007). Networks and tourism: Mobile social life. *Annals of Tourism Research*, 34(1), 244–262.

McCullough, M. E., Kilpatrick, S. D., Emmons, R. A., & Larson, D. B. (2001). Is gratitude a moral affect? *Psychological Bulletin*, 127(2), 249–266.

McPherson, M., Smith-Lovin, L., & Cook, J. M. (2001). Birds of a feather: Homophily in social networks. *Annual Review of Sociology*, 27, 415–444.

Murphy, P. E., & Murphy, A. (2004). *Strategic management for tourism communities: Bridging the gaps*. Clevedon: Channel View.

Nowak, M. A., & Roch, S. (2007). Upstream reciprocity and the evolution of gratitude. *Proceedings of the Royal Society of London B: Biological Sciences*, 274(1610), 605–610.

Ostrom, E. (2000). Collective action and the evolution of social norms. *Journal of Economic Perspective*, 14, 37–58.

Otake, K., Shimai, S., Tanaka-Matsumi, J., Otsui, K., & Fredrickson, B. L. (2006). Happy people become happier through kindness: A counting kindnesses intervention. *Journal of Happiness Studies*, 7(3), 361–375.

Pearce, P. L. (2011). *Tourist behaviour and the contemporary world*. Bristol: Channel View.

Pearce, P. L., & Lee, U. L. (2005). Developing the travel career approach to tourist motivation. *Journal of Travel Research*, 43, 226–237.

Saunders, R., Laing, J., & Weiler, B. (2014). Personal transformation through long-distance walking. In S. Filep & P. L. Pearce (Eds.), *Tourist experience and fulfilment: Insights from positive psychology* (pp. 127–146). New York: Routledge.

Simpson, B., & Willer, R. (2015). Beyond altruism: Sociological foundations of cooperation and prosocial behavior. *Annual Review of Sociology*, 41, 43–63.

Torche, F., & Valenzuela, E. (2011). Trust and reciprocity: A theoretical distinction of the sources of social capital. *European Journal of Social Theory*, 14(2), 181–198.

Tsvetkova, M., & Macy, M. W. (2014). The social contagion of generosity. *PloS One*, 9(2), e87275.

Tsvetkova, M., & Macy, M. W. (2015). The contagion of prosocial behavior and the emergence of voluntary-contribution communities. In M. Tsvetkova and M. W. Macy, *Social phenomena* (pp. 117–134). Dordrecht: Springer.

Wijesinghe, G. (2013). Can hospitality workers engage in virtuous practice in a commercial context? A study of virtue ethics and virtues of commerce. In H. Harris, G. Wijesinghe & S. McKenzie (Eds.), *The heart of the good institution: Virtue ethics as a framework for responsible management issues in business ethics* (Vol. 38, pp. 141–158). Dordrecht: Springer.

Willer, R., Flynn, F. J., Feinberg, M. W., Mensching, O., deMello Ferreira, V. R., et al. (2014). *Do people pay it forward? Gratitude fosters generalized reciprocity*. Working Paper, Department of Sociology. Stanford, CA: Stanford University.

Wilson, T. D., Centerbar, D. B., Kermer, D. A., & Gilbert, D. T. (2005). The pleasures of uncertainty: Prolonging positive moods in ways people do not anticipate. *Journal of Personality and Social Psychology*, 88(1), 5–21.

Zagzebski, L. T. (1996). *Virtues of the mind*. New York: Cambridge University Press.

# 10 The impact of tourism on the quality of life of local industry employees in Ubud, Bali

*Peita Hillman, Brent D. Moyle,*
*Betty Weiler and Deborah Che*

## Introduction

Quality of life (QOL) is a subjective phenomenon influenced by an individual's environment and experiences (Andereck, Valentine, Vogt & Knopf, 2007; Liburd, Benckendorff & Carlsen, 2012). Grounded in the discipline of psychology, QOL is often equated with life satisfaction, life progression or overall wellness (Moscardo, 2009). QOL may also be viewed from a community-wide perspective, with previous studies taking into consideration issues such as environmental quality, per capita income, life expectancy and other health and well-being (Andereck & Nyaupane, 2011; Cummins 1996; Uysal, Sirgy, Woo & Kim, 2015).

In the tourism field, QOL residents' are often asked how tourism affects the host community, specifically what changes have been evident in the surrounding environment as a precursor to understanding subsequent support for future tourism development (Carmichael, 2006; Meng, Li & Uysal, 2010). Host communities have a varying level of economic dependence on tourism, with studies having a tendency to occur in tourism-dependant localities (Michalkó, Bakucz & Rátz, 2013; Moscardo, 2009; Neal, Sirgy & Uysal, 2004). Existing literature presents an opportunity to provide insights into residents' QOL, especially when studies extend to understanding how tourism influences satisfaction, lifestyle or feelings of contentment or fulfilment (Andereck *et al.* 2007).

All the same, the breadth of QOL research in tourism has focused on the influence of tourism on the traveller (Filep, 2008). For tourists, participation in travel can result in the creation of memories that will last a lifetime (Nawijn, 2011). Studies generally conclude that fulfilling, positive travel experiences can leave the tourist with feelings of contentment and satisfaction and can sometimes deliver QOL outcomes that can be much more profound and even life changing (Benckendorff *et al.*, 2009; Dolnicar, Yanamandram & Cliff, 2012). If tourism can be used as a means for advancing the quality of life for the tourists, perhaps tourism can be a vehicle for extending these benefits and satisfaction to the host community (Filep, 2008; Lipovčan, Brajša-Žganec & Poljanec-Borić, 2014).

Despite a growing recognition of the importance of QOL for tourists and host communities, there is limited research actually exploring what QOL means for locals directly employed in the tourism industry (Hillman, Moyle & Weiler, 2015).

Arguably, QOL is an especially important component for host communities with limited options for economic development and thus a vulnerability to potential over-development, such as island communities (Oreja Rodríguez, Parra-López & Yanes-Estévez, 2008). Tourism is a part of many islands' identities, and without a sustainable industry driving economic development, often these communities have an uncertain future (Butler & Carlsen, 2011; Moyle, Croy & Weiler, 2010). The relationship between tourism and the quality of life of island communities is thus paramount.

The aim of this research is to identify what QOL means to residents directly employed in the tourism industry. Drawing on the region of Ubud in Bali, Indonesia, as a case study, the research sought to explore the link between tourism and QOL in a host community undergoing transition from agriculture to tourism. Specifically, this research seeks to unearth if locals with a direct economic attachment to tourism are more likely to respond positively about the influence of tourism on QOL, thus tapping into the effect of tourism on the local culture of Ubud.

Previous research on QOL from a host community perspective has tended to focus on the physical design of an area, often imposing western concepts such as urban sprawl and tax revenue rather than building QOL knowledge from the perspective of locals (Andereck *et al.*, 2007; Moscardo & Pearce, 1999). In contrast, this chapter seeks to explore what QOL actually means to locals directly employed in the tourism industry, in this case, residents of a small island community in a developing country. This case study of tourism and QOL in Ubud, Bali, moves beyond the traditional focus on resident attitudes and perceptions of social impacts, thus contributing to a better understanding of the connections between local employment in island tourism and QOL. The significance of this research is embedded in an in-depth understanding of a non-traditional island setting, which is a non-coastal location on an island where the primary economic driver is tourism. Adopting a case study of Ubud, which unlike coastal destinations is predominantly driven by cultural tourism, will limit the extent to which the findings are generalizable to other tourism or island settings.

## Literature review: conceptualising and measuring quality of life

The Organisation for Economic Co-operation and Development defines QOL as a measure of well-being and has identified several social indicators to enable an assessment of QOL to be undertaken: health status, work and life balance, education and skills, social connections, civic engagement and governance, environmental quality, personal security and subjective well-being (OECD, 2011). Individuals may be happier with life progression if they are satisfied with competing priorities in life, including work and family (Weiermair & Peters, 2012).

QOL research is multidisciplinary and emerged from social, behavioural, environmental and policy sciences over the past few decades (Uysal *et al.*, 2015). QOL can incorporate psychological, physiological and ecological factors that may be perceived differently by each individual in a community (Neal, Sirgy &

Uysal, 1999). Research on QOL outside of tourism has tended to focus on medical concerns (Petry, Maes & Vlaskamp, 2009), life stages (Llamosas & Vicente, 2015), leisure time (Maditinos, Papadopoulos & Prats, 2014) and environmental quality (Suwandee, Anupunpisit & Boonpen, 2013). These studies often focus on constructs such as happiness, subjective well-being, life satisfaction, resilience and health.

In the tourism field, QOL is often incorporated into studies focusing on sustainability (Weaver, 2012; Woo, Kim & Uysal, 2015), social impacts (Deery, Jago & Fredline, 2012) and costs and benefits (Cole, 2008; Hampton, 2005; Sutawa, 2012). Indeed, several authors have reported on the potential link between the economic, sociocultural and environmental impacts of tourism and QOL for host communities (Andereck & Jurowski, 2006; McCabe & Johnson, 2013; Michalkó *et al.*, 2013). Previous studies report that tourism has the capacity to influence residents' QOL and as such may affect support for tourism and associated future development (Andereck & Nyaupane, 2011; Jurowski, Daniels & Pennington-Gray, 2006). QOL research in tourism has developed a conceptual understanding of how impacts are internalised by the host community and how tourism impacts influence the day-to-day lives of locals (Benckendorff *et al.*, 2009).

Previous studies on QOL for host communities involved in tourism were often undertaken from an economic perspective (Moscardo, 2009). Within this literature, there is a common belief that increased economic benefits will improve QOL for host communities (Andereck & Jurowski, 2006). The economic focus of previous studies (Brunt & Courtney, 1999; Jurowski, Uysal & Williams, 1997; McGehee & Andereck, 2004) has been criticised by Woo *et al.* (2015), who state there is a lack of research on residents' perceived value of tourism as a predictor of QOL and whether or not it can improve community well-being in a destination. Similarly, other authors confirm that there are several community constructs to consider, including housing, neighbourhood, family, satisfaction with surrounding community, social life and employment (Grzeskowiak, Sirgy & Widgery, 2003; Sirgy & Cornwell, 2001). However, there is limited research, especially in a developing country context, exploring how locals who are employed in the tourism industry perceive the impacts of tourism on their surrounding environment and how this adds or detracts from QOL.

Previous literature suggests the impact of tourism on perceived QOL varies according to the destination, and thus there are no universal recommendations for developing and enhancing any benefits received (Pearce, 2008). The differences in perceived impacts to QOL have been found to fluctuate in response to the environmental setting in which tourism operates, the behaviour of tourists, patterns of travel, the expertise of tourism industry staff and the role that tourism plays vis-à-vis further development (Dredge & Jenkins, 2007). While studies have found that tourism improves the overall amenity of the destination and the mood of the locals by way of living in a place that is a desirable place to visit, the real beneficiaries of tourism who enjoy a higher QOL may be in the minority (Michalkó *et al.*, 2013).

Despite a growing recognition of the importance of QOL, there are few studies which focus exclusively on the subjective well-being of host community members with a direct economic connection to the tourism industry (Kerstetter & Bricker, 2012; Michalkó & Rátz, 2010). While work-life balance has been studied widely over the past two decades, only a few studies have focused on the QOL of tourism industry staff who can be subject to lower pay, shift work and low-status employment in an industry commonly seasonal in nature (Deery, 2008; Liburd *et al.*, 2012).

Consequently, the aim of the present study was to explore the meaning of quality of life for locals from Ubud with a direct economic attachment to the tourism industry. In the developing country context, coupled with the unique island culture of Bali, and Ubud in particular, this research does not impose pre-existing indicators that could potentially make assumptions that impose western definitions about what QOL means to host communities. Instead, this research presented respondents with an opportunity to inductively identify the core components of QOL, specifically seeking to extract their salient perceptions on the connection between tourism and QOL.

## Case study setting: Ubud, Bali, Indonesia

The island of Bali is located between Lombok and Java in the Republic of Indonesia (Hitchcock & Putra, 2007). Bali is considered a tourism paradise that boasts a range of accommodation choices from affordable resorts to luxury retreats, beautiful landscapes, friendly and welcoming people and attractive cultural offerings, including dance, music, art and cuisine (Rubenstein & Conner, 1999). In 2015, it was estimated that there were over nine million visitors to Bali, of which approximately four million were international visitors (Bali Government Tourist Office, 2016).

The community of Ubud, situated in the central region of the island, is widely regarded as the traditional cultural centre of Bali (Brata, 2014). Ubud is considered semi-rural and has been identified by previous studies as the destination in Bali most at risk of losing the very qualities that attract tourists to the region if development continues at its current pace (Sutawa, 2012). Visitors to Ubud can experience the famous Monkey Forest, Ubud Market, museums and walking tours of the rice paddies (Bali Tourism Board, n.d.).

Recently, Ubud has had its share of tourism development issues, with agricultural land sold to developers to construct more hotels, villas and restaurants for visitors (Sutawa, 2012). Concerns regarding the preservation of authentic culture in Ubud have also been raised with signs of cultural commodification, such as the mass production of arts and handicrafts and the use of traditional open-air spaces for commercial activity (Barker, Putra & Wiranatha, 2006; Brata, 2014). Previous literature has demonstrated that in destinations, particularly island settings, this commodification of culture for tourism purposes can result in tension amongst the host community (Cheer, Reeves & Laing, 2013; Moyle, Weiler & Croy, 2013) and potentially impact negatively on their QOL.

## Methods

Semi-structured interviews were conducted with 21 local tourism industry employees of Balinese descent in Ubud, Bali. This study employed a phenomenological approach where the participants articulated how they understood the concept of quality of life and whether this is influenced by tourism. Previous studies have recognised that local industry employees of shared ethnicity are well positioned to comment on how tourism influences QOL as opposed to residents not working in tourism, as they have a level degree of involvement with the industry and similar cultural backgrounds (Bohdanowicz & Zientara, 2009; Pizam, Milman & King, 1994).

Building on an approach from Simmons and Fairweather (2005), three stages were used to recruit and select participants for the research. First, an online search was conducted to identify key tourism businesses in the region. Second, a cross section of respondents from the variety of tourism-based businesses located in Ubud, such as restaurants, hotels, transport services and retail outlets, were identified to participate in the research at their place of employment. Third, purposive sampling was used via a Bahasa Indonesian speaking 'gatekeeper' (interpreter) who approached potential respondents and set up interviews from referrals from initial participants and contacts in the local tourism industry (Altinay & Paraskevas, 2008).

All participants were required to be 18 years of age or older, be of Balinese descent, be currently working in the tourism industry, have lived in the region for at least two years and, although an interpreter was present, have a competent level of English-language skills. To establish rapport, the core objective of the research was explained to respondents by the gatekeeper using the Bahasa Indonesian language (Walsham, 2006). This technique stimulated initial conversation at the beginning of each interview, which not only established rapport with respondents but also explained the researcher's own story, the context of the study and the cultural positioning. This approach assisted in achieving cross-cultural competency, where the ability to interpret the meanings from other cultures exists along with being able to provide accurate meanings to participants in return (Lustig and Koester, 1999).

After rapport was established, interviews commenced with four questions on QOL, with further probing questions designed to capture the aspects that needed to be in place to achieve QOL. These questions were adapted from studies, including, though not limited to, Filep (2008), Kayat (2002) and Walsham (2006). Participants were initially asked to provide their background; explain their involvement and connection to tourism, including length of time in the industry; and identify their current and previous roles. Questions also revealed perceived positive and negative impacts of tourism and explored the link between tourism and quality of life. Each interview lasted for between 30 and 60 minutes, depending on the time and language competency. Of particular relevance to this chapter, respondents were asked their perceptions on the influence of tourism on QOL as an individual, for family and for the host community of Ubud. Rather than suggesting how QOL could be achieved, such as statements about a good education, steady employment or general well-being, salient perceptions were elicited from respondents, thus building knowledge using a grounded approach.

Interviews continued until the point of saturation was reached, where no new themes were emerging from the data (Merriam, 2009; Yin, 1994). At the conclusion of the interviews, transcripts were analysed for data pertaining to the primary questions of QOL aspects followed by access to QOL for respondents, their families and their communities. These themes were then analysed to determine the frequency with which each theme emerged from the data. Coding density has been identified as an indicator of the importance of clear perceptions emerging from the transcript analysis (Corbin & Strauss, 2014). Pseudonyms were used to protect the anonymity of respondents. Each pseudonym was identified from an online directory of Balinese names; the letter of each person's pseudonym corresponded with the order in which they were interviewed where possible.

While there was opportunity for cultural or verbal misunderstandings, the researcher had visited the case study setting in excess of ten times previously and, as already noted, was accompanied by a gatekeeper/interpreter who resides in Bali. Interviews with locals revealed different perspectives, each with a different position regarding tourism (Takacs, 2003). The gatekeeper was present throughout the whole interview process to assist and clarify any aspects of the interview research stage that needed a local perspective. Selecting bilingual respondents who were residents of the region being studied and using open-response questions were strategies to reduce bias (He & van de Vijver, 2012). At the conclusion of most of the interviews, where feasible, the researcher and the gatekeeper would discuss the interview that had just taken place to review their initial impressions and additional information that the gatekeeper observed from the participant's body language or the comments made in Bahasa Indonesia while the interview was taking place. As the respondent had left the site of the interview, the gatekeeper was able to speak freely regarding his observations of the interview and was able to identify themes and patterns emerging from the interviews, such as the differences in views on QOL between younger and older respondents, with friendships being of particular importance amongst younger respondents.

## Results

Respondents included seven participants who were in the first year of work in the tourism industry and five who had been in their current roles between 10 and 21 years. Most (13) of the respondents worked in the central tourism area of the town, with the remaining (8) respondents' workplaces within a 15 minutes' drive from the centre of town. The gender of respondents was split fairly evenly, with 12 females and 9 males. Respondents were mostly well-educated, with ten having finished secondary school and five having completed university studies. In terms of marital status, again the sample was quite even, with 11 respondents married or widowed, while 10 were single. The single respondents were also the youngest

*Table 10.1* Summary of QOL themes raised by Ubud respondents

| Theme | Sub-theme |
| --- | --- |
| Family | Children |
| | Spouse |
| | Togetherness |
| | Quality time |
| Health | Well-being |
| Education | Affordability |
| Employment | Income |
| | Job opportunities |
| | Work/life balance |
| | Workplace relations |
| Friends | Socialising |
| Culture | Preservation |

participants. Of the 21 respondents, 12 had other family members working in tourism, mostly in hotels and bars and as drivers or spa owners.

When respondents were initially asked about their concept of QOL, *family* was the most common overarching theme to emerge from the data. When further probed, it became clear that four sub-themes within family were central to respondents' perceptions of QOL: children, spouses, togetherness and quality time (see Table 10.1).

Children emerged as one of the strongest themes for QOL. In Balinese culture, children are highly regarded as an essential part of family life. Having a family is desirable and a precursor to feeling happiness. Odmi, who works as a hotel all-rounder and has a husband and one infant child, stated, 'Big family and my children is, yeah, very good!' Quality time with family, including spending time together enjoying each other's company, was mentioned by several respondents as being central to maintaining QOL. Feeling loved by family members and being with extended family members on a daily basis is central to life in Ubud. Respondents had a tendency to live with several family members, often siblings, and they lived with two or three generations in the same home. As such, family time is essential in passing on cultural and family traditions to younger members and assisting with childcare.

Providing family members with an education that could generate career opportunities was identified by respondents as central to the concept of family and quality of life. While several respondents mentioned that the cost of education was high in Bali, they valued the difference that tourism made in their lives in providing increased earning and career opportunities in the industry, such as future promotions and management roles. For example, Anbeh, who has been married 15 years and has two children, mentioned that while education is a big cost and many of life's other essentials are expensive on the island, education is paramount to obtaining a good job and thereby improving QOL. Health was also identified as a central component in discussions surrounding family and QOL. For example,

Tanu, who works as a tourist driver and has a wife and two children, stated, 'Being healthy is number one for my family; if we are healthy we can do everything'.

Moving beyond the theme of family, trying to achieve and maintain a positive *work/life balance* and a *pleasant working environment* was also important to many respondents, particularly those in the early stages of their careers. Dimia, who was newly married and worked in sales administration in a luxury resort, explained that her full-time, office-based job in tourism allowed her regular daytime hours: 'I have to balance my job, my family, and also the social community; we always join the activities, so I have to balance the timing'. Pattem, who has a wife and three children and works in the front office of a hotel, also mentioned that to be in a stable job with good working conditions was important for his QOL: 'To be in set work, have a good relationship with co-workers and a good relationship with the boss, then everything is great, positive'. Enjoying harmonious relationships with others in the workplace was also highly valued by Anbeh: 'I have worked here for 17 years, the staff and my boss, we have a good team . . . we are friends'.

The majority of respondents interviewed worked in front-line roles within the tourism industry and seemed to enjoy communicating and socialising with the tourists on a daily basis. Jangha, a market seller, who was single and studying at university, enthused: 'From tourists coming here, I can earn while studying, speaking English, speaking Japanese, [and] speaking Mandarin'. Tanu mentioned, 'I like talking to tourists; we're more like friends really'. Respondents such as Nyoman, who was single and worked as a waiter at a popular tourist restaurant, also commented, 'I like that many tourists come to Ubud; they say it's beautiful and that there is good food!'

The importance of strong *friendships* was also recognised as important for achieving QOL, particularly amongst younger respondents, which previous studies have found is a natural priority for youth to achieve well-being before switching their focus towards coupling as their life progresses (Schueller, 2012; Tonon & Rodriguez de la Vega, 2014). This included friendships with both friends and family members and the interplay between the two groups. As Dewi, one of the youngest respondents who worked as a restaurant host, mentioned, through her job in tourism, she is able to be with her friends every day at her workplace: 'Something that makes me happy is when I get together with my family, I can walk around with my friends and then I come here to work with my friends'. Epana, a recent university graduate who worked in restaurant administration, explained,

> I have a lot of friends, they are kind and we can share things with each other, after being away for four years studying, I came back here to find my job and we are happy to meet each other again.

The key social themes of family, health and friendships nominated by respondents in this study confirm findings that strong, secure relationships are an important foundation upon which an individual can build towards achieving QOL (McCabe & Johnson, 2013; Ryff & Singer, 2000)

*Preserving the Balinese culture* was cited by several participants as being essential for QOL. Interest in Balinese culture from visiting tourists may contribute to the enhancement of cultural pride and identity. Dede, a tourism film-maker, noted, 'I want the next generation to still see this culture like it is today', and Rishi, a waitress confirmed, 'we get to showcase our culture to the tourists, which also brings money'. Ultimately, many respondents acknowledged that if culture is negatively affected, it will also have an impact on the appeal of the region to potential tourists. As Anbeh declared, 'I think we are boring that we like traditional but others like modern, but it's important to protect because [it is] why many tourists come to Ubud'. Ba'Mua, a widowed guesthouse owner with two children, supported this view of preservation: 'Culture is controlled and we must keep it traditional, because it's an asset for Ubud; when we cannot keep it traditional, I would worry that tourists will not come again'.

Respondents were also asked to distinguish between the influences of tourism on opportunities for QOL for them personally, for their families and for their communities. In terms of the *respondent's access to QOL*, the results were largely favourable, particularly in terms of long-term job security and career prospects. As Dimia stated, 'I need tourism; it can give more opportunities of course to my career'. Dewi concurred, 'Yes, for me, it makes it increase for my life because I have just graduated, so it has [improved] my life'. Tourism was seen as a means of climbing the career ladder for respondents such as Catur, a resort sales associate: 'Because, I know my career is now in here, I hope next I can do something. I can make my career higher than now'. There was an overall sense that respondents were pleased to be working in the tourism industry, even though respondents worked full time, six days a week; no concerns were expressed over tourism being unable to provide work/life balance (Deery, 2008). Observing tourists' enjoyment of Ubud and interacting with them on a day-to-day basis in their jobs made respondents feel intrinsically more satisfied. This supports findings in previous studies that when locals feel engaged and considered in the tourism industry, they are more likely to be welcoming and supportive of future visitors (Moyle *et al.*, 2010; Weaver & Lawton, 2013).

Improving *access to QOL for the respondents' families* was also valued. Ba'Mua noted, 'Because my business is about tourism, I get the salary, the money from tourism for my family and my life also'. However, seasonality of tourism and trying to provide for their families are still issues for all of those working in tourism in Ubud. Anbeh explained, 'We have a low season and high season; low season is January to April. May starts high season and then June, July, August; we have also the same for Christmas and New Year. We have high season, so the economy will drop in low season. My salary is also down'.

Feelings about tourism improving *access to QOL for the wider community* of Ubud were mixed. As Pattem commented, 'I think for me, it's good. Tourism is good, and if there is a lot of tourists, it's good for the people around Ubud; it's easy to get a job'. Epana mentioned, 'Yes – what I've seen from tourism has been good for the people here; local people get an opportunity to work in that field. They can work and then they know how to socialise with other people'.

Uri, a hotel owner felt strongly that the tourism industry presence has improved QOL for locals:

> When I first started working in tourism in the 1960s, Bali was very poor; the hotels then started, gradually, trying to upgrade the standard of life here. Life was poor; then with tourism life was better because there was money to send children to school, not just the people working in hotels, the side effects – the farmers, transportation. It's quite big the impact of tourism.

As mentioned, the respondents were mostly well-educated and a large proportion had children, which supports findings from previous studies that such residents are likely to be less critical in their attitudes towards tourism (Kuvan & Akan, 2005; Tosun, 2002). Overall, respondents had more positive than negative perceptions of the effects of tourism in their community, which some researchers have suggested will flow through to their personal satisfaction with their lives, for example, residents who respond favourably regarding the social impact of tourism will, in turn, positively influence their perceptions of their own social well-being (Andereck & Nyaupane, 2011; Nawijn & Mitas, 2012; Uysal, Perdue & Sirgy, 2012).

Even so, other respondents expressed concerns about the negative influences tourism can bring to their QOL and surroundings, particularly the increase in new hotels and restaurants. Ba'Mua noted that tourism doesn't necessarily give his family more opportunities: 'Money doesn't guarantee happiness, at the moment in Ubud doesn't feel that good effect yet; it's not that obvious that it's a better place'. Nina, a cashier observed, 'As I see it, Ubud is still good I think, but I don't know whether [it will stay that way]. I don't like the traffic jams, so many buildings'. The respondents' concerns over an increase in tourism development confirm previous findings in the literature that expansion will have a potentially negative effect on perceptions of QOL from the host community (Dolnicar *et al.*, 2012; Pratt, McCabe & Movono, 2015).

In terms of there being a link between tourism and QOL, respondents were divided. Anbeh responded that QOL for her means, 'I am happy with family, a little money, as long as there is enough to pay for school, for food'. When asked if tourism has affected her QOL, Anbeh explained that without steady levels of visitors, her income will suffer: 'I don't have another job, I just work for tourism, so for me it's income; my husband also works for, he's an artist, so no tourists – no income'. Gusi, a restaurant cashier also expressed support regarding a possible link citing her second job performing as a dancer in a hotel and the revamped Ubud Market as examples of tourism-induced improvements: 'Tourism brings an impact – a better opportunity for the town of Ubud'. These findings support previous research revealing improved QOL is evidenced through increased economic opportunities and a higher standard of living in a community (Andereck *et al.*, 2007; Benckendorff *et al.*, 2009; Puczkó & Smith, 2011). It is important to recognise, however, that increased economic benefits, including income, do not necessarily result in attaining a higher sense of well-being (Kahneman & Deaton, 2010; Rivera, Croes & Lee, 2015).

In addition, through the gatekeeper/interpreter, some respondents rejected the idea of a link between tourism and QOL. For example, two younger male respondents who were both employed as restaurant waiters stated, 'There's no influence, no impact – if he didn't work in tourism he would be a teacher; that's what his parents wanted him to do but he chose tourism instead' (Krishna). Lakshmi concurred, 'It doesn't really have to be like that. He says if there is tourism, the family will work in the tourism industry; if there is no tourism, they will do farming'. There is an overall feeling that the government authorities and the tourism industry could further enhance the well-being of Ubud residents, as evidenced in previous studies on island communities (Morgan, 2012; Moscardo & Murphy, 2016; Nunkoo & Ramkissoon, 2012), with a sharpened focus on tourism sustainability; community well-being strategies, including preservation of features central to QOL; and mindfulness of physical, social and environmental conditions.

## Discussion and conclusion

Similar to many island economies, the town of Ubud in Bali, Indonesia, is reliant on tourism as a development pathway. However, regardless of the economic contribution and number of visitors received, tourism has the potential to influence the QOL of individuals and communities (Butler & Carlsen, 2011; Oreja Rodríguez *et al.* 2008). This research found tourism was a predominantly positive influence on the QOL of locals employed in the industry. Positive perceptions stemmed from the job opportunities perceived as directly contributing to family togetherness as well as to the health and education of family members. In addition, positive work/life balance, enhancing friendships and preserving culture were all QOL themes mentioned by respondents. Respondents largely felt that tourism has not negatively affected Ubud's Balinese culture and that tourism is a potential vehicle that can ensure traditions are preserved for future generations.

The findings of this research support previous studies which indicated those residents who have frequent contact with tourists and/or are economically dependent on the tourism industry are more likely to be positive and supportive of tourism in their communities (Andereck & Nyaupane, 2011; Deery *et al.*, 2012). However, whilst participants responded mostly positively towards tourism's influence on QOL, sometimes it was questioned whether tourism was actually needed in order to achieve QOL. For instance, respondents such as Krishna and Lakshmi felt that if they didn't work in tourism, they would be willing and able to work in another occupation, such as teaching or farming, to earn the income necessary to achieve QOL, which suggests that tourism's ability to enhance QOL for these respondents is indirect (Croes, 2011; Uysal *et al.*, 2012).

While participants alluded to a number of the OECD's (2011) social indicators for QOL, with interviews specifically emphasising the importance of health, education, social connections and subjective well-being, the issue of personal security/the experience of crime did not emerge from the interviews. Crime was not raised by any of the respondents as a potential influence on QOL or as a risk posed by involvement in tourism, which is possibly a reflection of the stage of tourism development in the region compared to more developed areas in Bali (Altindag, 2014; West, 2015). However, the notion of *family* emerged through the course of conducting the interviews as the most important consideration for QOL in Ubud. This is a QOL indicator not specifically explored in the OECD list of social indicators. Important determinants of QOL for families which emerged from this research included children, spouses, togetherness and quality time.

In terms of limitations of the study, this research was conducted in a foreign country and in a culture that is different from the authors' Western backgrounds. To mitigate this limitation, positionality as a Western researcher was acknowledged to overcome preconceptions held by the interviewer or the respondents, as there may have been some misinterpretation due to cultural differences or unintended influences on responses through questions being asked in English. The impact was reduced by the presence of the gatekeeper, who explained and interpreted responses when required throughout the interview process.

Overall, this research found the lives of local industry employees appear to be enriched by the job opportunities and career prospects tourism offers, the health and educational benefits it brings to tourism workers and their families and the friendships formed at work with colleagues and tourists. Little concern was expressed regarding work/life balance or negative effects on the local culture. Tourism has the ability to improve QOL not only for the residents directly employed in tourism but also for their families. Replication with Ubud residents not employed in the tourism industry would add another important dimension to the current study. Future research is needed on what constitutes QOL for residents of other tourism destinations, both in developing and developed countries and in communities and regions of varying sizes and varying levels of tourism development, before conclusions can be drawn on the meaning of QOL to local residents and how QOL is affected by tourism development and activity. While tourism is acknowledged to enhance the lives and well-being of tourists worldwide, the focus needs to be on ensuring that the benefits of tourism extend to maintaining and enhancing access to QOL for host communities.

Finally, future research is also needed to explore whether tourism adds to or detracts from QOL for locals employed in different economic sectors, such as agriculture. Specifically, studies focused on residents' perceptions of tourism need to go beyond measuring attitudes to social impacts and enhance conceptual clarification surrounding what QOL actually means for host communities in order to add to the suite of tools used to ascertain if tourism is a sustainable development pathway, especially in island destinations.

# References

Altinay, L., & Paraskevas, A. (2008). *Planning research in hospitality and tourism*. New York: Routledge.

Altindag, D. T. (2014). Crime and international tourism. *Journal of Labor Research*, 35(1), 1–14.

Andereck, K. L., & Jurowski, C. (2006). Tourism and quality of life. In G. Jennings & N. Nickerson (Eds.), *Quality tourism experiences* (pp. 136–154). Oxford: Elsevier Butterworth-Heinemann.

Andereck, K. L., & Nyaupane, G. P. (2011). Exploring the nature of tourism and quality of life perceptions among residents. *Journal of Travel Research*, 50(3), 248–260.

Andereck, K. L., Valentine, K. M., Vogt, C. A., & Knopf, R. C. (2007). A cross-cultural analysis of tourism and quality of life perceptions. *Journal of Sustainable Tourism*, 15(5), 483–502.

Bali Government Tourist Office. (2016). *The Number of Foreign Tourist Arrivals to Bali by Month 2008–2015*. Retrieved 13 February 2016 from: http://www.disparda.baliprov.go.id/en/Statistics2

Bali Tourism Board. (n.d.). *Ecotourism (Nature Tourism) Ubud*. Retrieved 15 June 2015 from: http://www.balitourismboard.org/ubud.html

Barker, T., Putra, D., & Wiranatha, A. (2006). Authenticity and commodification of balinese dance performances. In M. Smith & M. Robinson (Eds.), *Cultural tourism in a changing world: Politics, participation and (re) presentation* (pp. 215–224). London: Channel View.

Benckendorff, P., Edwards, D., Jurowski, C., Liburd, J. J., Miller, G., & Moscardo, G. (2009). Exploring the future of tourism and quality of life. *Tourism and Hospitality Research*, 9(2), 171–183.

Bohdanowicz, P., & Zientara, P. (2009). Hotel companies' contribution to improving the quality of life of local communities and the well-being of their employees. *Tourism and Hospitality Research*, 9(2), 147–158.

Brata, I. B. (2014). Commodification of Telajakan at Ubud Village, Gianyar, Bali. *E-Journal of Cultural Studies*, 7(1), Retrieved 10 July from: http://ojs.unud.ac.id/index.php/ecs/article/view/8417

Brunt, P., & Courtney, P. (1999). Host perceptions of sociocultural impacts. *Annals of Tourism Research*, 26(3), 493–515.

Butler, R., & Carlsen, J. (2011). Conclusions and implications for sustainable island tourism. In R. Butler & J. Carlsen (Eds.), *Ecotourism series, number 8: Island tourism: A sustainable perspective* (p. 228). London: CABI Publishing.

Carmichael, B. A. (2006). Linking quality tourism experiences, residents' quality of life, and quality experiences for tourists. In G. Jennings & N. Nickerson (Eds.), *Quality tourism experiences* (pp. 115–135). Oxford: Elsevier Butterworth-Heinemann.

Cheer, J. M., Reeves, K. J., & Laing, J. H. (2013). Tourism and traditional culture: Land diving in Vanuatu. *Annals of Tourism Research*, 43, 435–455.

Cole, S. (2008). *Tourism, culture and development: Hopes, dreams and realities in East Indonesia*. Clevedon: Channel View.

Corbin, J., & Strauss, A. (2014). *Basics of qualitative research: Techniques and procedures for developing grounded theory*. Newbury Park, CA: Sage Publications.

Croes, R. R. (2011). *The small Island paradox, tourism specialization as a potential solution*. Saarbrucken, Germany: Lambert Academic.

Cummins, R. A. (1996). The domains of life satisfaction: An attempt to order chaos. *Social Indicators Research*, 38(3), 303–328.

Deery, M. (2008). Talent management, work-life balance and retention strategies. *International Journal of Contemporary Hospitality Management*, 20(7), 792–806.

Deery, M., Jago, L., & Fredline, L. (2012). Rethinking social impacts of tourism research: A new research agenda. *Tourism Management*, 33(1), 64–73.

Dolnicar, S., Yanamandram, V., & Cliff, K. (2012). The contribution of vacations to quality of life. *Annals of Tourism Research*, 39(1), 59–83.

Dredge, D. M., & Jenkins, J. M. (2007). *Tourism planning and policy*. Milton, QLD: Wiley.

Filep, S. (2008). Linking Tourist Satisfaction to Happiness and Quality of Life. *BESTEN Think Tank VIII*. Retrieved 24 August 2015 from: http://ertr.tamu.edu/files/2012/09/410_Filep.pdf

Grzeskowiak, S., Sirgy, M. J., & Widgery, R. (2003). Residents' satisfaction with community services: Predictors and outcomes. *Journal of Regional Analysis and Policy*, 33, 1–36.

Hampton, M. P. (2005). Heritage, local communities and economic development. *Annals of Tourism Research*, 32(3), 735–759.

He, J., & van de Vijver, F. (2012). Bias and equivalence in cross-cultural research. *Online Readings in Psychology and Culture*, 2(2). doi: 10.9707/2307-0919.1111

Hillman, P., Moyle, B. D., & Weiler, B. (2015). What does quality of life mean to locals employed in the tourism industry? A case study of Ubud, Bali. *Paper presented in CAUTHE Conference*, Gold Coast, 2–5 February, 2015.

Hitchcock, M. P., & Putra, N. D. (2007). *Tourism, development & terrorism in Bali*. Farnham: Ashgate.

Jurowski, C., Daniels, M. J., & Pennington-Gray, L. (2006). The distribution of tourism benefits. In G. Jennings & N. Nickerson (Eds.), *Quality tourism experiences* (pp. 192–207). Oxford: Elsevier Butterworth-Heinemann.

Jurowski, C., Uysal, M., & Williams, D. R. (1997). A theoretical analysis of host community resident reactions to tourism. *Journal of Travel Research*, 36(2), 3–11.

Kahneman, D., & Deaton, A. (2010). High income improves evaluation of life but not emotional well-being. *Proceedings of the National Academy of Sciences*, 107(38), 16489–16493.

Kayat, K. (2002). Power, social exchanges and tourism in Langkawi: Rethinking resident perceptions. *International Journal of Tourism Research*, 4(3), 171–191.

Kerstetter, D. L., & Bricker, K. S. (2012). Relationship between carrying capacity of small Island tourism destinations and quality-of-life. In M. Uysal, R. Perdue & J. Sirgy (Eds.), *Handbook of tourism and quality-of-life research* (pp. 445–462). Dordrecht: Springer.

Kuvan, Y., & Akan, P. (2005). Residents' attitudes toward general and forest-related impacts of tourism: The case of Belek, Antalya. *Tourism Management*, 26(5), 691–706.

Liburd, J. J., Benckendorff, P., & Carlsen, J. (2012). Tourism and quality-of-life: How does tourism measure up? In M. Uysal *et al.* (Eds.), *Handbook of tourism and quality-of-life research: Enhancing the lives of tourists and residents of host communities* (pp. 105–132). Dordrecht: Springer.

Lipovčan, L. K., Brajša-Žganec, N., & Poljanec-Borić, S. (2014). What is good for tourists should be good for residents too: The relationship between the quality of the touristic offer and subjective well-being of residents. *Tourism Analysis*, 19(6), 719–730.

Llamosas, J. S., & Vicente, V. C. (2015). Quality of life among community-dwelling elderly persons with a history of previous falls. *Fisioterapia*, 37(1), 3–8.

Lustig, M. W., & Koester, J. (1999). *Intercultural competence: Interpersonal communication across cultures* (3rd ed.). New York: Longman.

Maditinos, D. I., Papadopoulos, D., & Prats, L. (2014). The free time allocation and its relationship with the perceived quality of life (QOL) and satisfaction with life (SWL). *Procedia Economics and Finance*, 9, 519–532.

McCabe, S., & Johnson, S. (2013). The happiness factor in tourism: Subjective well-being and social tourism. *Annals of Tourism Research*, 41, 42–65.

McGehee, N. G., & Andereck, K. L. (2004). Factors predicting rural residents' support of tourism. *Journal of Travel Research*, 43(2), 131–140.

Meng, F., Li, X., & Uysal, M. (2010). Tourism development and regional quality of life: The case of China. *Journal of China Tourism Research*, 6(2), 164–182.

Merriam, S. B. (2009). *Qualitative research: A guide to design and implementation*. San Francisco: Jossey-Bass.

Michalkó, G., Bakucz, M., & Rátz, T. (2013). The relationship between tourism and residents' quality of life: A case study of Harkány, Hungary. *European Journal of Tourism Research*, 6(2), 154–169.

Michalkó, G., & Rátz, T. (2010). Measurement of tourism-oriented aspects of quality of life. *Journal of Tourism Challenges and Trends*, 3(2), 35–50.

Morgan, N. (2012). Time for 'mindful' destination management and marketing. *Journal of Destination Marketing & Management*, 1(1), 8–9.

Moscardo, G. (2009). Tourism and quality of life: Towards a more critical approach. *Tourism and Hospitality Research*, 9(2), 159–170.

Moscardo, G., & Murphy, L. (2016). Using destination community wellbeing to assess tourist markets: A case study of Magnetic Island, Australia. *Journal of Destination Marketing & Management*. doi: 10.1016/j.jdmm.2016.01.003

Moscardo, G., & Pearce, P. L. (1999). Understanding ethnic tourists. *Annals of Tourism Research*, 26(2), 416–434.

Moyle, B. D., Croy, W. G., & Weiler, B. (2010). Community perceptions of tourism: Bruny and Magnetic Islands, Australia. *Asia Pacific Journal of Tourism Research*, 15(3), 353–366.

Moyle, B. D., Weiler, B., & Croy, W. G. (2013). Visitors' perceptions of tourism impacts on Bruny and Magnetic Islands, Australia. *Journal of Travel Research*, 52(3), 392–406.

Nawijn, J. (2011). Determinants of daily happiness of vacation. *Journal of Travel Research*, 50(5), 559–566.

Nawijn, J., & Mitas, O. (2012). Resident attitudes to tourism and their effect on subjective well-being: The case of Palma de Mallorca. *Journal of Travel Research*, 51(5), 531–541.

Neal, J. D., Sirgy, M. J., & Uysal, M. (1999). The role of satisfaction with leisure travel/tourism services and experience in satisfaction with leisure life and overall life. *Journal of Business Research*, 44(3), 153–163.

Neal, J. D., Sirgy, M. J., & Uysal, M. (2004). Measuring the effect of tourism services on travelers' quality of life: Further validation. *Social Indicators Research*, 69(3), 243–277.

Nunkoo, R. & Ramkissoon, H. (2012). Power, trust, social exchange and community support. *Annals of Tourism Research*, 39(2), 997–1023.

Oreja Rodríguez, J. R., Parra-López, E., & Yanes-Estévez, V. (2008). The sustainability of island destinations: Tourism area life cycle and teleological perspectives: The case of Tenerife. *Tourism Management*, 29(1), 53–65.

Organisation for Economic Cooperation and Development. (2011). *Compendium of OECD well-being indicators*. Paris: Author.

Pearce, P. (2008). Understanding how tourism can bring sociocultural benefits to destination communities. In G. Moscardo (Ed.), *Building community capacity for tourism development* (pp. 29–40). London: CABI.

Petry, K., Maes, B., & Vlaskamp, C. (2009). Measuring the quality of life of people with profound multiple disabilities using the QOL-PMD: First results. *Research in Developmental Disabilities*, 30(6), 1394–1405.

Pizam, A., Milman, A., & King, B. (1994). The perceptions of tourism employees and their families towards tourism: A cross-cultural comparison. *Tourism Management*, 15(1), 53–61.

Pratt, S., McCabe, S., & Movono, A. (2015). Gross happiness of a 'tourism' village in Fiji. *Journal of Destination Marketing & Management*. doi: 10.1016/j.jdmm.2015.11.001

Puczkó, L., & Smith, M. (2011). Tourism-specific quality-of-life index: The Budapest model. In M. Budruk & R. Phillips (Eds.), *Quality-of-life community indicators for parks, recreation and tourism management* (pp. 163–183). Dordrecht: Springer.

Rivera, M., Croes, R., & Lee, S. H. (2015). Tourism development and happiness: A residents' perspective. *Journal of Destination Marketing & Management*, 5(1), 5–15.

Rubenstein, R., & Conner, L. H. (1999). *Staying local in the global village: Bali in the twentieth century*. Honolulu: University of Hawaii Press.

Ryff, C. D., & Singer, B. (2000). Interpersonal flourishing: A positive health agenda for the new millennium. *Personality and Social Psychology Review*, 4(1), 30–44.

Schueller, S. M. (2012). Positive psychology. In V. S. Ramachandran (Ed.), *Encyclopedia of human behavior* (pp. 140–147). San Diego: Academic Press.

Simmons, D. G., & Fairweather, J. R. (2005). *Understanding the tourism host-guest encounter in New Zealand: Foundations for adaptive planning and management*. Christchurch, New Zealand: EOS Ecology.

Sirgy, M. J., & Cornwell, T. (2001). Further validation of the Sirgy *et al.*'s measure of community quality of life. *Social Indicators Research*, 56(2), 125–143.

Sutawa, G. K. (2012). Issues on Bali tourism development and community empowerment to support sustainable tourism development. *Procedia Economics and Finance*, 4, 413–422.

Suwandee, S., Anupunpisit, V., & Boonpen, P. (2013). Quality of life and environment of communities along Saen Saeb canal: A guideline for reform (Phase II). *Social and Behavioral Sciences Symposium, 4th International Science, Social Science, Engineering and Energy Conference 2012 (I-SEEC 2012)*, Procedia – Social and Behavioural Sciences, Cha-Am, Thailand, 88, 212–219.

Takacs, D. (2003). How does your positionality bias your epistemology? *Thought & Action*, 19(1), 27–38.

Tonon, G., & Rodriguez de la Vega, L. (2014). The importance of friendship in the construction of positive nations. In H. Agueda Marujo & L. Miguel Neto (Eds.), *Positive nations and communities: Collective, qualitative and cultural-sensitive processes in positive psychology* (pp. 209–230). Dordrecht: Springer.

Tosun, C. (2002). Host perceptions of impacts: A comparative tourism study. *Annals of Tourism Research*, 29(1), 231–253.

Uysal, M., Perdue, R., & Sirgy, J. (Eds.). (2012). *Handbook of tourism and quality-of-life research: Enhancing the lives of tourists and residents of host communities*. Dordrecht: Springer.

Uysal, M., Sirgy, M. J., Woo, E., & Kim, H. L. (2015). Quality of life (QOL) and well-being research in tourism. *Tourism Management*, 53, 244–261.

Walsham, G. (2006). Doing interpretive research. *European Journal of Information Systems*, 15(3), 320–330.

Weaver, D. B. (2012). Organic, incremental and induced paths to sustainable mass tourism convergence. *Tourism Management*, 33(5), 1030–1037.

Weaver, D. B., & Lawton, L. J. (2013). Resident perceptions of a contentious tourism event. *Tourism Management*, 37, 165–175.

Weiermair, K., & Peters, M. (2012). Quality-of-life values among stakeholders in tourism destinations: A tale of converging and diverging interests and conflicts. In M. Uysal, R. Perdue & J. Sirgy (Eds.), *Handbook of tourism and quality-of-life research: Enhancing the lives of tourists and residents of host communities* (pp. 463–473). Dordrecht: Springer.

West, B. (2015). Dialogical history in a time of crisis: Tourist logics and the 2002 Bali Bombings. In B. West, *Re-enchanting nationalisms* (pp. 81–112). New York: Springer.

Woo, E., Kim, H., & Uysal, M. (2015). Life satisfaction and support for tourism development. *Annals of Tourism Research*, 50, 84–97.

Yin, R. K. (1994). *Case study research: Design and methods*. Thousand Oaks, CA: Sage.

# Part IV
# Positive tourism workers

# 11 Transformative guiding and long-distance walking

*Robert Saunders, Betty Weiler and Jennifer Laing*

## Introduction

The idea that people's lives can sometimes be changed for the better as a result of travel experiences appears frequently in the tourism literature (Reisinger, 2013a). Transformation through travel is generally understood as a personal change *outcome* that a participant associates with a significant tourism *experience* (Saunders, 2014; Saunders, Laing & Weiler, 2014); however, what counts as transformation through travel varies substantially. It can include increasing cultural or environmental awareness, stimulating inner psychological development or growth through transformative learning (Morgan, 2010) or permanently altering participants' values and behaviours in ways which promote sustainability (Lean, 2009). Moreover, the emerging field of transformative tourism (Lean, 2009; Reisinger, 2013b) highlights a growing focus on tourist experiences, including adventure travel activities, which are conceived and marketed as change inducing.

Adventure tours involving physical challenge and immersion in nature or history sometimes generate remarkable stories of personal transformation (Saunders, 2014). Studies of participant experiences often reveal an emergent sense of existential authenticity (Wang, 1999), but much less has been written about how and to what extent tour operators and guides actively plan and manage these events in order to enhance their impact and memorability, or to promote transformation (Saunders, 2013; Sharpe, 2005a). The 'choreographing' (Beedie, 2003) of adventure tourism activities can be expected to add to the physical demands and responsibilities of guides, but this too appears to be under-researched. Exploring how guides working in transformative tourism perform, cope with and manage their multiple roles is potentially important to their well-being and job satisfaction, and it may help operators better manage the quality of client experiences.

This chapter presents the results of a study exploring transformative tourism from the perspective of tour guides, focusing in particular on guided long-distance walks which are marketed as potentially 'life changing'. Long-distance walking (LDW) as a guided adventure tourism activity is increasingly popular and diverse, ranging from physically challenging tent-based treks to more comfortable supported walks using huts for accommodation. While the majority of commercial LDW tours are nature-based, an increasing number of culturally oriented long-distance walks have been developed in recent years, including trekking the Kokoda Trail in Papua New Guinea. The present study examined transformative guiding in both types of LDW tours. For the purposes of this study, a minimum duration of three days was used to ensure participants gained a sense of immersion in the setting and to allow time for guides to frame and manage participant experiences.

The first aim of the study was to explore *motivations* for becoming a LDW guide, including whether personal experience and understanding of transformation influences the ways guides work and their objectives for clients. The second aim was to explore the various *roles* guides adopt during long-distance walks, including how they mediate experiences and their meanings in ways that may foster transformation. Finally, the chapter explores the perceived *satisfactions and stresses* of being a transformative LDW guide, including guides' feelings about their work and the places they take clients.

## Synopsis of relevant literature

In order to understand the work of a tour guide within a transformative tourism context, we first review the literature on the range of roles played by guides. Second, we present theories and concepts relating to emotional labour from human resource management as a framework for considering the potential for both positive and negative consequences on guides. As Black and Weiler (2015, p. 41) note, while many studies have focused on the negative effects of emotional labour, 'there may be opportunities to study the positive consequences for tour guides, tourists, and other stakeholders'. As a third area of background to the study, we also review the literature on LDW as a tourism activity.

### *Guiding roles*

Research on tourist guiding reveals the evolution and elaboration of three overarching roles or spheres of activity in which guides are engaged. Cohen (1985) labels the two traditional guiding roles *pathfinding* and *mentoring* and notes that both are evident in the activities of many modern guides. Weiler and Black (2015) outline research which has further explored the complexities of these two roles and re-label them with the terms *tour management* and *experience management*, respectively, to better capture the breadth of their contemporary expression. In addition, Weiler and Black (2015) describe a third area of guiding activity that focuses on *destination and resource management*. This area embraces roles contributing to the sustainability of host communities and environments as identified by Weiler and Davis (1993) in the context of ecotourism and also includes job creation and economic sustainability as discussed by Pereira and Mykletun (2012). What a guide does in this third sphere appears to be less relevant to the transformation of individual clients than the first two spheres.

Tour management facilitates physical access and can be characterised primarily as group-focused leadership. In LDW, this role encompasses issues of safety, route selection and navigation, gaining permits to enter protected areas and the overall control of a group. Tour management can also involve complex logistical tasks in relation to local suppliers and communities, not all of which are evident to clients. Planning, preparation and various other aspects of tour management may be hidden, or taken for granted, and only noticed by participants when things go wrong.

In contrast, experience management focuses on the individual and involves presenting, interpreting and facilitating communication within and outside the group, including interactions with the setting. In many ways, experience management constitutes the core of the guide's role in transformative tourism, as it fosters engagement in a tour and mediates meaning and understanding (Weiler & Black, 2015) that can be critical to establishing a foundation for transformation. A skilful guide can enhance the impact and memorability of tour experiences in various ways (Tung & Ritchie, 2011). Adventure tourism experiences may be managed to heighten the perception of risk or to engender an appreciative communion with nature (Arnould & Price, 1993). Experiences may also be choreographed to promote a sense of authenticity (Wang, 1999) or to foster empathy and respect (Saunders, 2013). Here too process elements may remain hidden from clients. In some cases, as Arnould and Price (1993, p. 25) observe, 'the guide role is a demanding one fraught with illusion and role conflict'.

### *Emotional labour and the experience of being a guide*

Emotional engagement with clients is thought to be a key element of memorable experiences (Tung & Ritchie, 2011). However, fostering this depth of involvement can be challenging for guides. *Emotional labour* has been defined by Hochschild (1983, p. 7) as the 'management of feeling to create a publicly observable facial and bodily display' by workers to produce a preferred state of mind or response in clients. Hochschild's (1983) research suggests that *surface acting* (hiding real emotions or even 'faking' feelings) can generate a sense of estrangement and alienation, leading to a loss of job satisfaction.

Emotional labour can present particular challenges to adventure guides, who may be 'required to be in close proximity with clients, often over extended periods of time with few opportunities to retreat to "backstage" areas where they can relax and step out of their leader persona' (Black & Weiler, 2015, pp. 37–38). Previous research confirms that high levels of emotional labour can be required of adventure guides and that negative well-being outcomes can result (Ap & Wong, 2001; Mackenzie & Kerr, 2013; Sharpe, 2005b).

Operators sometimes seek purposefully to promote particular experiences or transformative outcomes (Saunders, 2013; Sharpe, 2005a). Guides may experience conflict or inauthenticity from cognitive or emotional dissonance, for example, where their attitudes or values (Rokeach, 1973) differ from those an operator requires to be espoused. Interestingly, Ryan (2002) suggests it is usually the intensity of such experiences that is of interest to the tourist rather than their purpose.

Guides have been found to adopt strategies to mitigate the stress of emotional dissonance, including periodic withdrawal from the group and self-talk (Sharpe, 2005b). To enhance guiding skills, Christie and Mason (2003) advocate training in the use of critical reflection. While this approach is not necessarily value-neutral, its focus on clients' own processing of experience may be important in fostering clients' transformations and may also help reduce issues of dissonance in guides.

Some research has identified positive effects of emotional labour on guides. For example, Torland (2011, p. 138) concludes that *deep acting* (where tour guides actually feel the emotions they express) helps 'to convey a sense of authenticity and a feeling of achievement in employees, thus leading to higher levels of job satisfaction'. However, there is little understanding of the relationships between the roles undertaken by guides as part of their work and the beneficial and potentially transformative outcomes for both guides and clients.

### *Long-distance walking as a tourism activity*

There is a growing body of research on LDW, including its dynamics (den Breejen, 2007), dimensions (Chhetri, Arrowsmith & Jackson, 2004) and experiences (Mills & Butler, 2005). Walking is often 'not so much an end in itself but rather a means to complex ends, to comprehensive experiences' (Kay & Moxham, 1996, p. 176). Edensor (2000) relates modern styles of walking to 'excursive walking' that arose during the Romantic era. He suggests that walking in the countryside allows people to recover their sensory capacities and that LDW in particular is focused on ideals of self-development and achievement.

While devotion to organised religion has waned in many western societies, interest in traditional pilgrimage routes, including walking-based pilgrimages, remains strong. As well as a tangible contact with history, these routes offer an embodied, grounded experience of place and scope for individual styles of spiritual searching (Slavin, 2003). In both secular and religious walking traditions, there are tendencies to follow in the footsteps of others (Pearce, 2011), literally and metaphorically 'constructing' paths and destinations.

Until recently, there was little detailed research on LDW as a tourism activity. A case study by den Breejen (2007) on the 152 km West Highland Way in Scotland investigated the dynamics of long-distance walkers' experiences. Participants reported finishing on an 'upward trend' of intensity and enjoyment related to strong relationships they forged with their surroundings and a sense of achievement they attained (den Breejen, 2007, p. 1426). Positive emotions, reduced effects of stress, enhanced well-being and a sense of personal growth have also been identified as outcomes from LDW (Crust, Keegan, Piggott & Swann, 2011).

Quinlan Cutler, Carmichael and Doherty (2014) explored the experiences and subsequent memories of a group of university students whose three-day, 43 km Inca Trail trek took them to Machu Picchu in Peru. Findings showed that the 'emotional, educational, and physical journey' of the trek eclipsed the experience of the destination, and became 'an important marker of identity and personal growth . . . related to the experience of pain and difficulty along the trail' (Quinlan Cutler *et al.*, 2014, p. 165). The roles of guides in these experiences are not discussed, although interactions with guides and porters are acknowledged as part of the experience.

Active roles of LDW guides in mediating experiences and their meanings are clearly evident in a study by one of the current authors regarding trekking the Kokoda Trail in Papua New Guinea (Saunders, 2013). Similarities are noted with choreographed experiences from other adventure activities such as white-water rafting (Arnould & Price, 1993). The war history of the Kokoda Trail gives it a unique emotional character which clearly adds to its memorability. The multifaceted experiential nature of guided LDW offers scope for further research (Pearce, 2011, p. 108), and the current study addresses a gap in the literature by focusing on the experiences of guides who lead walking tours that have been conceived and marketed as transformative.

## Method

This study uses Interpretative Phenomenological Analysis (IPA) to explore the experiences and perspectives of LDW guides. The main theoretical underpinnings of IPA are *phenomenology, hermeneutics* and *idiography* (Smith, Flowers & Larkin, 2009). Phenomenology focuses on studying individuals' experiences as they perceive them, particularly those they consider significant. Hermeneutics then questions how phenomena are evaluated by participants and elucidates their interpretation. Idiography is concerned with the particular, in the sense of both detail and context (Smith *et al.*, 2009). As a consequence, the voices of research participants are typically presented through rich and sometimes extended quotes.

## Data collection and sampling

IPA research generally involves small purposive samples and detailed contextual analysis. In this study, ten guides were selected from six Australia-based tour operators, each of which offers distinctly different LDW tours, but all of which market their tours as having the potential for participants to undergo 'life-changing' experiences. The tours ranged from nature-based walks in a range of Australian settings posing different degrees of challenge, to treks along the historic battlefield of the Kokoda Trail in Papua New Guinea. They were selected to reflect the range of guided LDW tours available within the Australasian region.

The number of participants was determined using the constant comparative method (Boeiji, 2002) to assess when additional interviews became redundant. In IPA, sample sizes of three to six participants are common. Nevertheless, it is important to 'provide sufficient cases for the development of meaningful points of similarity and difference between participants' (Smith *et al.*, 2009, p. 51).

Semi-structured, in-depth interviews were held with each guide, based around a schedule of questions which focused on three main topics: how interviewees first became involved in LDW and guiding, how they think their tours (including particular experiences they seek to facilitate) affect their clients and what guiding means to them (including any particularly memorable experiences they have had as guides). In IPA research, a flexible, conversational style of interviewing is used to elicit experiential details, narratives about significant events and insights into frames of understanding. The focus is on the lived experiences and meaning-making processes of interviewees.

## Analysis and interpretation

As mentioned previously, this study aims to explore motivations for becoming a guide, including whether personal experience and understanding of transformation influences the ways guides work and their objectives for clients. It also aims to explore the various roles guides adopt during long-distance walks, including how they mediate experiences and their meanings for clients. Finally, the satisfactions and stresses of being a guide are considered. These include guides' feelings about the places they take clients and the actions they take to promote transformative experiences.

Pseudonyms have been used for all participants in the study, and their employers are not identified. Analysis was carried out individually for each guide, following the methodology of Smith *et al.* (2009). Common themes were then identified and grouped into categories. In the analysis presented here, only themes which were evident in more than one-third of the relevant guides have been included. Conceptual categories present in more than two-thirds of the relevant guides are considered to be major themes (Smith *et al.*, 2009). Narratives have also been used to provide insights into what an experience or incident meant to the individual concerned. This involved looking beyond the narrative as a recapitulation of an experience and report of what occurred, to evaluate the meanings each narrator derived from events (Cortazzi, 1993; Labov & Waletzky, 1966).

## Findings and analysis

### *Becoming a guide*

Most interviewees were eager to expand upon how they first became a guide. Many of the guides interviewed indicated that their own personally significant experiences of LDW contributed to their decision to take up guiding. Affinities with LDW and being attracted by the settings of these walks were frequent themes. As well as enjoying trekking, the majority of guides indicated that they were attracted by the challenge of the work, and most felt that they had relevant transferrable skills from previous employment.

Another prominent theme associated with becoming a guide was congruent personal values. A deep interest in war history was evident in the three Kokoda guides, two of whom had family connections with the Kokoda Campaign. All expressed a strong sense of national identity based around Australia's military history and ascribed to associated personal values of mateship, courage and endurance. In most cases, nature-based walking guides indicated deeply held nature conservation values.

Motivations to change jobs and become a guide ranged from seeking more fulfilling employment and a general sense of dissatisfaction with a previous career, to being attracted to guiding after a particular life crisis or negative life experience. This aspect of becoming a guide is illustrated in the following section, which highlights transformations such as changes in life direction and improvements in life satisfaction evident in many of these guides.

## *Becoming a Kokoda Trail guide*

The Kokoda Trail is an arduous six- to ten-day trek through mountainous jungle that was a significant battlefield in the Pacific theatre of World War II. Jeff first undertook the Kokoda trek at a time of transition in his life. He had recently become a parent and had given up a part-time job in outdoor education to take on more reliable and better paid work. His new career involved long hours and stress. He found the sudden changes in his life disconcerting:

> Kokoda was a very significant event for me ... I had some family things happening ... There's a lot of time to reflect when you're walking, so you have a lot of time to think about things. I was able to reflect on what I was going through ...

An important realisation for Jeff was that he missed aspects of his previous outdoor education work. He saw an opportunity to combine his permanent job with an annual challenge: guiding a trek on the Kokoda Trail:

> I thought, maybe I could actually do this. I wouldn't mind being one of the guides ... To do something each year to create a goal for me to strive for, so that I'll have the fitness goal; I'll have a responsibility goal. I've taken that into this job.

In contrast, Neville has a military background. He first walked the Kokoda Trail about 15 years ago:

> The group I walked with were ex-special forces guys I'd served with, so there was a close bond regarding that ... Being with people you trust with your life was just very refreshing. And that's what knocked me about when I got off the track ... it shattered me.

Neville's experience of the Kokoda Trail highlighted a growing dissatisfaction with his work:

> I'd sit in the car park in the basement each morning psyching myself up to go in, and I was in tears sometimes ... As you walked in everyone would say

'Mate we've got a problem here boss . . . This guy's just quit . . . This client's just rung, they want that job finished by tomorrow morning . . . ' And it would just pour down on you. I was having counselling and all sorts of stuff.

The experience of trekking the Kokoda Trail caused Neville to question what he was doing with his life:

I was working virtually seven days a week at that stage. I'd get home at night and there'd be messages for me, and it never stopped. I was earning very good money, and I had a good car and all the crap that went with it, but on Kokoda it meant nothing. I suddenly stood back and thought 'actually this really isn't that important'.

In terms of the first aim of this study, for Neville in particular, becoming a Kokoda guide seems to relate to his own experiences on the Kokoda Trail. Guiding now gives him more of a sense of purpose than his previous job and involves less conflict with his personal values.

### *Becoming a nature-based, long-distance walking guide*

Themes of having an affinity for guiding and holding personal values congruent with those embodied in tour settings are also evident in the guides of nature-based, long-distance walks. Peter began guiding through his involvement with a conservation organisation during a break from his original career:

The guiding was so much fun I thought, 'well, I'll do a second year'. That was 12 years ago. It was hard to get back into the health industry once I'd, you know, tasted, well not just the tourism industry but eco-tourism. You know, with a strong environmental focus.

A theme of negative life experiences motivating change is particularly evident in Xavier, who runs a range of tours in remote outback areas of Australia. The lifestyle of his previous work had led him to alcohol and drug addiction, but taking time out in the wilderness helped him to recover:

It was a clean slate, literally, with pure rivers and lovely rainforests and untouched and unspoilt. So it was clearly a metaphor for a re-birth . . . When you've got drug-induced psychosis, moments of beauty are like pouring ointment on a blister.

Once he was free of his addictions, Xavier found that LDW also allowed him to be creative and to formulate new directions in his life:

The notion of the walks started when I was doing that big walk from Melbourne to Sydney . . . I was doing yoga in a grove of Mountain Ash, and

I thought, 'Christ, wouldn't this be amazing? To do trips that weren't just walking'.

The most frequent themes associated with becoming a nature-based guide are affinity with LDW, affinity with guiding and congruent personal values. The LDW experience also clearly had a transformative impact for these guides in that each moved into part-time or full-time guiding as a result of their LDW experience. To some degree, however, nature-based guiding seems to be more of a lifestyle choice, and the zeal and commitment to a particular set of values evident in some of the Kokoda guides seems to be less of a motivating factor for these people.

### Guiding roles during long-distance walks

Of the three role spheres of tour management, experience management and destination/resource management, the latter was largely absent from the interview data. A commitment to tour planning and management was universally evident, but only those leading physically demanding treks mentioned the importance of client preparation. Group training can begin to develop social bonds, but guides tended to encourage individual training programmes, particularly where their clients came from widely distant locations.

In contrast, experience management is evident in the responses of all guides, with themes of mediating cognitive and affective engagement being particularly common. Mediating clients' physical engagement with walking was also mentioned by almost all guides, although the strategies used to do this varied considerably. Operators clearly have different goals, depending on the style and setting of the walk undertaken, but few guides articulated these in any precise or prescriptive way, preferring to illustrate the kinds of outcomes that clients achieve on their walks. Clients' experiences, and sometimes the meanings of those experiences, are clearly important to guides. How aspects of experience management are used to mediate meanings for clients, engage them emotionally and perhaps facilitate life change can best be illustrated by guides' narratives, particularly in relation to the Kokoda Trail.

### Mediating experience and facilitating life change on the Kokoda Trail

On the Kokoda Trail, client experiences are frequently choreographed and influenced by guides in order to enhance their effect. Neville makes use of his military background to 'bring history to life' when he picks up apparently authentic objects that remain on site:

> I've fired virtually all of the infantry weapons that were used in the Kokoda Campaign, so I understand them when I talk to my trekkers. I can pick up the remains of a Bren Gun, and I can talk about it. It's a weapon I've actually fired. So I guess there's a significance there.

One element strongly evident in the narratives of the three Kokoda Trail guides is their awareness of the trek's emotional impact, not just on trekkers but also on themselves:

> I get groups in tears, and I've got tears pouring down my face. You know, I'm emotional about it now. It's a very emotional place (Neville).

All three Kokoda guides are self-aware about their emotional engagement and manipulate the affective component of their treks by using rituals to choreograph clients' experiences. Alan understands that this adds to the memorability of the experience:

> I use a lot of poetry. You first do a factual briefing at a site, what happened there, different people that were involved. But I'll always finish with a poem. You'll suddenly notice a group . . . there's tears running down the faces . . .
>   They will forget what I said, they'll forget what I did, but they'll never forget how I made them feel.

In contrast, Jeff prefers to feel self-controlled at all times and is reluctant to display his emotions:

> Selfishly I try to do some things that I know will be enough for the people that I've got there to feel, to satisfy them, but not enough to upset me too much. It's a funny thing to say, but I want to make sure that their experience is good . . . and they're not worried about me being upset . . . We've got a series of poems, but we pick and choose which ones we want to use . . . I actually ask, 'Does anyone else want to read this?' So the group read them back and that works really well.

Alan also uses the emotional engagement of trekkers to motivate their physical performance:

> Every trip I carry dog tags from diggers who fought on the track, and after about two to three days I might, if someone's struggling, I might ask them 'would you like to wear this dog tag?' And suddenly someone who was close to finishing will go 'wow, I can keep going'.

The most overt claim regarding the personal transformation of clients was made by Alan, who said in response to a question about what he likes about his job, 'you get to change people's lives'. What Alan counts as personal change is 'becoming a better person'. He encourages his clients to make contact with Kokoda veterans when they return home, to visit and talk with them. Alan also indicated that one of his goals is to have the Kokoda Trail recognised by Australians as the most important campaign of the Pacific theatre of World War II and to give it a status similar to that of the Gallipoli Campaign of World War I.

Alan clearly tries to mediate clients' experiences in order to stimulate emotional engagement, which he sees as making the experience more memorable. But he also encourages personal reflection and specific follow-up actions which can add a sense of meaning or purpose well after the trek has ended and may also help foster transformation.

*Mediating experience and facilitating life change on nature-based walks*

Nature-based walking guides interviewed for this study used less intense strategies of experience management than those evident on the Kokoda Trail. In broad terms, nature-based walking guides rely on clients' sense of immersion in the environment to generate memorable and potentially transformative experiences. Nevertheless, overt choreography of experience is often used, with pre-dawn treks to iconic peaks in order to watch the sun rise being popular. Peter explained how his guides are trained to foster a variety of experiences:

> We give the guides a bit of direction . . . I mean, for example, one of the things they do on day five of the walk, there's just a gorgeous patch of rainforest and there's some waterfalls, and most of the guides get the guests to split up and basically walk through that section on their own.

Peter explained that separating the walkers stops them from chatting idly and tends to create a greater sense of mindfulness at special places. On the other hand, Peter also recognises that social aspects of the guiding role are also vital, which is something he promotes during meals in the huts at night:

> It's a big priority of the guides to get the group to bond, not only because it just, it enhances the experience but it's going to make the job a hell of a lot easier as a guide too, if they all have fun, getting on really well together.

On his outback tours, Bill conducts a meditation session every morning, beginning just before dawn. He believes that focusing on the direct experience of the desert sights and sounds, and feeling the breeze that often precedes dawn, helps people to savour their experience and begin each day relaxed and positive. A ritual on these trips is that nobody speaks until after the meditation session has finished. Bill also encourages participants to use 'walking meditation' during the day:

> Rhythm and breathing are integral to meditation, and walking at a comfortable pace over an extended period of time can stimulate that kind of experience. The process of walking meditation is much the same as all meditation. It is about losing the sense of self, allowing the things you observe to pass by without conscious thought and without distracting your focus of awareness.

Dave is passionate about the national park and has an extensive knowledge of its geology, flora, fauna and history. He enjoys interacting with his clients and facilitating their cognitive awareness of the natural environment. Dave is also aware of the power of wilderness to affect people:

> Many people write to us to tell us about their experience – how it has been the best thing they have ever done.

In general, the nature-based walking guides seemed less intentional about mediating personal change in their clients. Dave believes that any such change comes from within the client:

> Sometimes people are searching for something, you know they are. Other times people don't even know they are looking for something, but they are open to things when they happen. They've got to be ready for it. You can't transform someone who isn't ready for it.

Xavier encourages reflection through creative writing, usually after his clients have been immersed in the environment and their own thoughts for many hours. He invites people to share some of their writing, but does not force this, as he says it is often the most private writing that is most powerful and important. Xavier spoke of personal transformation as being 'core business but not overt business' on his tours and claimed that it is not unusual for participants to make major life decisions at the end of his tours.

In terms of the second aim of this study, it appears that nature-based guides tend to focus on the intensity of experience (Ryan, 2002) as a key to fostering transformation. This contrasts with the Kokoda guides (particularly Alan and Neville) who seem more committed to the Kokoda experience having a meaning and a purpose.

### *Outcomes and benefits of being a guide*

Enjoyment and pleasure in what they do, place attachment and a sense of purpose and connection to something worthwhile are consistent themes associated with guides' feelings about their work. As a source of satisfaction for guides, the most prominent theme was helping others to experience or achieve something they find significant, which as indicated at the outset of this chapter is a definitive aspect of transformative tourism. Guiding also often generates positive feedback from clients, which is appreciated by all guides.

### *Outcomes and benefits of being a guide on the Kokoda Trail*

All three Kokoda guides expressed a strong personal connection with the Trail. Alan consciously aims to communicate this to others:

> I deeply love the place, and I want to pass on, in 10 days, that passion and that love of the place to other people.

For each of the Kokoda guides, there is also an important sense of achievement. For Neville, the achievement is often a vicarious one:

> I'm proud of myself . . . knowing that personally I've got this group through, seeing their joy when they come through those arches, especially ones where I know that it's very significant for family reasons. It's an experience they'll never forget. I've been a paramount part of that.

Jeff finds the leadership aspects of his guiding role particularly satisfying:

> I look forward to it every year. It's a milestone each year that I aim for . . . I still find it a really exciting thing, that I'm the leader. I've got responsibilities. So far . . . everyone has been really happy. And I've come away with this personal satisfaction because, you know, I can do this. . . No matter what else gets me down in my life, or whatever, I keep thinking back 'well shit, I did that thing: that's pretty impressive'.

In some ways, Neville sees being a Kokoda guide as the culmination of growth and development throughout his working life. It uses his knowledge and capacities, and it directs those personal strengths towards something he finds meaningful and worthwhile:

> I guess it's a fulfilment . . . I'm 60 in a couple of months' time. And I couldn't have done this job 10 years ago . . . I'm seeing this job as a culmination of things and my training and experiences and being mature and things that have all come together with this job.

Overall, there is a strong sense of satisfaction among the Kokoda guides interviewed, reflecting a belief that what they do is worthwhile for clients, for the local community and for the perpetuation of the memory of those involved in the Kokoda Campaign of World War II. Underlying this satisfaction is a belief in the significance of the Kokoda story and a personal commitment to the symbolic meanings it holds.

*Outcomes and benefits of being a guide on nature-based walks*

Nature-based walking guides also derive a sense of purpose and connection to something worthwhile from their work. Peter emphasises the importance of providing opportunities to people who otherwise wouldn't experience wilderness settings:

> We're able to give a higher level of service and a higher level of comfort, which in turn attracts a different clientele . . . a big part of our philosophy is the importance of getting those people that otherwise wouldn't get into the wilderness out there.

For Tanya, there is a special satisfaction in seeing her clients reach destinations they find challenging. Having climbed the highest peaks of most continents, Tanya feels she understands the importance of achievement and recognises her role in facilitating that:

> I try to imagine what it was like when I first got involved, and it was quite profound. So, you know, trying to really be a guide but also empathise with my trekkers' feelings and experiences. So you've got to be a guide at one level, but also you need to be at their level, where you're enjoying it and you're fascinated and it's scary and you're vulnerable and all that. But I love that; I just get so excited about it.

Tanya is also conscious of her wider support team and what they get out of her tours. She spoke at length about her Sherpa team in Nepal and what guiding means to them:

> The young guys on my support team are university students and it's great for them to interact with us, you know, me and the clients. Great to practice their English . . . It's great for their confidence and their maturity. They're only in their early 20s but they are lovely guys and they really grow and develop, especially with a good manager . . . who gives them responsibilities . . . They love it, and it's good money for them that helps them through their studies. Their families are incredibly proud of them.

While the nature-based walking guides interviewed for this study vary in the kinds of outcomes they seek, all demonstrate a sense of purpose and connection to something they feel is worthwhile and gain satisfaction from helping others achieve things they find significant.

In terms of the third aim of this study, guides clearly find their work satisfying and generally accept any stresses of working with clients as part of the overall challenge of their work. All guides also appreciate the positive feedback they receive from clients. Many encourage tour participants to provide testimonials that are then used on websites promoting future treks. Xavier in particular indicated that he valued clients' stories about their 'inner journeys' and felt that those, more than stories about the environment or the quality of the catering on his trips, showed that he was doing his job well. Testimonials may be an important way that future clients' expectations are shaped and appropriate market segments are selected.

## Discussion and conclusion

The findings of this study deepen our understanding of guiding roles and emotional labour in the context of LDW. With respect to the former, all guides interviewed for this study are clearly passionate about their work and are committed to enhancing the experience of their clients. They also see potential for LDW to help people make changes in their lives. Guides do this primarily by focusing on the experience management dimensions of their work. Tasks associated with tour management and destination/resource management, while necessary, are clearly insufficient for fostering transformative LDW experiences.

The work of Seligman (2002, 2011) is introduced here as a unifying thread that links the findings of the study's three aims: the motivations for becoming a LDW guide, the roles adopted by LDW guides and the positive impacts of guiding on LDW guides. For example, the Kokoda guides seem particularly committed to generating an emotional impact in their clients and forging connections to the war history of the area. Seligman's (2002) concepts of engagement and the meaningful life are evident here, and engagement in the facilitation of experience and meaning for clients clearly contributes to a sense of meaning for guides themselves. For participants in the current study, guiding long-distance walks seems to promote all three elements of what Seligman (2002) describes as *authentic happiness*: the pleasant life, the engaged life and the meaningful life. Importantly, it also offers opportunities to facilitate these elements in other people.

Guides interviewed in this study all demonstrated positive emotions about their work. For some, there was also a strong sense of achievement and to some extent the development of relationships with clients and with the local people who constitute their support teams. If, as Seligman (2011) has conjectured, positive emotion, engagement, relationships, meaning and achievement are the five key elements which promote flourishing, then these guides are enhancing their own well-being while potentially assisting their clients to do likewise.

Interestingly, while emotional labour is clearly evident in the narratives of all three Kokoda guides, a need to manage the resulting stress is really only evident in Jeff's strategy of asking clients to read poems rather than doing so himself. While all three Kokoda guides seem to share a set of values that are aligned with those expected by their operators, a degree of emotional dissonance is evident in Jeff. Theories such as emotional labour can help identify directions for future research, and further consideration of ways to enhance the capacities of guides to deal effectively with the emotional pressures of their work may be useful in guide training.

Alan's way of drawing out personal reflections and encouraging clients to process their experiences during their trek is reminiscent of the approach encouraged by Christie and Mason (2003). Alan also suggests specific tasks, such as finding Kokoda veterans in nursing homes and talking with them about their experiences, which extend engagement in the Kokoda story beyond the trek. This seems to be an intuitive response on Alan's part, but is also clearly something that can be taught to other guides. Alan also seems to address the embodied, cognitive and emotional (affective) domains of his clients, perhaps because of his background in the field of education and training. Again, these are skills and approaches that can usefully be taught to other guides.

Nature-based walking guides seem to share a set of values aligned to nature conservation so that any deep acting that might be required is essentially an expression of their own attitudes and beliefs. As reported elsewhere (Mackenzie & Kerr, 2013; Sharpe, 2005b), the effects of deep acting on guides' job satisfaction seem to be mostly positive. To the extent that this also enhances guides' sense of doing something meaningful and worthwhile (Seligman, 2002), it is likely to contribute to their overall well-being.

Positive psychology seems to be particularly valuable in providing the link between the motivations for becoming a guide, the benefits of guiding and the roles played by guides. Emotional labour seems to influence the strategies used by some guides, with deep acting being used by the Kokoda guides who are strongly committed to the meanings and values they associate with that setting. Consideration of the different spheres of a tour guide's roles has highlighted the centrality of experience management, particularly for facilitating life-changing experiences of clients and positive thoughts and feelings among guides about their work. These findings together with further research in this area may help inform the recruitment, selection, training and development and performance management and thus the job satisfaction and retention of tour guides.

For many guides, it seems that helping others to achieve their goals, to engage with a sense of meaning and to help them to grow and develop are important motivators for becoming a guide, as well as a source of significant satisfaction with their work. These guides appear to gain a sense of meaning in life out of influencing others, perhaps even transforming them in some deep sense, beyond ensuring they have a safe and pleasant trip. In doing this, they tend to draw on significant experiences which have enhanced meaning in their own lives.

# References

Ap, J., & Wong, K. K. F. (2001). Case study on tour guiding: Professionalism, issues and problems. *Tourism Management*, 22(5), 551–563.

Arnould, E. J., & Price, L. L. (1993). River magic: Extraordinary experience and the extended service encounter. *Journal of Consumer Research*, 20, 24–45.

Beedie, P. (2003). Mountain guiding and adventure tourism: Reflections on the choreography of the experience. *Leisure Studies*, 22, 147–167.

Black, R., & Weiler, B. (2015). Theoretical perspectives on tour guiding. In K. Bricker & H. Donohoe (Eds.), *Demystifying theories in tourism research* (pp. 31–45). London: CABI.

Boeiji, H. (2002). A purposeful approach to the Constant Comparative Method in the analysis of qualitative interviews. *Quality and Quantity*, 36(4), 391–409.

Chhetri, P., Arrowsmith, C., & Jackson, M. (2004). Determining hiking experiences in nature-based tourist destinations. *Tourism Management*, 25, 31–43.

Christie, M. F., & Mason, P. A. (2003). Transformative tour guiding: Training tour guides to be critically reflective practitioners. *Journal of Ecotourism*, 2(1), 1–16.

Cohen, E. (1985). The tourist guide: The origins, structure and dynamics of a role. *Annals of Tourism Research*, 12(1), 5–29.

Cortazzi, M. (1993). *Narrative analysis*. London: The Falmer Press.

Crust, L., Keegan, R., Piggott, D., & Swann, C. (2011). Walking the walk: A phenomenological study of long distance walking. *Journal of Applied Sport Psychology*, 23(3), 243–262.

den Breejen, L. (2007). The experiences of long distance walking: A case study of the West Highland Way in Scotland. *Tourism Management*, 28, 1417–1427.

Edensor, T. (2000). Walking in the British countryside: Reflexivity, embodied practices and ways to escape. *Body and Society*, 6(3–4), 81–106.

Hochschild, A. R. (1983). *The managed heart: Commercialization of human feeling.* Berkeley: University of California Press.

Kay, G., & Moxham, N. (1996). Paths for whom? Countryside access for recreational walking. *Leisure Studies*, 15, 171–183.

Labov, W., & Waletzky, J. (1966). Narrative analysis: Oral versions of personal experience. In J. Helm (Ed.), *Essays on the verbal and visual arts: Proceedings of the 1966 Annual Spring Meeting of the American Ethnological Society* (pp. 12–44). Seattle: University of Washington Press.

Lean, G. L. (2009). Transformative travel: Inspiring sustainability. In R. Bushell & P. Sheldon (Eds.), *Wellness tourism: Mind, body, spirit, place* (pp. 191–205). New York: Cognizant.

Mackenzie, S. H., & Kerr, J. H. (2013). Stress and emotions at work: An adventure tourism guide's experiences. *Tourism Management*, 36, 3–14.

Mills, A. S., & Butler, T. S. (2005). Flow experience among Appalachian Trail thru-hikers. In J. G. Peden & R. M. Schuster (Eds.), *Proceedings of the 2005 Northeastern Recreation Research symposium; Bolton Landing, NY*. Gen. Tech. Rep. NE-341 (pp. 366–370). Newtown Square, PA: U.S. Forest Service, Northeastern Research Station.

Morgan, A. D. (2010). Journeys into transformation: Travel to an 'Other' place as a vehicle for transformative learning. *Journal of Transformative Education*, 8(4), 246–268.

Pearce, P. L. (2011). *Tourist behaviour and the contemporary world.* Bristol: Channel View.

Pereira, E. M., & Mykletun, R. J. (2012). Guides as contributors to sustainable tourism? A case study from the Amazon. *Scandinavian Journal of Hospitality and Tourism*, 12(1), 74–94.

Quinlan Cutler, S., Carmichael, B., & Doherty, S. (2014). The Inca Trail experience: Does the journey matter? *Annals of Tourism Research*, 45(1), 152–166.

Reisinger, Y. (2013a). Connection between travel, tourism and transformation. In Y. Reisinger (Ed.), *Transformational tourism: Tourist perspectives* (pp. 27–32). Wallingford, UK: CABI Publishing.

Reisinger, Y. (2013b). *Transformational tourism: Tourist perspectives.* Wallingford, UK: CABI Publishing.

Rokeach, M. (1973). *The nature of human values.* New York: Free Press.

Ryan, C. (Ed.). (2002). *The tourist experience.* London: Continuum.

Saunders, R. E. (2013). Identity, meaning and tourism on the Kokoda Trail. In A. Norman (Ed.), *Journeys and destinations: Studies in travel, identity, and meaning* (pp. 23–45). Newcastle upon Tyne: Cambridge Scholars Publishing.

Saunders, R. E. (2014). *Steps towards change: Personal transformation through long-distance walking.* PhD thesis. Melbourne, VIC: Monash University.

Saunders, R. E., Laing, J., & Weiler, B. (2014). Personal transformation through long-distance walking. In S. Filep & P. Pearce (Eds.), *Tourist experience and fulfilment: Insights from positive psychology* (pp. 127–146). London: Routledge.

Seligman, M. E. P. (2002). *Authentic happiness: Using the new Positive Psychology to realize your potential for lasting fulfillment.* New York: Free Press.

Seligman, M. E. P. (2011). *Flourish: A visionary new understanding of happiness and well-being.* New York: Free Press.

Sharpe, E. K. (2005a). Delivering communitas: Wilderness adventure and the making of community. *Journal of Leisure Research*, 37(3), 255–280.

Sharpe, E. K. (2005b). Going above and beyond: The emotional labor of adventure guides. *Journal of Leisure Research*, 37(1), 29–50.

Slavin, S. (2003). Walking as spiritual practice: The pilgrimage to Santiago de Compostela. *Body & Society*, 9(3), 1–18.

Smith, J. A., Flowers, P., & Larkin, M. (2009). *Interpretative phenomenological analysis*. Los Angeles: Sage Publications.

Torland, M. (2011). Effects of emotional labor on adventure tour leaders' job satisfaction. *Tourism Review International*, 14, 129–142.

Tung, V. W. S., & Ritchie, J. R. B. (2011). Exploring the essence of memorable tourism experiences. *Annals of Tourism Research*, 38(4), 1367–1386.

Wang, N. (1999). Rethinking authenticity in tourism experience. *Annals of Tourism Research*, 26(2), 349–370.

Weiler, B., & Black, R. (2015). *Tour guiding research: Insights, issues and implications*. Bristol: Channel View.

Weiler, B., & Davis, D. (1993). An exploratory investigation into the roles of the nature-based tour leaders. *Tourism Management*, April, 14(2), 91–98.

# 12 Co-creation and experience brokering in guided adventure tours

*Susan Houge Mackenzie and John Kerr*

## Introduction

Tour guiding has changed considerably in recent decades. Traditional tour guiding, which primarily focuses on helping clients understand destinations, is evolving towards 'co-created' tours that also require guides to facilitate intragroup or intrapersonal experiences (Weiler & Black, 2015a, b). Co-creation models of tour guiding highlight the immense potential for guides to enhance, or detract from, tourists' experiences depending on how they 'broker' physical access and encounters. For example, guides can broker physical access to local culture through site selection and group movements, as well as through local food, stories and music choices (Weiler & Yu, 2007). Guides also broker local cultural understandings by translating language and interpreting behaviours (Scherle & Nonnenmann, 2008). In addition, the way in which guides choreograph tours (Beedie, 2003) may broker empathy for local peoples, cultures and natural environments.

Co-creation models of tour guiding propose that guide and tourist experiences are interwoven and therefore cannot be examined independently. Recent literature suggests that, rather than evaluating tourist and tour guide experiences independently, reimagining guided tours as co-created and interdependent may be increasingly relevant and practical (e.g. Beedie, 2003; Weiler & Black, 2015b). In addition, Weiler and Black (2015a) argue that current social trends, such as the demand for more engaging, personalised and meaningful experiences and technological trends, such as increased use of information technologies to facilitate tourist experiences, are changing the role of tour guides in the twenty-first century. These authors outline how guides now act as 'experience brokers' across four domains (i.e. physical access, encounters, understanding and empathy) and emphasise the need for guides to be flexible towards diverse tourists with unique expectations. In contrast to traditional guided tours in which (a) guides are primarily in control, (b) tourists act as passive recipients of information and (c) the focus is on enjoyment, co-created tours require shared control, customised communications and focus on creating enjoyable *and* meaningful tourism experiences (Weiler & Black, 2015a; see Table 12.1). This model appears particularly useful for examining guided adventure tours that offer greater opportunities for guide-client interactions and customisation. Typical target markets for co-created tours

*Table 12.1* A typology of guided tours, tour guiding communications and tourist outcomes (adapted from Weiler & Black, 2015a)

| Type of guided tour | How tour group is perceived by guide | How guide is perceived by tour group | Guide's communication style | Tourist outcomes |
|---|---|---|---|---|
| Traditional | Audience (passive and reactive) | Entertainer/ presenter (guide control) | Commentary/ script | Enjoyable |
| Experience-focused | Actors (passive or active) | Choreographer (guide control) | Experience brokering: *encounters, understanding, empathy* | Enjoyable, memorable |
| Customised/ personalised | Co-creators (pro-active) | Co-creator (shared control) | Variable: *Customised to groups, individuals and contexts* | Enjoyable, memorable, meaningful |

include 'millennials' (born circa 1980–2000, Strauss & Howe, 2000) and environmentally responsible and pro-active travellers (Weiler & Black, 2015a). Given the symbiotic nature of co-created tours, effective experience brokering also holds the potential to foster optimal experiences for tour guides as well as tourists.

Despite the potential for effectively brokered co-created tours to foster enjoyment and meaning for guides and clients alike, work-related stressors amongst tourism workers may undermine the success of these initiatives. For instance, emotional, aesthetic and performative labour result from social expectations regarding appropriate emotional expression, aesthetic presentation and performative aspects of guiding work (e.g. Hochschild, 1983; Witz, Warhurst & Nickson, 2003). Studies indicate that emotional labour may be more prevalent for frontline tourism workers generally, and adventure guides specifically, because of unique service demands and diverse interpersonal interactions (e.g. Arnould, Price & Otnes, 1999; Constanti & Gibbs, 2005; Guerrier & Adib, 2003; Holyfield, 1999; Sharpe, 2005; Zapf, 2002). Adventure workers' demanding lifestyles and intensive co-worker interactions can negatively affect interpersonal relationships, work-related anxiety, burnout and turnover (e.g. Houge Mackenzie & Kerr, 2013b; Marchland, Russell & Cross, 2009). Moreover, clients often expect adventure guides to display a narrow range of positive emotions (Buckley, 2010; Jonas, 1999), while suppressing feelings such as anger, fear, boredom or aggression. These expectations, coupled with heightened risks in adventure settings, may exacerbate stress and negative emotions for adventure guides (e.g. Houge Mackenzie & Kerr, 2013c, 2014). In light of these findings, and the well-documented negative effects of emotional labour and stress on employees' well-being generally (e.g. Brotheridge & Grandey, 2002; Erickson & Wharton, 1997; Liu, Perrewe, Hochwarter & Kacmar, 2004; Lv, Shi & Hui, 2012; Pugliesi, 1999; Zapf & Holz, 2006), understanding the factors that facilitate (or detract from) successfully co-created tours and brokering may optimise guide and client experiences.

As co-creation models emphasise *enjoyment* and *meaning* as defining characteristics, this investigation drew upon psychology frameworks related to optimal experiences and motivation (i.e. self-determination theory and reversal theory) to analyse elements that either enhanced or detracted from co-created adventure tour experiences across each of the 'experience-brokering' domains proposed by Weiler and Black (2015a). Their four domains of *physical access, encounters, understanding* and *empathy* were evaluated on one of the world's most popular guided adventure tours: the Inca Trail in Peru. Two psychological theories were applied throughout data analysis to identify potential features of effective (or ineffective) experience brokering. The following section will briefly outline these psychological theories and explain their relevance to co-created guided adventure tourism experiences.

## Review of psychological literature

Self-determination theory (SDT) is a 'meta' theory with a number of sub-theories that identify links between different types of motivation and optimal experiences. Amongst other things, SDT outlines social and cultural factors that facilitate or undermine individual well-being and quality of experience and functioning (Ryan & Deci, 2000). Basic psychological needs theory, the SDT sub-theory applied in the current study, proposes that humans have innate psychological needs for *autonomy, competence* and *relatedness*. The degree to which these three psychological needs are supported or thwarted has been found to significantly impact key aspects of well-being and optimal functioning, such as sustained motivation, optimal engagement, performance and creativity (Deci & Ryan, 2012). Notwithstanding robust empirical support for SDT across many domains, including education, health, sustainability, leisure and business (see Deci & Ryan, 2012 for review), this theory is largely absent from tourism studies. Given the potential for SDT to improve our understanding of tourists' and guides' behaviours, motivations and experiences, the authors applied this theory to (a) enhance theoretical bases for data analysis and (b) provide practical recommendations for improving co-created adventure tourism experiences.

Another psychological theory that has only recently been applied to explain optimal adventure experiences is reversal theory (RT) (Houge Mackenzie, Hodge & Boyes, 2011, 2013; Houge Mackenzie & Kerr, 2013a, c). RT provides insights regarding dynamic motivational and emotional states associated with optimal, or non-optimal, experiences. For example, Houge Mackenzie *et al.* (2013) analysed phases of motivations and emotions during adventure recreation experiences from a RT perspective in order to better predict antecedents of optimal experiences. Briefly, RT explains the structure of experience and resulting emotions by identifying opposing pairs of motivational states. It proposes that an individual's current frame of mind (i.e. *meta*motivational state) dictates how they interpret somatic feelings and interpersonal transactions (Apter, 2001) and thereby can be used to predict emotional experiences.

Reversal theory posits that four pairs of opposing motivational states influence our felt emotions. Table 12.2 outlines the key characteristics of each state. In the

*Table 12.2* Opposing motivational state pairs in reversal theory (adapted from Houge Mackenzie & Kerr, 2013c)

| Telic: *serious, outcome-oriented, arousal-avoidant* | Paratelic: *playful, process-oriented, arousal-seeking* |
|---|---|
| Conformist: *rule-abiding* | Negativistic: *rebellious* |
| Mastery: *domination-oriented* | Sympathy: *relationship-oriented* |
| Autic: *self-focused, concern for self* | Alloic: *other-focused, concern for others* |

*telic state*, a person feels serious, goal oriented and arousal avoidant, while feeling spontaneous, playful and arousal-seeking in the opposing *paratelic state*. In the *conformist state*, a person feels compliant and agreeable, while feeling rebellious, unconventional and defiant in the opposing *negativistic state*. A person in the *mastery state* is competitive and dominating, while desiring harmony and cooperation in the *sympathy state*. A person in the *autic state* is egoistic and concerned with the self, while feeling altruistic and concerned with others in the *alloic state*. Regular *reversals* between these paired motivational states are predicted to produce significant changes in a person's motivations and emotional experiences. RT has been developed across a range of disciplines, including sport, exercise and adventure recreation (Apter, 1992; Chirivella & Martinez, 1994; Cogan & Brown, 1999; Pain & Kerr, 2004), but it has rarely been applied in tourism.

In summary, the current investigation drew upon SDT and RT constructs to evaluate co-created adventure tourism experiences across Weiler and Black's (2015a) four key domains: physical access, encounters, understanding and empathy. This approach incorporated both *static* (i.e. enduring psychological needs) and *dynamic* (i.e. fluctuating motivational states and reversals) motivational perspectives to evaluate factors that contributed to, or detracted from, optimal co-created adventure tourism experiences. Identifying these factors was intended to yield practical recommendations for enhancing tourist and guide experiences.

## Method

Tour guiding in Cusco, the gateway to Machu Picchu, has previously garnered the attention of tourism scholars in relation to interpretation and training issues. McGrath (2007), for example, identified the need for guides in this region to move beyond the transmission of facts to focus on fostering positive affective states that promote mindfulness and meaning amongst visitors. The current investigation evaluated the impact of tour guiding approaches on clients' affective states and psychological experiences during a four-day 50 mile/75 kilometre guided trek through the Andes Mountains in southern Peru. The trek followed the Inca Trail from Cusco to Machu Picchu. These ruins are a United Nations Educational,

Scientific and Cultural Organization World Heritage site and Peru's most visited tourist destination. Trek highlights include overlooking Machu Picchu from the Sun Gate at dawn and from Huayna Picchu, a peak above the ruins.

In order to identify key affective states as they unfolded during the tour, the first author and autoethnographer (AE) participated in this adventure trek as a tourist and participant observer. She was accompanied by her partner and a mutual friend who provided additional insights into psychological effects of tour guiding approaches. During the trek, autoethnographical data was privately recorded daily. Data consisted of diary entries, field notes and experiential diagrams that visually summarised key events and accompanying motivational and emotional changes. The AE's experience in psychological research, outdoor activities, adventure guiding and Spanish language provided an opportunity to act as an informed participant observer and prospectively document key aspects of tour guiding that enhanced or detracted from co-created adventure tourism experiences.

This methodological approach was replicated from a study of motivational and emotional patterns during a multi-day mountaineering tourism climb (Houge Mackenzie & Kerr, 2012), which demonstrated the unique perspectives and insights provided through autoethnographical analyses of tourism experiences. A central distinction between autoethnography and traditional methodologies is that researcher biases and reflexivity are openly acknowledged and discussed in autoethnography. In contrast to ethnography, in which researchers attempt to become insiders, autoethnographers are insiders who provide unique insights into personal and emotional life-worlds (Ateljevic, Pritchard & Morgan, 2007). Despite the unique perspectives that autoethnography can yield, scholars continue to debate acceptable methodologies within this form of inquiry as well as appropriate evaluation criteria and ethical issues (e.g. Anderson & Austin, 2012; Tolich, 2010). Autoethnographical data is informed by the AE's past experiences and cultural values and thus is inherently limited due to its situated and constructed nature (Houge Mackenzie & Kerr, 2013c). Despite the critiques and limitations of this approach, critical literature and tourism studies have demonstrated the effectiveness of this methodology in advancing knowledge of tourist behaviour (e.g. Beedie, 2003; Buckley, 2012; Hall, 2004; Jonas, Stewart & Larkin, 2003).

Anderson's (2006) autoethnographical research guidelines and qualitative analysis protocols (Denzin & Lincoln, 2005) were followed to ensure the integrity of the data collection, analysis and interpretation. In line with analytical autoethnography approaches (Anderson, 2006), concepts from SDT (e.g. Deci & Ryan, 2012) and RT (Apter, 2001) were used to interpret the AE's psychological experience during the trek. Following psychological data analysis, guides' experience-brokering effectiveness was assessed across Weiler and Black's (2015a) four domains: physical access, understanding, encounters and empathy.

In order to better situate the reader within the AE's dynamic psychological experiences, the results and discussion section begins with chronological first-person diary excerpts. Following a brief narration of the diary material, theoretical data interpretations in relation to RT and SDT psychological constructs are provided.

The section concludes with an evaluation of experience brokering across Weiler and Black's (2015a) domains.

## Results and discussion

### *Diary data excerpts*

Evening prior to departure:

- *Annoyed with guides/company . . . Problems accepting payment . . . Staff were unhelpful/patronising.*
- *I started to wonder if this trip was a big rip-off – too expensive for what they were offering? Would it just be like Disneyland?*
- *We were not placed in the same group as our mates as requested. Instead put into a group who* [appeared to be] *slow/unfit.*

Day 1 morning (bus trip and start of trek):

- *Very early AM pick up and had to drive all around Cusco . . . felt like time was being wasted unnecessarily.*
- *Felt ripped off – the breakfast was not included. Instead you were taken to a town where you had to buy breakfast from one of the 'tourist' shops there . . . More or less forced to eat in 'their' restaurant . . . there were A LOT of people there.*
- *Negative interactions with other tourists . . . Example: other tourists not waiting in line to enter the trail.*
- *Frequent stops on the way up to the first camp . . . We wanted to keep going.*
- *Felt very frustrated that we had to keep stopping and waiting for slower members and getting held up by slower groups in front of us as well.*
- *Just wanted to get out away from people and walk on my own on the trail.*

Day 1 afternoon/evening (first camp):

- *Played football with the guides and locals – we won . . . felt bonded to other players . . . Our guide Estefan[1] was pretty excited.*
- *Great dinner and food. Felt very happy socialising and eating*

Day 2 (trekking and second camp):

- *Just wanted to get there . . . to the top of the biggest climb.*
- *Bored when waiting around at stops . . . listening to commentary.*
- *Did not want to be a part of group/socialise. Enjoyed most walking down alone from the summit after passing the big groups of people and the sun came out and sky cleared a bit more.*
- *A bit bored waiting at camp for others to finish hiking.*
- *The second night was in a beautiful valley . . . The food was amazing.*
- *Felt serene and happy to explore on my own a bit that evening as moon came out. We taught the porters to play the card game Uno.*

Day 3 (trekking and third camp):

- *Enjoyed the walk . . . got away from the group a bit . . . fantastic lunch.*

- *Felt we had to rush down a bit to get in front of people so we wouldn't be stuck behind them again.*
- *Lots of steps to go down . . . very physically uncomfortable.*
- *Feelings of guilt as the porters carrying massive packs went flying past us in an effort to set it* [the evening camp] *all up for us . . .* [they had] *poor footwear.*
- *Felt not right that* [the porters] *seemed almost like second-class citizens, despite the fact that they supposedly got paid well and our company focused a lot on porter welfare and protection . . . made me feel uncomfortable . . . this relationship.*
- [This evening] *we listened to all the porters tell their stories and had to decide how much we wanted to tip them. So that was a very uncomfortable process of deciding* [on a tip] *with 20 other people.*
- *Very put off by the campsite for night three . . . commercialised 'bar' area, loud music, power lines running through hills, etc.*

Day 4 (arrival to Machu Picchu through Sun Gate):
- *Up at 3 a.m. and waited in line until 5:30 a.m. in the rain* [without shelter].
- *We literally ran to Machu Picchu* [due to poor weather and to avoid crowds].
- *I couldn't see anything at first when we got there. Only our second day of rain in South America and it was the day we came through the Sun Gate in the morning to gaze down at Machu Picchu.*
- *We ran to* [get ticketed access to] *Huayna Picchu, which is the huge steep climb straight up a mountain with very slippery steps . . . no one else in our group did it.*
- [After driving down from Machu Picchu into town we felt] *angry we had to wait for seven hours in town for the bus without any food provided.*
- [I felt] *'Negativistic'* [reversal theory transactional state] *when trying to enter a restaurant that wanted to charge us just to enter.*
- *Very annoyed at the mandatory tipping issue . . . I didn't want to be told how much and who to tip – that should be my decision . . . tips were an issue.*
- [I felt] *'self-focused'* ['autic' reversal theory transactional state] *when waiting in line for ages.*

As evidenced in the diary excerpts, pre-trek interactions with the adventure company and guides were disappointing. Several administrative and organisational difficulties led the AE to experience negative hedonic tone (e.g. frustration). These included lack of available payment methods and clients' concerns that they were being overcharged. The guides' unpleasant attitudes during these interactions heightened the AE's negative feelings. Ignored requests to trek in a group with friends of similar trekking ability also fostered a negative affective state prior to trip departure. The AE and her two companions were assigned to a large group consisting of 17 friends travelling overseas together who appeared to lack trekking experience and physical fitness.

The AE's frustration and negative affective state continued during the first morning of the trek. During the pre-dawn pickup, she was excited to begin the trek. However, her excitement waned after travel delays due to numerous pickups of trekkers in other groups joining the large bus, followed by a mandatory stop in a different town for breakfast. The previously undisclosed breakfast stop accompanied by, what the AE and companions perceived to be, an inflated fee increased her negative affect and feelings of rebelliousness. Many hours after the initial pickup, they arrived at the Inca Trail entry, where the volume of tourists waiting to enter and guides' disorganisation surprised her. The abundance of visitors coupled with guides' lack of instructions led to unpleasant interactions with other tourists. Once the AE's group entered the trail, slower groups in front and guides' mandatory 'catch up' stops for slower group members intensified the AE's feelings of frustration and resentment.

At the start of day two, the AE was highly goal oriented in terms of wanting to trek briskly and in relative solitude. Therefore, anything that inhibited her progress resulted in negative feelings, such as boredom. Conversely, she enjoyed the freedom to walk ahead of the larger crowds and experience some of the trail in quiet reflection. These pleasant feelings continued into the evening of day two when she appreciated the beautiful location of the campsite and the provision of ample free time for moonlit exploration of the area. Although it appeared unplanned, there were also enjoyable opportunities for social interactions and games with the guides and porters.

The day three trail section was very physically demanding. Notwithstanding, the AE continued to experience pleasant affective states because she was allowed to walk ahead of large groups and set her own pace. The physically challenging nature of this segment also initiated a shift from her self-focused, goal-oriented mental state to an 'other-oriented' 'sympathetic' state in relation to the porters. The AE reported feeling guilty about how hard the porters were working, with seemingly insufficient footwear and equipment for carrying large packs for tourists. Although she had selected the trekking company based on their porter welfare policy that described fair pay and work conditions, she experienced negative feelings when confronted by the reality of the porters' situation. Ironically, in the evening of day three, her unpleasant feelings stemmed from the manner in which the guide choreographed a lengthy meeting designed to elicit sympathy for porters, which culminated in a group debate regarding how much to tip the porters. In addition to these interpersonal interactions, the commercialised camp environment detracted from the AE's positive experiences on the third trekking day.

According to the AE's guide, Estefan, arriving above the Machu Picchu ruins on day four through the Sun Gate at sunrise was the Inca Trail highlight. However, day four was cloudy and rainy. Although the Machu Picchu visit data were characterised by neutral or positive affect in comparison to earlier entries, the highly anticipated Sun Gate experience did not meet the AE's expectations. Factors that appeared to detract from a more positive or meaningful experience included a long pre-dawn wait in the rain to enter the trail, lack of visibility and encounters with tourists who had arrived at the Sun Gate earlier by taking a pre-dawn bus to the site. Conversely, the AE's narrative of her challenging climb up Huayna Picchu suggested a sense of pride at accomplishing something few others completed. After touring Machu Picchu, she descended by bus into the nearest town to wait for the evening train to Cusco. Her diary excerpts after leaving Machu Picchu reflected negative affective states, which contrasted starkly with her earlier affective experiences. For example, in a local restaurant, she reported feelings of rebelliousness and anger in response to staff-imposed food and beverage selections, mandatory spend per person and the prescribed gratuity.

*Theoretical interpretations: self-determination theory and reversal theory*

As outlined in the introduction, self-determination theory proposes that experiences are optimised when basic psychological needs (BPN) for autonomy, competence and relatedness are fulfilled. Autonomy-supportive environments in particular are related to a range of positive outcomes, such as enhanced learning, engagement and enjoyment (e.g. Deci & Ryan, 2012). Reversal theory constructs explain how rapid shifts, or 'reversals', in emotions and hedonic tone can occur due to motivational state changes. In reversal theory, these changes are triggered by *environmental events, frustration or satiation* (e.g. Apter, 2001).

The AE's diary data demonstrate several instances in which BPN fulfilment, or thwarting, and motivational state reversals directly influenced her affective experience throughout the four-day trek. For example, on day one, her goal-oriented, serious (telic-conformist) motivation reflected a desire to begin the trek at the start of the day and travel at her own brisk pace. As her needs for autonomy (e.g. personal choice) and competence (e.g. goal attainment) were thwarted, she underwent a motivational reversal to serious and rebellious (telic-negativistic) states that resulted in negative hedonic tone. As she continued trekking on day one, she remained self-focused and unconcerned about other trekkers, while seeking solitude and freedom to hike at her own pace (autic-mastery: 'just wanted to get out away from people and walk on my own on the trail').

The AE's psychological states at camp one in the afternoon directly contrasted with her morning experiences on the trail. Her motivational experience greatly improved as a result of reversing to the playfully competitive (mastery) state accompanied by heightened arousal during the football game ('played football [soccer] with the guides and locals – we won!'). This experience fulfilled BPN for competence and relatedness and brought about several reversals. First, she reversed from a serious (telic) to playful (paratelic) state and reported positive social interactions ('felt bonded to other players . . . felt very happy socialising and eating'). These data suggested reversals from the self-focused (autic and mastery) states she experienced during the trek, to pleasant other-focused and relationship-oriented (alloic and sympathy) states evidenced by feelings of camaraderie following the game. These data highlighted the positive affective states she experienced as a result of (a) BPN fulfilment and (b) reversals precipitated by engaging, meaningful interpersonal interactions.

Further motivational reversals were evident in day three data. As was typical for the AE while trekking, she reported serious, goal-oriented (telic), self-focused (mastery) states. Despite the physical challenges of this section, feelings of satisfaction and enjoyment stemmed from the freedom to trek unhindered, which fulfilled BPN for autonomy and competence ('enjoyed the walk . . . got away from the group a bit'). However, as she observed porters at work during the trek, negative affect emerged. Feelings of guilt due to her perception that porters were being overworked for the benefit of tourists ('guilt at the porters carrying massive packs and flying past us in an effort to set it all up for us . . . felt not right, they seemed almost like second-class citizens') suggested reversals from self-focused (autic) to other-focused (alloic) states and from mastery to sympathy states, resulting in an unpleasant motivational experience. In reversal theory, guilt is an unpleasant emotion associated with the other-oriented (alloic) and sympathy states. This negative experience may have also resulted from a thwarted need for relatedness.

Day four data revealed a significant change in the AE's hedonic tone due to a reversal from the conformist to the serious (telic) state after climbing Huayna Picchu. The climb was a positive psychological experience that fulfilled all three BPN, but after the bus trip to the base town followed by a seven-hour wait for the Cusco train, she became angry ('angry we had to wait for seven hours in town for the train without any food provided'). Anger, and potential feelings of resentment, were directed toward the tour company and guide, which also negatively affected interactions with restaurant staff regarding mandatory cover charges and gratuities ('felt like I didn't want to be told how much and who to tip – that should be my decision'). In reversal theory, anger is an emotion related to the serious (telic) and negativistic states with accompanying levels of high arousal. The AE's thwarted need for autonomy and reversals to the telic and negativistic states lead to the tour concluding with an unpleasant affective experience.

Reversal theory and self-determination theory may synergistically explain how to maximise positive psychological experiences and minimise negative ones. While SDT provides a 'macro-level' explanation of how BPN fulfilment can enhance experiences, reversal theory analyses provide dynamic 'micro-level' explanations of how adventure experiences can be optimised by either (a) preventing reversals to states associated with negative hedonic tone or (b) facilitating reversals to states associated with positive hedonic tone. In adventure contexts, for instance, high arousal levels are associated with excitement in the playful *paratelic* state, whereas high arousal leads to anxiety in the serious *telic* state. SDT and RT analyses also highlighted avenues for improving tour guiding practices. For example, in the present case, analyses indicated that eliminating long waits prior to and during the trek and providing more freedom of choice with regard to (a) personal challenges, (b) pacing, (c) walking companions and (d) gratuity decisions may have decreased reversals to negative affective states and improved the AE's overall psychological experience considerably. In the following section, data analyses focus specifically on guides' experience-brokering practices and outcomes.

*Brokering adventure tourism experiences*

In addition to identifying psychological aspects of optimal adventure tour experiences, investigators evaluated Weiler and Black's (2015a) domains of experience brokering in a co-created adventure tour. As optimal tour experiences hinge upon successful brokering, Inca Trail tour guides' effectiveness in brokering physical access, encounters and understanding was examined (Weiler & Black, 2015a). Although these brokering domains inherently overlap, they are discussed separately for clarity.

*Brokering physical access*

Tour guides broker physical access to important sites by organising and controlling tourist groups. The AE's diary excerpts show repeated frustration at being 'held up' by slower trekkers, or having to wait for slower trekkers in her group to catch up. The issue may have stemmed from management-level decisions to form large tour groups with varying abilities and fitness levels, or ignorance of participant abilities. To improve this aspect of experience brokering, tour companies and guides could obtain basic information regarding clients' fitness, abilities, previous experience and desired pacing. Collecting more client information, either verbally or through registration questions, would allow guides to customise tours and thereby optimise client experiences. For instance, grouping trekkers of comparable ability levels seeking similar challenges and pacing could decrease frustrations for both quicker and slower walkers. In addition, 'staggered' start times based on estimated pace could also enhance group cohesiveness and positive experiences by reducing frustrations from encounters with other groups. This approach could also prevent slower groups from feeling pressured by faster trekkers seeking to pass them.

A key element of physical access brokering on the Inca Trail is arrival to Machu Picchu through the Sun Gate at dawn. Guides make this experience as memorable as possible through careful choreography and clear efforts to successfully broker physical access to the Sun Gate (i.e. having the group queue up from 3:00 to 5:30 a.m. to ensure clients could enter the trail upon opening). Data suggested that this brokering strategy, along with rain obscuring the much-anticipated view, detracted from the culminating experience. Although weather conditions are beyond guides' control, brokering could be refined through enhanced timing and departure arrangements and/or providing shelter. For example, visitors' experiences might be enhanced if guides issued morning departure tickets (on a rotational basis amongst companies) and/or set up tarpaulins or temporary protection from wind and rain.

*Brokering encounters*

Weiler and Black (2015a, b) draw on a range of empirical studies to highlight the importance of guides brokering social interactions between tourists and host communities. In the current study, two examples of successful social brokering were identified: (1) the football game staged on day one (evening) with guides and locals and (2) playing cards with porters on day two (evening). These activities, which appeared to foster optimal experiences for both tourists and locals, embodied the concept of co-creation insofar as guides and clients played equally active roles in shaping these opportunities. Data also highlighted unsuccessfully brokered social encounters wherein the AE felt uncomfortable or taken advantage of during the trek. It is noteworthy that data from negative social interactions lacked the key co-creation elements (e.g. active, meaningful engagement) that fostered successful encounters.

Negotiating clear economic arrangements and providing sufficient information and perceived choices in advance of a tour may help guides improve social brokering. For instance, negotiating flat-rate service charges with hosts (e.g. restaurant or shop owners) and educating tourists in advance of these arrangements might ensure tourists and hosts have shared expectations and understandings. This brokering would maintain minimum spend levels for local businesses, while avoiding negative emotions due to unexpected fees and uncomfortable social encounters. Guides could use a similar approach to broker intragroup and porter interactions. For instance, building gratuities for porters and guides into the total trip price might be more effective than asking 20 diverse people to determine an appropriate gratuity while camping. These brokering approaches might benefit guides, porters and tourists by avoiding unnecessary awkwardness and anxiety on tour.

Despite the absence of research on 'within-tour mediation' (Weiler & Black, 2015a, p. 366), data analysis reinforced Weiler and Black's (2015a) contention that guides' roles include mediating intragroup encounters. In the current study, this was evidenced by the AE's lack of meaningful connection with other group members (aside from her two travelling companions) throughout the trip. The tour company or guides may have missed an opportunity to broker positive intragroup social encounters by (a) assigning friends to different trekking groups and (b) not offering more intragroup and interpersonal social activities. Intentionally brokering positive, meaningful interactions amongst group members in a pre-trek meeting or at the outset may optimise intragroup experiences during the trek. Intragroup encounters could also be effectively brokered through thoughtful group creation that considers trekkers' requests and tourists' diversity. Carefully considering diverse cultural norms and perspectives may improve group dynamics. Guides could also enhance social brokering by scheduling time for co-created (e.g. less structured, informal, playful) activities amongst tourists, guides, porters and locals.

### Brokering cultural understanding

Tour guides are ideally positioned to broker cultural understanding (Weiler & Black, 2015a, b). Although Estefan (the AE's primary guide) was multilingual, had friendly rapport with locals and provided informed historical interpretations, data lacked evidence of effective cultural brokering. These data directly contrasted with findings from a similar investigation by the authors (Houge Mackenzie & Kerr, 2016). Their Colca Canyon study illustrated how guides can effectively broker many opportunities for trekkers to personally engage with local people and understand local culture in a meaningful way. The AE in that study reported highly positive affect resulting from friendly, authentic encounters with local hosts during daily dinner preparations and a one-room museum visit. These co-created sociocultural interactions allowed the AE to experience local customs, values, and behaviours first-hand, which optimised her psychological experiences. In contrast, the current study exemplified Weiler and Black (2015a, b)'s concern that guides may unwittingly inhibit cultural understanding by failing to broker sufficient opportunities for meaningful cultural understandings and/or by providing insufficient contextual information.

*Brokering empathy*

This form of brokering is conceptually less developed than the previous three (Weiler & Black, 2015a). Essentially, guides can broker empathy amongst tourists as well as host communities. In day three data, the AE expressed guilt and sympathy for porters due to their job demands. These feelings resulted from witnessing them rush ahead over challenging terrain to set up camp while carrying large loads with poor footwear. Although it was surprising to find that her empathy did not resurface during the evening gratuity discussion, data indicated this might have been due to how guides conducted this meeting. Despite the empathy evoked 'organically' for porters during the trip through unchoreographed interactions, there are a number of reasons guides may have ineffectively brokered empathy in structured contexts.

On evening three, before asking the group to determine an appropriate gratuity, guides asked every porter (approximately 20) to speak. While storytelling has great potential to broker empathy, the meeting length coupled with porters' scripted, factual speeches and obvious discomfort hindered meaningful engagement and empathy. Arguably, one way guides could enhance empathy brokering in this context would be to help porters craft and deliver effective, personalised stories and to improve both tourists' and porters' language skills. Small changes in meeting choreography might also improve empathy brokering. For example, breaking trekkers and porters into smaller informal groups with translators may have facilitated more meaningful co-created experiences for everyone. Smaller groups can enhance rapport and facilitate personalised encounters. In addition, providing leadership or structure to the large group debate regarding gratuities could enhance tourists' experiences. As suggested earlier, setting a flat-rate service charge for porters might negate this issue.

It is important to note that although these strategies may enhance *tourist* experiences, they may not necessarily enhance *porter* experiences. In addition to the discomfort associated with addressing a large group in a second language, porters may have also found this approach to personal storytelling demeaning, particularly when linked to gratuities. Thus the most effective way to improve empathy brokering may be for guides to first consult the host community (or in this case the porters) regarding their desired processes and outcomes. Respecting the self-determination of host communities through consultation and inclusion should be a primary priority for operators of co-created tours. This approach will enhance empathy brokering processes and benefits for both tourists and hosts.

Effectively brokered encounters, such as the evening meeting with porters, have immense potential to broker cultural understanding and empathy between tourists and hosts. However, successful brokering requires that the motives for these encounters extend beyond economics. Rather, guides should strive to foster meaningful social interactions and empathy using processes that maintain the integrity and dignity of host communities. Successfully brokering these encounters may help optimise tourism experiences not only for individual tourists but also for guides, other trekkers, porters and the host community.

## Conclusion

Tour guiding is changing rapidly in response to tourist demands for unique, customised experiences that provide meaning and enjoyment for participants (Weiler & Black, 2015a, b). Adventure guides not only provide safety and destination information, but they are increasingly challenged to facilitate optimal intragroup or intrapersonal experiences. Applying psychological theories of motivation and emotion, such as self-determination theory and reversal theory, may enhance tourism practices and theoretical analyses in tourism studies. Linking these principles to the four experience-brokering domains proposed by Weiler and Black (2015a) may further optimise co-created adventure tour experiences. Evidence from this autoethnographical exploration suggests that scholars and practitioners may benefit from using co-creation guided tour models, which highlight the interdependence and importance of optimal guide and tourist experiences to inform tourism research and practice.

## Note

1  All names are pseudonyms.

## References

Anderson, L. (2006). Analytic autoethnography. *Journal of Contemporary Ethnography*, 35, 373–394.
Anderson, L., & Austin, M. (2012). Auto-ethnography in leisure studies. *Leisure Studies*, 31(2), 131–146.
Apter, M. J. (1992). *The dangerous edge: The psychology of excitement*. New York: Free Press.

Apter, M. J. (Ed.). (2001). *Motivational styles in everyday life: A guide to reversal theory.* Washington, DC: American Psychological Association.

Arnould, E., Price, L., & Otnes, C. (1999). Making magic consumption: A study of white-water river rafting. *Journal of Contemporary Ethnography, 28*, 33–68.

Ateljevic, I., Pritchard, A. & Morgan, N. (Eds.). (2007). *The critical turn in tourism studies.* New York: Routledge.

Beedie, P. (2003). Mountain guiding and adventure tourism: Reflections on the choreography of the experience. *Leisure Studies, 22*, 147–167.

Brotheridge, C. M., & Grandey, A. A. (2002). Emotional labor and burnout: Comparing two perspectives of 'people work'. *Journal of Vocational Behavior, 60*(1), 17–39.

Buckley, R. C. (2010). Communications in adventure tour products: Health and safety in rafting and kayaking. *Annals of Tourism Research, 37*(2), 315–332.

Buckley, R. C. (2012). Rush as a key motivation in skilled adventure tourism: Resolving the risk recreation paradox. *Tourism Management, 33*, 961–970.

Chirivella, E. C., & Martinez, L. M. (1994). The sensation of risk and motivational tendencies in sports: An empirical study. *Personality and Individual Differences, 16*(5), 777–786.

Cogan, N., & Brown, R. (1999). Metamotivational dominance, states and injuries in risk and safe sports. *Personality and Individual Differences, 27*(3), 503–518.

Constanti, P., & Gibbs, P. (2005). Emotional labour and surplus value: The case of holiday 'reps'. *Service Industries Journal, 25*(1), 103–116.

Deci, E. L., & Ryan, R. M. (2012). Motivation, personality, and development within embedded social contexts: An overview of self-determination theory. In R. M. Ryan (Ed.), *Oxford handbook of human motivation* (pp. 85–107). Oxford: Oxford University Press. doi: 10.1093/oxfordhb/9780195399820.001.0001

Denzin, N. K., & Lincoln, Y. S. (Eds.). (2005). *The Sage handbook of qualitative research* (3rd ed.). Thousand Oaks, CA: Sage.

Erickson, R. J., & Wharton, A. S. (1997). Inauthenticity and depression: Assessing the consequences of interactive service work. *Work and Occupations, 24*(2), 188–214.

Guerrier, Y., & Adib, A. (2003). Work at leisure and leisure at work: A study of the emotional labour of tour reps. *Human Relations, 56*(11), 1399–1417.

Hall, M. (2004). Reflexivity and tourism research. In J. Phillimore & L. Goodson (Eds.), *Qualitative research in tourism* (pp. 137–155). London: Routledge.

Hochschild, A. R. (1983). *The managed heart: Commercialization of human feeling.* Berkeley: University of California Press.

Holyfield, L. (1999). Manufacturing adventure: The buying and selling of emotions. *Journal of Contemporary Ethnography, 28*, 3–32.

Houge Mackenzie, S., Hodge, K., & Boyes, M. (2011). Expanding the flow model in adventure activities: A reversal theory perspective. *Journal of Leisure Research, 43*(4), 519–544.

Houge Mackenzie, S., Hodge, K., & Boyes, M. (2013). The multi-phasic and dynamic nature of flow in adventure experiences. *Journal of Leisure Research, 45*(2), 214–232.

Houge Mackenzie, S., & Kerr, J. H. (2012). A (mis)guided adventure tourism experience: An autoethnographic analysis of mountaineering in Bolivia. *Journal of Sport & Tourism, 17*(2), 125–144.

Houge Mackenzie, S., & Kerr, J. H. (2013a). Beyond thrill-seeking: Exploring multiple motives for adventure participation. *Journal of Outdoor Recreation, Education, and Leadership, 5*(2), 136–139.

Houge Mackenzie, S., & Kerr, J. H. (2013b). Can't we all just get along? Emotions and the team guiding experience in adventure tourism. Special edition of *Journal of Destination Marketing and Management*, 2(2), 85–93.

Houge Mackenzie, S., & Kerr, J. H. (2013c). Stress and emotions at work: Adventure tourism guiding experiences in South America. *Tourism Management*, 36, 3–14.

Houge Mackenzie, S., & Kerr, J. H. (2014). The psychological experience of river guiding: Exploring the protective frame and implications for guide well-being. *Journal of Sport & Tourism*, (ahead-of-print), doi: 10.1080/14775085.2014.967796

Houge Mackenzie, S., & Kerr, J. H. (2016). Positive motivational experience over a three-day outdoor adventure trek in Peru. *Journal of Adventure Education and Outdoor Learning*, (accepted for publication).

Jonas, L. (1999). Making and facing danger: Constructing strong character on the river. *Symbolic Interaction*, 22(3), 247–267.

Jonas, L. M., Stewart, W. P., & Larkin, K. W. (2003). Encountering Heidi: Audiences for a wilderness adventurer identity. *Journal of Contemporary Ethnography*, 32(4), 403–431.

Liu, Y., Perrewe, P. L., Hochwarter, W. A., & Kacmar, C. J. (2004). Dispositional antecedents and consequences of emotional labor at work. *Journal of Leadership and Organisational Studies*, 10(4), 12–25.

Lv, Q., Shi, X., & Hui, J. (2012). Emotional labor strategies, emotional exhaustion, and turnover intention: An empirical study of Chinese hotel employees. *Journal of Human Resources in Hospitality & Tourism*, 11(2), 87–105.

Marchland, G., Russell, K., & Cross, R. (2009). An empirical examination of outdoor behavioral healthcare field instructor job-related stress and retention. *Journal of Experiential Education*, 31(3), 359–375.

McGrath, G. (2007). Towards developing tour guides as interpreters of cultural heritage: The case of Cusco, Peru. In R. Black & A. Crabtree (Eds.), *Quality assurance and certification in ecotourism* (pp. 364–394). Wallingford, UK: CABI.

Pain, M. T., & Kerr, J. H. (2004). Extreme risk taker who wants to continue taking part in high risk sports after serious injury. *British Journal of Sports Medicine*, 38, 337–339.

Pugliesi, K. (1999). The consequences of emotional labor: Effects on work stress, job satisfaction, and well-being. *Motivation and Emotion*, 23(2), 125–154.

Ryan, R. M., & Deci, E. L. (2000). Self-determination theory and the facilitation of intrinsic motivation, social development, and well-being. *American Psychologist*, 55, 68–78.

Scherle, N., & Nonnenmann, A. (2008). Swimming in cultural flows: Conceptualising tour guides as intercultural mediators and cosmopolitans. *Journal of Tourism and Cultural Change*, 6(2), 120–137.

Sharpe, E. K. (2005). 'Going above and beyond': The emotional labor of adventure guides. *Journal of Leisure Research*, 37, 29–50.

Strauss, W., & Howe, N. (2000). *Millennials rising: The next great generation*. New York: Vintage Original.

Tolich, M. (2010). A critique of current practice: Ten foundational guidelines for autoethnographers. *Qualitative Health Research*, 20, 1599–1610.

Weiler, B., & Black, R. S. (2015a). The changing face of the tour guide: One-way communicator to choreographer to co-creator of the tourist experience. *Tourism Recreation Research*, 40(3), 364–378, doi: 10.1080/02508281.2015.1083742

Weiler, B., & Black, R. S. (2015b). *Tour guiding research: Insights, issues and implications*. Bristol, UK: Channel View.

Weiler, B., & Yu, X. (2007). Dimensions of cultural mediation in guiding Chinese tour groups: Implications for interpretation. *Tourism Recreation Research*, 32(3), 13–22.

Witz, A., Warhurst, C., & Nickson, D. (2003). The labour of aesthetics and the aesthetics of organisation. *Organisation*, 10(1), 33–54.

Zapf, D. (2002). Emotion work and psychological well-being: A review of the literature and some conceptual considerations. *Human Resource Management Review*, 12(2), 237–268.

Zapf, D., & Holz, M. (2006). On the positive and negative effects of emotion work in organisations. *European Journal of Work and Organisational Psychology*, 15(1), 1–28.

# Part V

# Conclusions and future directions

# 13 Synthesising positive tourism

*Sebastian Filep, Jennifer Laing
and Mihaly Csikszentmihalyi*

## Introduction

Following the launch of positive psychology within tourism studies (Filep, 2009; Pearce, 2009), investigations in this emerging field have mainly focused on mapping out and delineating characteristics of optimal tourist experiences with some limited discussions of positive and healthy communities (Nyaupane & Poudel, 2012). In an earlier volume, it was concluded that the PERMA theoretical model of flourishing (positive emotions, engagement, relationships, meaning and achievement) neatly fits diverse outcomes of tourist experiences (Filep & Pearce, 2014). It was argued that such taxonomies, models, frameworks and integrative devices help researchers better understand the value and the complexity of tourism phenomena despite the hurdles of diversity of tourist experiences. Although the PERMA model was developed by Seligman (2011) as a generic model of human flourishing and a lifestyle model, its value to tourist experience research is now well documented (Saunders, Laing & Weiler, 2014). This volume has further developed the knowledge on optimal tourist experiences, but goes beyond the tourist in that it has also documented research on worker well-being and host community well-being through the lenses of positive psychology. In the following sections, we attempt to synthesise the core research findings of the book and highlight the authors' theoretical contributions. We do this in the following manner, following the style of the earlier, related Filep and Pearce (2014) volume. We sought inductively derived generalisations among our studies. The approach adopted amounted to a listing, albeit a listing where the items were delineated on the basis of their apparent relevance. Having benefited from our exposure to the studies in positive psychology, we then linked these listed themes, where possible, to some existing classification schemes. The themes are highlighted under each of the three pillars of positive tourism. We begin with the findings of the research studies that deal with tourist experiences.

## Tourist experiences, DRAMMA and PERMA

The positive tourist experiences section integrated positive psychology theories to offer readers fresh perspectives on tourists' romantic relationships (de Bloom,

Geurts and Lohmann), tourists' humour (Pabel), tourists' sensory experiences (Matteucci) and meaningful tourist experiences (Packer and Gill). For example, Pabel's investigation drew on the work of humour in positive psychology (Martin, 2007) to identify in what ways humour affected tourist experiences. Humour is broadly defined as the production and perception of a communication or act which induces an emotional state of mirth or exhilaration (Ruch, 2008). Through her focus group investigation with tourists at four tourism settings in Australia, she found that humour made it easier for tourists to start a conversation with others and acted as a successful ice breaker and initiator in building relationships. Matteucci similarly highlighted the value of hedonic experiences. In his study of flamenco tourists in Spain, he drew upon positive psychology works on savouring (Bryant, Chadwick & Kluwe, 2011) to explore tourists' sensory experiences and highlighted the role of the body and the senses in tourist experiences. Other contributors offered a more eudaimonic perspective to the study of positive tourist experiences. Packer and Gill's work explored vacations as a source of meaning. Qualitative data captured using a photo-elicitation technique revealed general sources of meaning that become more important on vacation, the specific sources of meaning that are inherent in vacation and the ways in which vacations themselves can be a source of meaning. De Bloom and colleagues, in a quantitative exploration of tourism and love, stressed the value of romantic relationships in tourism. In a longitudinal study of summer vacations of 35 Dutch workers, they investigated if and how tourist experiences affect romantic relationships and happiness during holidays. Their results indicated that vacationing not only enables working people to spend quality time with their partners but also enhances working people's romantic relationships in terms of relationship satisfaction and relatedness.

New perspectives on hedonic and eudaimonic well-being of tourists were also presented in chapters by Voigt and Csikszentmihalyi and Coffey. Voigt's study aimed to determine the benefits sought by wellness tourists and to explore whether the content of these benefits can be described as distinctly hedonic or eudaimonic. The study employed an interdisciplinary mixed-method approach to examine the concepts of hedonic and eudaimonic well-being on three different levels in the context of wellness tourism: the experiential, the motivational and the global levels. It was concluded that with regard to all three levels of well-being, there were distinct differences between the three groups of wellness tourists. Csikszentmihalyi and Coffey proposed a new theoretical model of tourist motivation grounded in the distinction between hedonic and eudaimonic well-being and presented ideas for measurement and application of this new model. The work expands on the previous, psychological tourist motivation theories, especially the earlier motivation models grounded in humanistic psychology and the works of Maslow (Pearce, 1982; Pearce & Lee, 2005).

Overall, the research studies on positive tourist experience correspond with the themes of the recently proposed framework that explains major psychological mechanisms which leisure experiences trigger to promote well-being (Newman, Tay & Diener, 2014). These psychological mechanisms are detachment-relaxation, autonomy, mastery, meaning and affiliation (DRAMMA). The DRAMMA themes relate well to the Seligman's (2011) PERMA themes. For example, the work by de Bloom and others relates to the relationships pillar of PERMA and also the affiliation pillar of DRAMMA; Packer and Gill's work fits in with the meaning element of both DRAMMA and PERMA. PERMA was also employed fully in a study by Laing and Frost. This was a study of well-being dimensions experienced by tourists in a dark Australian commemorative event context. The results suggested that attending a dark commemorative event, in this case two exhibitions forming part of the Centenary of World War One, resulted in outcomes that resembled PERMA dimensions: positive emotions, engagement, relationships, meaning and achievement. A sixth well-being dimension, identity, was also revealed in the investigation which was linked to eudaimonic well-being. Some key similarities between DRAMMA and PERMA and the corresponding chapter contributions are highlighted in Table 13.1.

While the aforementioned experiences relate mainly to outcomes of tourist experiences, Voigt's chapter and Csikszentmihalyi and Coffey's work on motivation also fit the DRAMMA and PERMA classification. Their motivation themes, for example, link in well with the aforementioned themes, both the eudaimonic elements (e.g. meaning from DRAMMA and PERMA) and the hedonic elements (e.g. positive emotions from PERMA). Overall, it is evident that optimal tourist experiences, according to the studies in this volume, are defined by eudaimonic characteristics, such as meaning and relationships, and to a slightly minor extent, hedonic characteristics such as positive emotions. Importantly for future research, this finding suggests that a hedonic conceptualisation of tourist well-being is a limited and an inadequate conceptualisation. It does not capture the subjective value of the tourist experience and its complexity, while PERMA and DRAMMA

*Table 13.1* Positive tourist experiences based on DRAMMA and PERMA

| DRAMMA (Newman et al., 2014) | PERMA (Filep & Pearce, 2014; Seligman, 2011) | Examples of corresponding contributions in this volume |
|---|---|---|
| Detachment-relaxation | Positive emotions | Matteucci on tourists' sensuality and savouring; Pabel on tourist humour |
| Autonomy/mastery/ meaning | Engagement | Laing and Frost on PERMA applied to dark tourism and events |
| Affiliation | Relationships | De Bloom and others on tourists' love |
| Meaning | Meaning | Packer and Gill on tourists' meaningful experiences |
| Mastery/autonomy | Achievement | Laing and Frost on PERMA applied to dark tourism and events |

serve as more useful frameworks and thus allow for broader appraisals of tourist experiences.

## Tourist–host relationships, social ties and temporary social capital

The second pillar of positive tourism, positive host communities, was addressed through contributions by Hillman, Moyle, Weiler and Che, and Glover and Filep. Positive psychology literature that relates to communities still does not have an established history, unlike the research on individual flourishing (Marujo, Neto & Miguel, 2014). Veenhoven (2014) explains that this lack of research is due to the traditional focus of positive psychology on the individual and subjective well-being as opposed to the collective well-being. There are, nonetheless, notable contributions on positive communities. Lambert, Passmore and Holder (2015) highlight the value of positive psychology in education with numerous school-based programs that shift emphasis from the individual to the collective good (Garcea & Linley, 2011); positive education is in fact a well-developed sub-field of positive psychology (Lambert *et al.*, 2015). Another exception is the tradition of research on national policy aligned with well-being indicators (Helliwell, Layard & Sachs, 2012). A tourism example of this line of work is research on the Bhutanese tourism sector (Teoh, 2012) on gross national happiness (GNH).There are also recent initiatives in which positive psychology is proposed as a vehicle for social change (Biswas-Diener, 2011); however, Lambert *et al.* (2015) remind us that the focus on collective happiness and well-being, while gaining traction in positive psychology, still needs further development.

In the tourism field, there is minimal work that aligns positive psychology theories and concepts to the study of host community issues. A notable exception is the research on appreciative inquiry, a strength-based methodological tool from positive psychology, which has been used in studies with communities affected by tourism development. Nyaupane and Poudel (2012) have found it to be an effective and epistemologically sound tool to gain a better understanding of rural population's knowledge, needs and priorities in a study of conservation, livelihood and tourism development in rural host communities located in Nepal. This volume further contributes to the body of knowledge on host communities from a positive psychology perspective, with authors reporting on the value of social ties between tourists and hosts and amongst locals at a tourism destination. The chapter by Hillman and others, through a cross-cultural research study of Balinese host community members who are employed in the tourism sector, highlighted the quality of social ties that are generated through tourism leading to interpersonal flourishing (Ryff & Singer, 2000). Similarly, Glover and Filep's examination of acts of kindness by hosts provided to tourist hikers in a nature-based tourism setting revealed the temporary social capital that is built in these interactions between strangers. The chapter added to the contemporary positive psychology literature on kindness and gratitude (Emmons & Crumpler, 2000).

More work is needed on community well-being, interpersonal flourishing and social capital through the lenses of positive psychology. Collectively, however, the findings in this section demonstrate the relevance of social ties and bonding as major indicators of well-being in tourist–host interactions. The strength of social ties is, according to Moos (2003), the key to enhancing the well-being and individual flourishing of community members. Taylor and Stanton (2007) remind us that social bonds are one of the most important psychological resources in times of need. The psychological value of these ties, albeit sporadic and temporary, is easily overlooked in more macro discussions of community well-being, such as tourism development literature (Sharpley & Telfer, 2002).

## Tour guide experiences: autonomy, challenge and social interaction

The third pillar of positive tourism relates to workers in the tourism sector, both management-level workers and those employed in lower-ranked positions. The focus is on individual well-being of tourism workers, in which tourism work is broadly defined to include jobs in numerous sectors of the industry from the accommodation sector (e.g. hotels, motels, hostels) to a suite of jobs in the transportation sector (e.g. airlines, cruise ships, coaches), the distribution sector (e.g. tour wholesalers, travel agents) and other sectors of the tourism industry. Some time ago, in a major discussion of the status of work in tourism, Baum (2007) pointed to four major environmental developments that have had an impact on employment in contemporary tourism globally: the impact of global and social forces on perceptions of work and careers, the impact of information communication technologies on work and employment in tourism, changing interpretations of skills within tourism and the increasingly diverse nature of the tourism workforce in developed countries. Importantly, Baum (2007) also highlighted poor working conditions and absenteeism and stressed the transient nature of many tourism jobs at a global level. Those factors have put a strain on the individual well-being of workers in the global tourism industry. The topic of individual well-being of tourism workers has received more recent attention in the literature, with streams of studies on negative aspects of emotional labour (emotional dissonance and burnout) in hindering employee well-being (see for example Saito, Irving, Packer & Solnet, 2015). Major research on well-being of workers drawing from positive psychology literature or its related sub-field of positive organisational scholarship (Cameron, Dutton & Quinn, 2003) is, however, to the best of our knowledge, missing. Within positive psychology, of particular interest is the work on job-related well-being. This includes research on job satisfaction, job involvement and organisational commitment (reflections on how employees view their jobs) (Turner, Barling & Zacharatos, 2002). Job-related well-being has been shown to lead to positive mental health outcomes of employees and to affect employees' overall life satisfaction. Job-related well-being is arguably especially relevant in industries typified by long hours, relatively low pay and highly competitive environments, as is the case with the global tourism industry. Workers are searching for meaningful work that underlines their efforts in an era of constant competition and a mentality that often favours profits over the welfare of people (Turner *et al.*, 2002). Turner *et al.* (2002) highlight three conditions that affect job-related well-being: autonomy and a sense of control in performing a job, challenging work and the opportunities for social interaction.

The findings of the studies in this volume conducted by Houge Mackenzie and Kerr, and Saunders, Weiler and Laing correspond with these three conditions identified by Turner and others. The exploration was on tour guides and their well-being in two different nature-based tourism contexts. Autonomy and sense of control, as well as opportunities for social interaction feature strongly, while the theme of challenge was present to a lesser extent. Houge Mackenzie and Kerr's investigation drew upon self-determination theory and reversal theory. Their data reinforced Weiler and Black's (2015) argument that tour guides' roles include mediating intragroup encounters. It was further revealed that guides may have missed an opportunity to broker positive intragroup social encounters by not offering more intragroup and interpersonal social activities which would have enhanced the overall job-related well-being. Saunders and others drew from Seligman's theories (2002, 2011) of authentic happiness and PERMA to highlight that the most important source of satisfaction for tour guides was helping others to experience or achieve something they find significant by having the control and ability to do so. The research study included interviews with long-distance walking guides and was informed by conceptual models from the tour guiding literature and theories from human resource management and positive psychology. Enjoyment and pleasure in what the guides did, place attachment and a sense of purpose and connection to something worthwhile are consistent themes associated with guides' feelings about their work. In a nutshell, the findings of both studies support the following contention by Turner *et al.* (2002, p. 717):

> One of the most important ways of improving the experience of work is to design jobs so as to encourage workers to engage actively with their tasks and work environment. By providing workers with autonomy in performing their jobs, challenging work and the opportunity for social interaction, we encourage them to exert choice and to feel competent. It is this form of work design that maximises employee effectiveness and well-being.

These kinds of work designs fit the domain of the now well-established experience economy paradigm in tourism (Pine & Gilmore, 1998). This is the idea that those who work in tourism are not simply selling goods and services, but rather selling experiences and often co-creating those experiences with tourists themselves. Within the tourism and positive psychology research field, these work design practices that heavily stress the value of meaningful social interactions, co-creation and a degree of challenge in a work environment have been documented in situations that involve the consumption and production of humour (Pearce & Pabel, 2015).

The conceptual contribution that authors made in this volume, therefore, by and large extends and adds to the previous work in the positive psychology and tourism field. Some brand-new contributions were also made, such as those that relate to our new understandings of love in tourist experiences, kindness of strangers in tourist–host interactions and the application of self-determination theory and reversal theory in a tourism worker/tour guide experience context. It is also pleasing to see cutting-edge contributions by several early career researchers, many of whom have conducted research in this field as PhD candidates. This augers well for the future of research on positive tourism. There are, nonetheless, limitations that are worth noting for readers of the volume. Most of the studies reported in the volume were conducted in western contexts involving researchers and research respondents from Australia, New Zealand, North America and European countries. This is a reflection of the geographical location where most of the authors are based. As research clusters of positive psychology develop across Asia, the Middle East, Africa and South America, and considering the importance of inbound and outbound tourism from these regions, the need for cross-cultural initiatives in this field is substantial. We were further limited by the scope of some investigations. For example, the well-being section on tourism workers only covers one type of tourism worker – namely, tour guides and their experiences. Only one contribution related to events, despite their importance in tourism, which reflects the need for more research on the links between events and positive psychology (Filep, Volic & Lee, 2015). Relevant works in the domain of positive psychology as they relate to host communities, for example, through applications of appreciative inquiry, were equally beyond the scope of the studies reported in the volume. Despite the limitations, we offer some final thoughts and conclusions that the readers of the volume may wish to consider.

## Conclusions

The volume demonstrates that eudaimonic themes, such as autonomy, affiliation/relationships, meaning and mastery, are strong features of positive tourism. Positive emotions help define optimal tourist experiences, however, the eudaimonic themes seem to feature more prominently across the three pillars of positive tourism. Eudaimonia (where daimon is the *true self*) is Aristotle's view of flourishing: the highest human good involving virtue and the realisation of one's potential. Eudaimonia has links to the work from humanistic- and psychodynamic-oriented psychologists, such as Jung (1955) and Maslow (1968). Ryff and Singer's (2008) work is seminal in the development of eudaimonic well-being. Their concept of psychological well-being includes six characteristics: self-acceptance, personal growth, relatedness, autonomy, relationships, environmental mastery and purpose in life. We see similarities between these elements of psychological, eudaimonic well-being and the themes uncovered in the volume. The findings related to the pillars of DRAMMA, PERMA and the results from the studies in the remaining sections of this volume imply the need to re-think the way tourism has traditionally been seen by the public and presented in some academic circles and by the media. The studies in the volume challenge the view of tourism as a fundamentally frivolous, insignificant and hedonic social phenomenon. Despite the authors' original contributions, we still do not know enough about the nature, intensity and durability of eudaimonic tourist experiences; about what a eudaimonic destination may look like; or about eudaimonic well-being of tourism workers. Studies on eudaimonic tourist experiences are, nonetheless, slowly emerging in the broader body of tourism and positive psychology literature (Matteucci & Filep, 2015; Voigt, Howat & Brown, 2010).

There are now calls for a comprehensive research agenda on eudaimonia in tourism research (Sirgy & Uysal, 2017). The eudaimonic themes that have been uncovered in this volume address the recent criticism of tourism and positive psychology research that states that it focuses exclusively on hedonic tourism contexts, where positive emotions are experienced (Nawijn, 2016). The chapter by Laing and Frost particularly addresses this point, highlighting the role of PERMA in the context of dark tourism and dark events. While we disagree with Nawijn's (2016) claim that there has been an exclusive focus on hedonic contexts in tourism, we recognise the overall hedonic emphasis in positive psychology research and the more limited, eudaimonic tradition of scholarship. We have not attempted to create a model of positive tourism to round off this volume. In part, this recognises some of the gaps in research in this field highlighted earlier. This would be a logical and welcome next step in the development of positive tourism. Instead, we have sought to emphasise the importance of eudaimonic research in tourism and point the way forward for future studies. We look forward to seeing further work that builds upon the research showcased herein, both from the contributors and beyond.

In creating the concept for this volume, we were conscious of the large body of work that has criticised and warned against tourism development. We canvas this work in the opening chapter and will not repeat what was said there. Nevertheless, we feel it is important to reiterate in this conclusion that while we acknowledge the negative outcomes of tourism that have occurred, both recently and through the ages, it is not the whole story. As the contributors' work suggests, tourism can and does bring many benefits to people around the globe, both personal and collective. To ignore or overlook this is to only tell half the story. Instead, we challenge researchers to continue to build on the theories and frameworks on positive tourism presented in this volume in order for us to better understand the true impact of tourism on our lives.

## References

Baum, T. (2007). Human resources in tourism: Still waiting for change. *Tourism Management*, 28(6), 1383–1399.

Biswas-Diener, R. (Ed.). (2011). *Positive psychology as social change*. Dordrecht: Springer.

Bryant, F., Chadwick, E., & Kluwe, K. (2011). Understanding the process that regulate positive emotional experience: Unsolved problems and future directions for theory and research on savouring. *International Journal of Wellbeing*, 1(1), 107–126.

Cameron, K., Dutton, J., & Quinn, R. (2003). Foundations of positive organizational scholarship. In K. Cameron, J. Dutton & R. Quinn (Eds.), *Positive organizational scholarship* (pp. 3–13). San Francisco: Berrett-Koehler.

Emmons, R., & Crumpler, C. (2000). Gratitude as human strength: Appraising the evidence. *Journal of Social and Clinical Psychology*, 19, 56–69.

Filep, S. (2009). *Tourists' happiness through the lens of positive psychology.* PhD thesis, James Cook University, Townsville, QLD, Australia.

Filep, S., & Pearce, P. (Eds.). (2014). *Tourist experience and fulfilment: Insights from positive psychology.* New York: Routledge.

Filep, S., Volic, I., & Lee, I. (2015). On positive psychology of events. *Event Management*, 19, 495–507.

Garcea, N., & Linley, P. (2011). Creating positive social change through building positive organizations: Four levels of intervention. In R. Biswas-Diener (Ed.), *Positive psychology as social change* (pp. 159–174). Dordrecht: Springer.

Helliwell, J., Layard, R., & Sachs, J. (2012). *World happiness report.* General Assembly of the United Nations, New York: The Earth Institute.

Jung, C. (1955). *Synchronicity: An acausal connecting principle.* London: Routledge and Kegan Paul.

Lambert, L., Passmore, H., & Holder, M. (2015). Foundational frameworks of positive psychology: Mapping well-being orientations. *Canadian Psychology: Special Issue on Positive Psychology*, 56(3), 311–321.

Martin, R. A. (2007). *The psychology of humor: An integrative approach.* Burlington, MA: Elsevier Academic Press.

Marujo, A., Neto, H., & Miguel, L. (Eds.). (2014). *Positive nations and communities: Collective, qualitative and cultural-sensitive processes in positive psychology.* Dordrecht: Springer.

Maslow, A. (1968). *Toward a psychology of being* (2nd ed.). New York: Van Nostrand.

Matteucci, X., & Filep, S. (2015). Eudaimonic tourist experiences: The case of flamenco. *Leisure Studies.* doi: 10.1080/02614367.2015.1085590

Moos, R. (2003). Social contexts: Transcending their power and their fragility. *American Journal of Community Psychology*, 31, 1–13.

Nawijn, J. (2016). Positive psychology in tourism: A critique. *Annals of Tourism Research*, 56, 151–153.

Newman, D. B., Tay, L., & Diener, E. (2014). Leisure and subjective well-being: A model of psychological mechanisms as mediating factors. *Journal of Happiness Studies*, (15), 555–578. doi: 10.1007/s10902-013-9435-x

Nyaupane, G., & Poudel, S. (2012). Application of appreciative inquiry in tourism research in rural communities. *Tourism Management*, 33(4), 978–987.

Pearce, P. (1982). *The social psychology of tourist behavior.* Oxford: Pergamon Press.

Pearce, P. (2009). The relationship between positive psychology and tourist behaviour studies. *Tourism Analysis*, 14(1), 37–48.

Pearce, P., & Lee, U. (2005). Developing the travel career approach to tourist motivation. *Journal of Travel Research*, 43, 226–237.

Pearce, P., & Pabel, A. (2015). *Tourism and humour.* Bristol, UK: Channel View.

Pine, B., & Gilmore, J. (1998). Welcome to the experience economy. *Harvard Business Review*, 76(4), 97–105.

Ruch, W. (2008). Psychology of humor. In V. Raskn (Ed.), *A primer of humor* (pp. 17–100). Berlin: Mouton de Gruyter.

Ryff, C., & Singer, B. (2000). Interpersonal flourishing: A positive health agenda for the new millennium. *Personality and Social Psychology Review*, 4(1), 30–44.

Ryff, C., & Singer, B. (2008). Know thyself and become what you are: A eudaimonic approach to psychological well-being. *Journal of Happiness Studies*, 9, 13–39.

Saito, H., Irving, G., Packer, J., & Solnet, D. (2015). The staff break room as an oasis: Emotional labour, restorative environments and employee well-being in the hospitality industry. In E. Wilson & M. Witsel (Eds.), *CAUTHE 2015 conference proceedings: Rising tides and sea changes: Adaptation and innovation in tourism and hospitality* (pp. 694–696). Gold Coast, QLD: School of Business and Tourism, Southern Cross University.

Saunders, R., Laing, J., & Weiler, B. (2014). Personal transformation through long-distance walking. In S. Filep & P. Pearce (Eds.), *Tourist experience and fulfilment: Insights from positive psychology* (pp. 127–146). New York: Routledge.

Seligman, M. E. (2002). *Authentic happiness: Using the new positive psychology to realize your potential for lasting fulfillment.* New York: Free Press.

Seligman, M. E. (2011). *Flourish.* Sydney, Australia: Random House.

Sharpley, R., & Telfer, D. (2002). *Tourism and development: Concepts and issues.* Clevedon, UK: Channel View.

Sirgy, J., & Uysal, M. (2017). Developing a eudaimonia research agenda in travel and tourism. In J. Vitterso (Ed.), *Handbook of eudaimonia research.* Dordrecht: Springer.

Taylor, S., & Stanton, A. (2007). Coping resources, coping processes, and mental health. *Annual Review of Clinical Psychology, 3,* 377–401.

Teoh, S. (2012). The ethics platform in tourism research: A Western Australian perspective of Bhutan's GNH tourism model. *Journal of Bhutan Studies, 27,* 34–66.

Turner, N., Barling, J., & Zacharatos, A. (2002). Positive psychology at work. In C. Snyder & S. Lopez (Eds.), *The handbook of positive psychology* (pp. 715–730). Oxford: Oxford University Press.

Veenhoven, R. (2014). Preface. In A. Marujo, H. Neto & L. Miguel (Eds.), *Positive nations and communities: Collective, qualitative and cultural-sensitive processes in positive psychology* (pp. 7–8). Dordrech: Springer.

Voigt, C., Howat, G., & Brown, G. (2010). Hedonic and eudaimonic experiences among wellness tourists: An exploratory inquiry. *Annals of Leisure Research, 13,* 541–562.

Weiler, B., & Black, R. (2015). *Tour guiding research: Insights, issues and implications.* Bristol, UK: Channel View.

# Index

For Product Safety Concerns and Information please contact our EU
representative GPSR@taylorandfrancis.com
Taylor & Francis Verlag GmbH, Kaufingerstraße 24, 80331 München, Germany

www.ingramcontent.com/pod-product-compliance
Ingram Content Group UK Ltd.
Pitfield, Milton Keynes, MK11 3LW, UK
UKHW021613240425
457818UK00018B/541